DATE			

D1270911

RANCHO MIRAGE

RANCHO

MIRAGE

An American Tragedy

of Manners, Madness,

and Murder

ARAM SAROYAN

Barricade Books Inc.
NEW YORK

Published by Barricade Books Inc.
61 Fourth Avenue
New York, NY 10003

Distributed by Publishers Group West
4065 Hollis
Emeryville, CA 94608

Printed in the United States of America

Library of Congress Cataloging-in-Publication Data

Saroyan, Aram.
    Rancho Mirage: an American tragedy of manners, madness and murder /
by Aram Saroyan.
        p. cm.
    ISBN 0-942637-95-X: $18.99
    1. Sand, Andrea. 2. Murderers—California—Palm Springs—Biography.
3. Women murderers—California—Palm Springs—Biography. 4. Murder—
California—Palm Springs—Case studies. I. Title.
HV6248.S327S37 1993
364.1'523'0979497—dc20   93-15903
                                                          CIP

9 8 7 6 5 4 3 2 1

TO GAILYN

"The discovery of truth is prevented most effectively, not by the false appearance things present and which mislead into error, not directly by weakness of the reasoning powers, but by preconceived opinion, by prejudice, which as a pseudo *a priori* stands in the path of truth and is then like a contrary wind driving a ship away from land, so that sail and rudder labour in vain."

—Arthur Schopenhauer

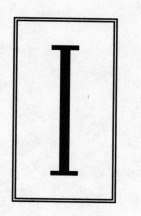

I

1

"What a mouth she's got on her, Foy. It would scare a truck driver."

"She curses?"

"Curses is a mild word for what she does. You should meet her."

"Why would I want to meet her?" Florence said. "Why in the world would I ever want to meet her?"

"You know this has nothing to do with us. I feel like an anthropologist."

"That's a ten-dollar word for paying a whore, Bob," Florence said.

"Stop."

He was sitting in his wheelchair by the kitchen phone. Andrea had gone to the doctor, his doctor, about her stomach cramps. He guessed Florence was sitting correctly in her den, trying to make sense of him, the poor woman.

"This you'll be interested in, Foy. I've got something else that goes into the book I'm going to write. Or should I send it to 'Ripley's Believe It Or Not'?"

"I don't want to do this, Bob. Did it ever occur to you that this might be painful for me?"

"That's why I want you to hear this," he said. "It won't be. I want you to know something interesting."

"Which is?"

"In the morning, when she wakes up, she has no face."

"No face?"

He heard a car skidding fifteen floors below down on Wilshire.

"That's right, nothing. Tabula rasa, this girl. I'm used to you and Sylvia, and you both have faces when you wake up. You are you, and Sylvia is Sylvia. Andrea is not anybody. I don't recognize her until after she's put on her makeup. It's very endearing in a way. I'm living with nobody."

"Why are you so happy, then?"

"I've told you. She's the most beautiful girl I've ever seen. She really is flawless..."

"Except that she has no face."

"She has one...after she does her makeup."

Andrea came in the front door and dropped onto one of the white Roche Bubois sofas in the living room.

Bob lowered his voice. "Guess who just walked in....Why won't you let me take you to lunch?"

"This is ugly. Don't you see that?"

"Florence, don't rain on my parade. I'm sixty-eight years old, and I've done my best..."

"What about me? And Sylvia?"

"I said I want to take you to lunch."

"Did Marxer ask you to get undressed?" Bob asked her when he wheeled into the living room.

"Yes and he thinks I'm crazy. He told me to just die."

"Oh, come now."

Estrelle, the maid, *was* poisoning her, because Bob was perfectly OK, and when Estrelle served them, she didn't bring a serving dish to each of them so they could serve themselves. She brought their plates with the food already on them.

Estrelle had also made a comment when she'd come across Andrea arranging the vitamins—a good One-a-Day, vitamins C and E, etc.—that she'd started Bob on.

"Poison?" Estrelle said and looked at her sharply.

"Vitamins," she answered. "*Vitamins*."

People had auras, and the color of their auras was like the color of their thoughts. Marxer had a shit-colored aura, and that was because that was what he was, a dried-up piece of shit.

She lay on the sofa breathing and feeling exhausted. It was practically dinnertime, and she was supposed to sit down and have Estrelle poison her and act like it was OK, because otherwise she was crazy and she knew Dr. Marxer would tell Bob his opinion of her.

"She's crazy," he'd say.

At dinner, Estrelle brought two plates to the table. Small pieces of veal, asparagus with hollandaise, and sliced boiled potatoes. Andrea looked at the food, and then at Bob, who was smiling at her like he was holding his cock under his napkin. She was hungry.

She took a sip of water.

"Dig in, my dear," Bob said as he raised a piece of veal to his mouth.

"I don't feel well when I eat this food, Bob," she said, wanting to leave a little marker in history, in case she died soon. Bob would remember. She would plant a little flag in his mind, or it would be like the story of Hansel and Gretel where they left a trail of bread crumbs to the cottage.

"So I understand," he said to her.

Estrelle was in the kitchen now, covering any tracks she'd made on her way to committing the perfect crime.

Andrea cut a small piece of veal. She took it in her mouth and chewed it. While she was chewing, she cut another piece of veal. She took the second piece into her mouth and chewed and swallowed it. She looked out to the living room and the windows that overlooked Wilshire Boulevard. It was sunset and the windows were full of light that didn't come very far into the room. Maybe she *was* crazy, and Estrelle was just making nice dinners for her and Bob.

Something horrible took hold of her stomach. She pushed back her chair and tried to stand, but wasn't going to be able to, and sat down on the carpet. She couldn't speak for a moment and just looked at the table legs while this horrible thing was trying to make her insides turn into metal or something.

Bob moved from the table over to her side, pushing her chair aside. He sat in his wheelchair with his napkin on his lap. Was his cock out? She didn't know and didn't care. He was looking at her, but she couldn't turn to look at him because the movement might kill her.

"Andrea? Are you all right?"

Sure, Bob, fine.

"Estrelle is trying to kill me." She said it to him like a character in a police series on TV just before she dies and the cop is holding her in his arms as she takes her last breaths: The maid with the big knockers...check the herbs...

"I'm leaving here, Bob. I'm not going to live here anymore." She stopped speaking because of her stomach.

If she didn't move out, she would die. That was the end of the story. Sometimes your body told you what to do before your brain could figure it out. Your brain might never be able to figure it out. But then your body realized if you didn't leave, you were going to die.

2

After Andrea moved into a little one-room apartment across the street from Bob's condo in the Comstock, she would still see him in the evenings but had the option of getting away when she had to. At night in bed, she loved it when he rubbed her back, and it often put her to sleep. But then she'd wake up with him wanting to cuddle. She'd fall back to sleep only to have it happen again and then wouldn't be able to go back to sleep. If it was around her period, she had to have some space, which Bob couldn't understand, and she would go into the guest room to try to get away or go back across the street, which pissed him off.

11 AM

Dearest Andrea—

After you left—I sat here very quietly and went over in my mind *all* of the things you said—and the things we discussed.

Conclusion (and I was 1/2 asleep!)—

(1) About last night—I was *totally* wrong. Simply a failure to read your intentions and not realizing that you were not deserting our room—but that you needed a good sleep and the peace of your room. You said that you had tried very hard to accommodate to my way of living and thinking—I hadn't thought a lot about that—but I agree that you have—I have toward you too but I must understand and do more (yesterday's picture taking and loving were all and everything I could expect.) Also, as you said, you have made a big and successful effort to make this a happy, clean, and well kept home—THANKS HONEY!!! I must do my part too!!

(2) We should both work in our own way to keep "Love" alive and *ever present*! It eases the way over the "bumps." We both have so much to give to each other to foolishly lose our way over really minor details like your getting up in the nite and going to your room, *or,* on my part wanting a small "snuggle" when we first go to bed. And participating in the intimacy of your baths and the wonderful free and easy way you have been with me in your "nudity." All of this I treat with respect and I love you for it. *Please* go on as you have and I *will cooperate*—because I care, and I dislike friction just as much as you do.

A great part of any problem we have, is getting you well and strong—Don't you agree? So we will do it!!

If you could realize that at this time and for a while, while the novelty has not worn off, I am having a very difficult time with "sex." In a short time it will become less, I'm sure. But right now because you are so pretty in every way, I have lots of trouble handling it! Please try to understand and give what you can of yourself. *Yesterday was perfect.*

I will do all possible to do away with your tensions, worries and doubts. I urgently want you to feel *secure—financially*, *emotionally* and in every way you may need.

Finally, I am not just another man in your life, I am offering you a permanent commitment which will be a beautiful experience for you— more and more as time goes on

Please join me in "Love" to make it all come true—

All my Love
Bob

$$\boxed{3}$$

Ronald Reagan was in a motorcade down on Wilshire one afternoon in late September. Andrea's mother and stepfather, Robert and Ellen Scott, visiting from New Jersey and staying in the Comstock apartment's guest bedroom, stood at the living room windows and watched the candidate go by in an open car, waving.

Robert Sand had invited the Scotts after Andrea had moved out and taken the little apartment across the street. He had fired the maid, invited Andrea's two grown-up sons, Guy and Douglas, for dinner along with their mother, and proposed to her several times. He'd also asked Florence to finally put through their divorce, which had been pending for a long time. Andrea hadn't said yes, but it looked like he would get his way. The immediate problem was that she could hardly keep any food down. Whatever the source of her illness—and maybe Estrelle *had* been poisoning her—she was a sick, pale shadow of herself.

Bob Scott, a seventy-year-old retired auto-parts tester for General Motors, thought Mr. Sand was a decent and obviously very successful man. When he and Ellen got off the plane at LAX, instead of seeing Andrea waiting for them, there was a young guy in a uniform and a hat who held up a cardboard sign that said "Mr. & Mrs. Scott." When they saw him, he greeted them and led them outside to a stretch limosine, where Mr. Sand and Andrea, as dressed up as Bob Scott had ever seen her, were waiting in the back.

The only thing that bothered him about the man was that when they watched television, which was pretty much all that went on at the apartment, Sand would have the channel changer in his hand and just when Bob Scott would be getting involved in a Lakers game or just getting interested in something on Donahue, Sand would switch channels.

Andrea's stepfather kept having to stop his mind and then start over again on a new channel. He'd make a polite grunt when he was really jolted, but Sand paid no attention, just seemed very preoccupied.

Bob lay down the remote on the table and wheeled away to his bedroom. A moment or two later, Andrea followed.

"Do you want to take a walk?" Bob Scott asked Ellen.

"I might need to help her with dinner."

"Why don't you see?"

Ellen stood up and walked back to the master bedroom and knocked.

"Oh, fuck!" Bob said on his bed.

Andrea was startled even though the door was locked. "Yes?"

"Andrea?"

"Yes, Mom."

"Bob wants to take a walk. Are you going to need some help with dinner?"

"Let's take them out tonight," Bob said to Andrea.

"That's OK, Mom," Andrea called to her mother in a light tone. "Bob's going to take us all out tonight."

When Mrs. Scott returned to her husband, Reagan was on the news talking and smiling about something, as if he knew a wonderful secret.

After the Scotts returned to New Jersey, Bob wanted Andrea to have her clothes off almost all the time they were alone or to wear just some little apron. He was filling up a scrapbook with nude Polaroids of her.

She had taken colonics and was getting back an appetite, and Bob kept proposing to her, which sometimes sounded fine but other times sounded a little off. But she knew marrying Robert Sand would give her security.

"I'm an old man," he said to her one evening while they watched the presidential debate. "I won't be around that long, and I'll see that you're well taken care of..."

Reagan looked over at Jimmy Carter, who was speaking, and said, "There he goes again..."

"I'm going to do a codicil to my will and leave you $150,000," Bob said.

That made her feel good. She'd sold her condo in the Valley and had more than $70,000 in the bank. She'd bought herself a brand new white Toyota Celica with $13,000 from the town-home sale. She was doing better but was beginning to get close to her period again, and it worried her because it was hard to get away from him.

$$4$$

Bob and Andrea drove down to Palm Springs together, Andrea at the wheel of his black Mercedes 450 SL. He and Florence had looked at condos there just before she threw him out. Someone had seen him coming out of a house, maybe. Maybe someone had seen him *in* a house. God knows. Florence was old, and he was too. Almost too old to be doing any of this with this high-strung blond who was like some kind of flower child under it all, but also had a temper and some kind of problem with her period.

She liked to drive, so he'd let her. She wanted the feeling of authority maybe—she was a little hard to pin down. It was like chasing a butterfly that would up and fly away each time you approached.

The Comstock condo was confining for her, too.

It was sunny and nice, and she'd gotten the eyeball from about a hundred guys. The car was gorgeous and when they pulled up at a gas station, the attendants raced out to take care of them like they were movie stars, which didn't happen to her in the Celica.

They followed the middle-aged lady who was their real estate agent to the condo in Rancho Mirage, at the Springs Country Club. Right across the street was the Eisenhower Medical Center, home of the Betty Ford Clinic, where a lot of people Andrea knew had gone to dry out.

The condo was perfect. It had two big bedrooms and a den, a pool across the street, golf and tennis, and all these tan happy older couples.

"I love it," she said to Bob while the real estate lady was outside the sliding door on the patio in the sunshine with the fairway beyond.

He smiled and nodded in his wheelchair. "We'll get married and move down here."

"Oh, Bob, it's just what we need!"

"Well, there may be some problems. I'll have to sell the apartment."

"There aren't any problems. We're going to buy this, Bob. I'll put some of my condo money in..."

"My rich girlfriend..."

She turned around and walked to the kitchen, and he followed her.

"It's perfect."

"You won't be bored?"

"Bob, I always wanted to learn to play tennis," she said, frowning at him.

$$5$$

Sylvia pulled up to a red light at Rodeo and Wilshire, realizing she was confused, angry, a million things at once, and there were all these other cars around, also stopped for the light or turning onto Wilshire from Rodeo. Everybody was going about their business, and she was sitting in her car waiting for the light to change because there were rules to obey, anyway.

She was on her way to see her father at the Comstock to get a check for $6,000 for a horse she wanted to buy, a horse named Sabrina Fair at the Malibu Riding and Tennis Club, that might provide her with another life to live now that she was divorced.

Her mother had a problem. She went on worshiping her father, even though they were now almost divorced and she'd even gone as far as insisting they sell the house in Hancock Park, that big beautiful house, a dream house to anyone who didn't happen to live in it.

For as long as she remembered, her father had taken a sedative every afternoon at 4:00. He would go to sleep at 4:30 and be up at 5:45 for dinner at 6:00 sharp. But she kept remembering one afternoon when she was fifteen or sixteen, and they lived on Homewood Drive in Brentwood. He must have waited too long before he started upstairs for his bedroom suite, and the sedative must have come on very heavily. Sylvia was doing her homework in the family room, and she could see him sort of trip and fall down slowly on the stairs and not move. Was he dead? she wondered. But she didn't move, something held her in a kind of paralyzed thrall. Eventually, after what seemed quite a long time, she saw him stand up and, leaning heavily on the railing, climb the stairs to his room, his nap.

The traffic flowed again. Her father had been so glamorous to her when she was a girl, like Cary Grant or George Hamilton. She wasn't exactly sure what it was that made her so angry at him now, when he worshiped the ground she walked on and had spoiled her so badly she seemed to be nothing but a big pile of jello inside. She hadn't done the right things either, and in one more day she was going to be thirty-seven years old.

The maid let her in. Sylvia and her mother had taken great care in furnishing the Comstock condo for Bob, right down to the Tiffany tableware. It hadn't mattered that her parents were separating, and their lives were so complicated. She and her mother and her father all loved each other. She knew that was true.

Her father seemed happy to see her and invited her into his library, where he wrote out a check for $6,000. It was, she knew, a lot of money. Was it enough that she needed to be nice to him? Her father was giving it to her for her birthday.

"Darling," he said after handing her the check, "I'm going to marry Andrea."

She stood in the doorway. She hadn't met Andrea and didn't want to, but had heard all about her from Florence, who had heard all about her over the phone with Bob.

"You don't really believe she loves you, do you?" Sylvia asked.

"No, I'm not that stupid," he said looking up at her. "But she's good to me, and she's what I need right now."

He didn't want to make too big an issue of it, just give her the news, which might be a little less of a pill because he was buying her the horse.

$$6$$

The Sand Door and Plywood people occupied one pew at the Little White Church just off Sunset in Westwood, while Andrea's friends, fast Hollywood types, along with her two grown sons and their women, occupied another across the aisle. Fred Kopplin, the number two man at the company, noted a couple of other tall good-looking blondes with older men. At one point just before the ceremony began, Jeanette Nelson, the wife of John Nelson, the company's sales manager, whispered in Fred's ear, "This is amazing!"

Having been with the company for thirty-five years, Fred was probably the least surprised of them all. After all, he was the one who had the keys that unlocked either end of the corridor—dubbed the "decompression chamber" by the employees—that led to Mr. Sand's private office. Fred had also been given the job of making withdrawals from the company account when Mr. Sand needed cash, which was a weekly occurrence. On one occasion when Mr. Sand asked him to withdraw $4,000—it was usually $1,000—Fred had finally dared to say something. For years he and John Nelson had agreed that the company's real problem was that Mr. Sand could never be counted on to reinvest a significant portion of his profits, which left the business cash poor.

"You know, Mr. Sand," Fred had said, "you'd almost think you had a secret life."

Mr. Sand actually became upset, denying it more vehemently than Fred had seen him respond to anything before. Usually his boss remained cool no matter what.

"Why would you think a thing like that, Fred? Why?"

But Fred was a loyal employee who had worked hard for decades, harder than he had ever seen Mr. Sand himself work, and that was as far as it went. Over the years he'd seen too many people let go for one reason or another, in essence having rubbed Mr. Sand the wrong way.

The buy-out agreement, worked out by Garthe Brown, Mr. Sand's lawyer, involving Fred and John Nelson and Fred Gwynn, the manager of the Fresno branch, who wasn't attending the wedding, had only happened at the insistence of the California Bank. The bank had extended Mr. Sand a million-dollar line of credit and had never even met the man. It was Fred and John who represented the company to the bank, and one day the man they dealt with there, Al Bolton, said that there was concern over Sand's continuous withdrawals. Even though there was no question the business was in good shape, the bank needed reassurance Fred and John were going to be there permanently doing what they did, otherwise it would have to pull back.

Mr. Sand's lawyer came into the picture then and set up the buyout to mollify the bank. Fred and John worked harder than ever, plowing their own profits right back into the company, and Mr. Sand made more money than ever. At the same time, Garthe Brown told Mr. Sand not to show up so often at the office or he'd jeopardize his social security checks. So Mr. Sand was coming in less and less.

In the ten years he'd been sales manager for the Sand Door and Plywood Company, John Nelson had had maybe five conversations with Sand. He knew that Fred had even urged the man to inquire once and a while about how John was doing, how business was going. But Sand never had, and so he'd been surprised to get a call from him the other evening, saying how much he hoped John and Jeanette would make it to his wedding. Sand even mentioned that the Little White Church had an organ—John was unaware Sand knew of his interest in music—and that he'd hired someone especially to play it for the ceremony.

The bride looked a little pale and wan, a beauty who, Nelson supposed, had known better days. She wasn't, in any case, his type, as Sand himself wasn't a man he'd ever have much in common with.

The first time Nelson had seen Sand in his office was right after Fred had told him he'd been hired and then led him through the two locked doors. There was this tall good-looking guy behind this desk in this huge room with a plush, deep red carpet, dark walnut paneling, and not a single window. Nelson had been in offices all around the country and never seen anything even remotely like it. It was the kind of place you might have expected to have your fortune told.

There was a reception at the Comstock condo after the ceremony. Bob, sitting in his wheelchair, told Elva Kopplin how beautiful he thought Andrea was, as the two of them watched her a few feet away, and how he just loved the way she walked. Elva didn't see anything particularly remarkable about the way Andrea walked but of course didn't say so to Mr. Sand. Then he told her that Andrea was going to get him to walk again, and Andrea looked over at them and said, "Uh-hunh. I'll give him something to get out of his chair for!"

Everybody laughed at that one, but to Elva it was like watching one of those television movies. It really wasn't like real life, with neighbors and relatives and report cards and fevers and dinners with leftovers.

It was a life, unlike hers and Fred's, where money was no worry. Where what you did was based on what you felt like doing at any given moment and not what needed to be done to get along and survive.

There was a photographer taking pictures, and Mr. Sand was helped up out of his wheelchair and stood up and put his arm around Andrea and leaned a little on her while the photographer's flash went off. And Elva could see in that moment that Andrea was trembling with the weight of such a big man as Bob Sand.

Downstairs as she and Fred were waiting for their tan Oldsmobile 88, a baby blue Cadillac pulled up, and one of the tall blond ladies got into the driver's seat and an older man got in beside her in the passenger's seat, and when the car drove away, Elva saw that the license plate read FOXYLDY.

"I'll bet Mr. Sand ends up at the bottom of a pool," she said to Fred.

7

In the beginning he had loved her to sit in his lap and would cuddle her and talk with her for hours about everything, but that had stopped a while ago along with the straightforward kind of sex they had started out having together. But on their wedding night, Andrea wanted to have normal intercourse and made sure Bob was so excited by what she wore and the way she acted that he eventually let go of his usual ideas for getting himself off—which seemed to involve less and less direct physical contact with her—and got down to business. It was good to know it was still possible.

Driving down to Palm Springs the next day, Bob in the Mercedes got ahead of Andrea in the Celica, and the next thing she knew she didn't know if she'd lost him or he'd lost her, and it made her very worried and spoiled what could have been the nicest day of her life, moving into her new house with her new husband.

When she got to Palm Springs, she couldn't find the real estate office and finally pulled over and phoned from a telephone in a Denny's. Bob was already there, and she started crying on the phone.

"I didn't know where you were, Bob!"

"I'm sorry, my darling," Bob said softly. "I'm so used to you knowing what you're doing, I just assumed you were right behind me or that you knew the way."

"Well, I didn't."

The next morning, when Andrea woke up in the big bed in the master bedroom with the sun shining outside and nothing but birds and every so often an airplane sound, she really thought she should pinch herself to make sure she was real.

Bob wasn't in bed with her. She got up quietly and snuck out to peek into the living room. There he was, sitting in his wheelchair in the middle of the big room that wasn't completely furnished, and he looked like the saddest man in the world, his lip hanging down the way it did when he felt bad. She went back into the bedroom to figure out something to wear to cheer him up. She put an outfit together and then went out to the living room very quietly to wait for him to find her with his eyes.

8

They bought a large mirror for the living room. The man who came to install it was cute and asked if he could have a glass of water. When Andrea brought it over to him, he thanked her and was smiling when Bob came in and threw a fit.

"Get out of here! We're not taking the mirror."

The man didn't know what the matter was, but eventually he took the mirror back out to his truck and drove away.

Bob liked to discover her in an outfit and notice that she wasn't wearing panties.

"You've been a bad girl," he'd say.

Then she'd have to lay across his lap to be paddled with one of her own exercise boards. If he did it too hard, Andrea stopped him, but she loved that she could make him so happy and excited by doing it. Sometimes when she wouldn't let him paddle her a little harder, he'd get sad, but she didn't want him to get into giving her real pain.

One afternoon when the maid was working in the house, Bob asked Andrea to take a bath just as the maid was about to clean the bathroom.

When Andrea refused, Bob said he wanted a divorce and was going to call his lawyer. She was shocked that he would react like that but didn't say anything. After sulking a long time, Bob seemed to forget about it and didn't bring it up again.

He sent her one of the cute cards he liked, letting her know he was treating her to four tennis lessons at the club. But he practically wouldn't let her go out by herself except to play tennis and would usually show up at the court in the three-wheeler Andrea had bought for him and shout encouragement. But when she made mistakes, he'd sometimes get mad.

"Andrea, that was pathetic!" he shouted at her one morning.

She wanted to tip him over in his three-wheeler.

He liked to take her shopping and buy sexy outfits and nightgowns for her while the salesgirl encouraged them. She'd come out in something, her nipples visible through the material, and the salesgirl would look pleased, and Bob, Andrea knew, was turned on.

The minute they got in the door at home, he wanted her in the outfit, and if they were going out, he'd sometimes come before they left.

They went to lunch at the Springs Country Club with Herb and Betty Hawkins, a handsome older couple who lived at the Springs. Herb had made a lot of money in real estate, and Betty was very active at her church. She invited Andrea to go to church and then to one of her church groups. Betty was beautiful, almost like a blond older sister.

The women in the church group were all terribly nice older ladies and made a fuss over Andrea, going on about how young and pretty she looked. But when she got home after the second Bible study meeting, Bob told her he didn't want her getting involved with Betty Hawkins and her church activities.

Almost every night they watched "The Newlywed Game" together and tried to answer the questions about each other, since they were newlyweds, too.

Most of the time their answers were wrong. Sometimes they watched the news, which was full of the new president, Ronald Reagan.

Bob picked out an outfit for her. Short white pants, and white high heels, and a very skimpy white top. Then he told Andrea he wanted her to take the Mercedes and drive around and pick up a man and fuck him for $100 and drive back and show Bob the money.

She drove around and could see all sorts of men who wanted to fuck her. Then she went to Ann Taylor and bought a blouse.

When she drove home, she told Bob she had picked up a South American who took her to the Palisades Motel and fucked her doggy-style and then had her blow him. She showed Bob $100 of her own money. He started beating off as she told him.

There were Mexican gardeners tending the grounds at the Springs, and Bob got upset if they got too close while Andrea sunbathed on the terrace.

"Go on, move on!" he shouted at them and looked irritated.

One afternoon when they were at the pool across the street—Bob in his wheelchair, Andrea stretched out full length in her bikini on a plastic pool chaise—a young Mexican gardener was working a few feet away.

"Take off your top," Bob whispered beside her.

First, he got all hot and bothered when they came around on the patio, and then he wanted her to take off her bikini top in front of one.

"No!" she answered and looked at him.

He was so strange.

That night she knew what was coming. He sat up in bed while she performed until he got off. She was standing naked at the foot of the bed.

"Man Number One," Bob said. "Remember that waiter at the restaurant last night who seemed to be so smitten with you?"

Some young boy he got pissed about...

"Remember?"

She nodded.

"Man Number One, step in please. Go on, let him see what you've got..."

She moved for him.

"Oh, but look," Bob said, "his cock's too small. I'm sorry, you'll have to find someone else. Andrea needs a big cock."

"Mmmhmm," she said.

"All right, Man Number Two," Bob said. "Remember the man at the next table when we had lunch with Herb and Betty Hawkins?"

A young businessman, maybe.

"Oh, look, Andrea. He has a *big* cock and he wants you to suck it. Look at it..."

She turned around.

"Oh, wow...I don't know if I can get it in, Bob, it's too big..."

"He's very impatient, Andrea. If you suck it properly, you'll be able to relax. He's desperate!"

"Bob, it's going to be a stretch just fitting it in..."

She got on her knees.

"All right, now. Here we have Man Number Three, the Mexican gardener from the pool today. He's young and good-looking, but Andrea, now that he's seen your ass, he's going to have to fuck you in the ass. He won't settle for anything else."

She leaned against one side of the bed, down from him, while the imaginary Mexican fucked her in the ass, and she made faces to show she was scared and it was painful.

"Oh, God, it hurts! I can't take it anymore! He's going to kill me, Bob! He's going to rip me, and I'm going to die!"

Bob was coming.

One evening Bob and Andrea came home tipsy from dinner at the Springs Country Club. They were both laughing and joking and got into the shower together, where Bob, as he liked to do, urinated on Andrea. Then he wanted Andrea to urinate on him, but it was hard for her to do it.

In bed afterwards, she got a piece of paper and a pencil and, using a copy of *Penthouse* as a backing, wrote out a contract Bob dictated to her:

1. Sex whenever appropriate & needed and acceptable between both of us.
2. Posing nude one roll a week, one roll a month outside
3. Do exercizes in nude
4. take baths in nude
5. Walk around nude casually as much as possible
6. Take shower with Robert twice a week, if traveling extra. Or disability like sprained ankle.
7. One Golden shower a week

8. In hot wheather wear no underwear & ask for spanking

Given willingly with Love,
For Robert Clark Sand
From his Darling wife
Andrea Claire Sand

9. P.S. Once a month do side show dancing

He'd told her that what she did for him took his mind off his pain. He said he had multiple sclerosis and had only a little more time to live. He'd given her a beautiful home and a beautiful lifestyle, and if he wanted her to use the exercise bike in the nude, Andrea didn't mind, although sometimes she thought Mexicans were looking in from the grounds at her.

Her son Guy's old girlfriend, Carmen, with whom Andrea had grown close and treated practically as her own daughter, came to visit with her husband Mike and their little boy. Mike wanted to plug the Nintendo into the TV set to keep the little boy busy.

"You're going to break the television doing that!" Bob told him, and Mike stopped.

They all went swimming while Bob watched TV. When they came back to the house, Mike went into the guest bedroom bathroom. Andrea was standing inside with a towel around her but dropped the towel and stood naked in front of him.

"Excuse me," he said and left the bathroom.

Andrea was cooking dinner, wearing a nice conservative dress she'd bought at Ann Taylor, a dark blue dress, and feeling happy and loving toward Bob, because her life now allowed her to be the kind of grown-up person who lived where she was living.

Bob wheeled in holding his Polaroid and asked her to lift up her dress. She lifted it.

"Higher!" he said.

She lifted her dress to the mid-thigh area. Then he wanted her to take off her underwear. She'd insisted on wearing panties that day.

"No," she said, "I'm cooking dinner. I'm making a healthy meal for you with love. Leave me alone."

"You bitch!" Bob yelled and threw the camera onto the floor.

For the rest of the evening, he sulked until she agreed to let him paddle her and then did it hard.

Guy came to visit with his wife, Yolanda, and their little boy, Aaron, Andrea's first grandchild, who was just six months old.

When they were having lunch in the dining room together, Bob pushed away from the table in his wheelchair and mumbled under his breath loud enough for Guy to hear, "I don't want all these people around here." Guy also noticed a hole in the second bedroom door where it looked like someone had kicked it in.

"Don't be surprised if something happens to me," Andrea said to Guy that afternoon when they were alone on the patio.

"If it's that bad, Mom," Guy said, "let's get in the car and leave right now."

"I have $50,000 of my own money invested in this house, I can't leave," Andrea said.

It exasperated Guy. Since he was a boy, he'd always tried to tell his mother the right thing to do, but usually she would only pretend to listen and then do exactly what she wanted.

Bob bought Andrea a golf cart but would never let her use it. He said there were men who would see her swinging a club and want to fuck her.

"Bob, I'll wear a dress down to my ankles," she said. "Just let me hit one medium bucket of balls."

When he wouldn't change his mind, she decided to go anyway. But when Bob saw she was leaving the condo, he came after her in the wheelchair swinging a fireplace iron.

Andrea ran out of the house and kept running all the way to Cathedral City, where she stopped and went into a coffee shop.

She was wearing her golf outfit with a short white skirt and had no money on her. There was a group of men sitting around a table. She asked them if she could borrow a dime for a phone call, explaining that she and her husband had had a fight.

"Sure," a man said and handed her a dime. Another man asked her to join them for a cup of coffee.

She sat down at the table, and a third man asked if she'd like to go to a party with them. Andrea said she had to make her call.

At the phone by the restrooms, she called her mother collect in New Jersey, but nobody was home. Then she couldn't think of anyone else to call, so she called Bob. He said everything was all right, and he'd come to pick her up.

Andrea's mother and stepfather came out from New Jersey for a visit, and Bob said that maybe he'd invite them along on their car trip to Portland to visit Bob's mother. Every day Andrea would ask him if it was OK to invite them, but he kept putting her off, and finally he said they'd take them next time.

Then he didn't want her to drive her parents to LAX.

"You might get into an accident and die," he said.

"But Bob, that might happen when I'm driving to Portland."

"But I'll be with you."

She had to take her elderly mother and stepfather to the bus station.

Andrea told Bob they needed to go to a marriage counselor—they'd seen one named Dr. Brudo briefly in L.A.—but Bob didn't want to discuss the things he knew Andrea wanted to discuss and promised not to ask her to do a lot of sessions on the trip to Portland.

He sometimes liked to have her lie on her stomach on their bed and tie her arms and legs to the bedposts. Then Man Number One, Two, or Three would come in and fuck her in the ass. She dreaded it when she knew another session was coming, which was now sometimes two and three times a day. Sometimes she was supposed to kill Bob's ex-wife, Florence, which she would pretend to do with a real knife, using ketchup for blood, or if she was having her period, smearing her own menstrual blood over herself.

She wanted him to be happy, but more and more of her time was taken up acting out fantasies, and she practically didn't have a moment to herself.

Then one night when she was tied to the bedposts, a real man got on the bed and fucked her in the ass. She was almost sure it happened because a few days later she saw a Polaroid Bob had taken of it. She tore up the picture.

They'd put the Wilshire condo up for sale with a friend of Sylvia's, Nina Rhodes, who came down to visit when she got an all-cash offer for close to the $500,000 they were asking, bringing some papers for Bob to sign.

Nina was impressed with Bob, who resembled a good-looking Eisenhower, with that army haircut and white hair. He wore a yellow shirt and golf pants.

Andrea took Nina on a little tour of the house and told her how wonderful Bob was and how happy they were together, and how she had him on vitamins and was working to get him walking again. But it seemed all too clear to Nina what sort of woman Andrea was and why she would be married to a man like Robert Sand.

The three went to lunch at the Springs Country Club. Although Bob seemed to be embarrassed that he needed the help, Nina was impressed with Andrea's strength and competence handling him, getting him into and out of the Mercedes and his wheelchair, and wheeling him up a ramp to the restaurant.

At lunch, Bob did everything he could to portray Andrea as a Pollyanna who roller-skated, swam, and played tennis, and yet was there for him morning, noon, and night. Nina noted that for someone involved in so much outdoor activity, Andrea seemed a little pale and wondered whether she wasn't going in more for *indoor* activities when she was away from Bob.

For some reason, Andrea was adamantly opposed to Bob accepting the offer Nina had brought and, much to Nina's surprise, he turned it down. She doubted she could get him a better one.

Nina knew Bob was trying to impress her with the wholesome quality of his relationship with Andrea because Nina's sister Suzanne was a close friend of Sylvia's, and Sylvia hadn't let Bob see his granddaughter, Alexandra, on whom he doted, since his marriage.

After lunch, they drove home. In the garage, Bob accidentally scraped the side of the car with his wheelchair, leaving a mark on the Mercedes.

"God! Look what you've done! How could you do that? You try to do things too fast..." Andrea was livid but quickly caught herself because of Nina and backpedaled.

1

On Wednesday, May 13, the television news was full of the pending air traffic controllers' strike and President Reagan's warning to the union that he wouldn't permit it to go on. Andrea fell asleep on the sofa after dinner and then woke up and went into the bathroom to take off her makeup and get into her nightgown. Her breasts felt swollen and ached, and she knew she was close to her period. She had a tennis clinic at eight the next morning and wanted to get a good night's sleep.

She got into bed around 9:30 and fell asleep quickly. A little after eleven, Bob woke her to tell her that Douglas was on the phone.

Her younger son needed money for a root canal, which Andrea promised to send him. After she got off the phone, she and Bob watched "The Newlywed Game" together and then went to bed. Bob was soon asleep and began to snore. Andrea couldn't get back to sleep. She woke Bob to tell him his snoring was keeping her up, but he only went back to sleep and started snoring again. She woke him again, and this time he allowed her to go into the second bedroom.

She knew he wanted a session—she'd refused him all day—and he wasn't in a good mood. They'd just returned from visiting Bob's mother in Portland, and he'd been very demanding when they stopped at hotels on the way up and back.

In the guest bedroom, which Andrea had decorated for herself, she called Bob on his line and told him she loved him and appreciated his being thoughtful about letting her get some sleep.

★ ★ ★

Two Springs security guards, Stanley Booker and Raul Cortez, arrived together in response to the alarm at 6 Brandeis Court a little before four on the morning of Thursday, May 14. Booker, a seventy-year-old Englishman, went to the front door. Finding it slightly open, he rang the bell. A blond woman came to the door wearing a dark robe, obviously very disturbed. She was holding her chest and told Booker she was feeling pains there and shortness of breath. He asked if she'd had these pains before. When she said that she had, he advised her to sit down in the living room and radioed for an ambulance.

After a moment, the woman told Booker there had been a man in the house and that he'd run out through the sliding glass door in the living room. Booker thought maybe the shock of seeing the man had given the woman a heart attack.

The woman asked Booker to go outside and see if he could find the man, so he went to the back of the living room. Behind the closed curtains, he found the sliding glass door open about eight inches. He checked the patio outside but didn't see anything and returned to the living room.

After another moment, having difficulty speaking, the woman stood up and led Booker by the hand to the master bedroom.

The room was spattered with blood, and the security officer saw the bloody body of an old man, a big man, nude except for a tee shirt, lying on his right side next to the bed. Booker immediately radioed the Springs Security Control Center to call the sheriff. After the woman washed her hands, the officer escorted her to the second bedroom and asked her to sit down on the bed. When the woman asked him to call Betty Hawkins, another Springs resident, and tell her what had happened, he went outside.

Peter Rode, an attendant employed by the Springs Ambulance Service, arrived a little after four and was shown to the body of Robert Sand by Booker. Rode checked Sand's vital signs and found none. He placed Sand's left hand back where it had been. Sand's eyes were fixed and dilated, and the attendant noted there was a piece of skin missing from his ear. Rode moved Sand's tee shirt and could see wounds on his rib cage, across his back in the shoulder area, and what he thought might be a bullet wound to the head. He estimated Sand had been dead for two hours or more. Sand was blue in his lower extremities, and his earlobe, tongue, and lips were also blue. The temperature of his skin was cool, and it had a pale ashen appearance.

At 4:13 Deputy Darryl Czajkowski was the first to arrive on the scene from the Indio Sheriff's Department, having requested en route that Sergeants Robert Kirby and Terry Burdo also respond. Instructing Cortez and Booker to remain outside, Czajkowski followed Kevin Bell, another Springs ambulance attendant, back to the master bedroom, where the deputy met Rode.

Rode pointed out various wounds on Sand and noted a bloodstained blue towel under the dead man's head. The deputy then escorted the attendant out of the room, using his baton to keep the bedroom door slightly ajar.

At 4:20 Sergeants Kirby and Burdo arrived and were briefed by Czajkowski. Inside the residence, Kirby noticed and pointed out red spots on the tile floor of the foyer and on the white carpet in the hallway.

The three went back to the master bedroom. Before the sergeants left the room, they instructed Czajkowski to resecure the room and prevent any others from entering the residence.

Sergeant Burdo contacted the Indio station and requested that an investigator and an identification technician respond to the scene. Sergeant Kirby asked Czajkowski to check the perimeter of the house and then get statements from all subjects at the scene. Czajkowski walked around the residence but didn't come across anything.

Standing with Booker outside, Czajkowski asked if he'd touched anything in the house. Booker said that he hadn't, adding that Mrs. Sand said she'd only pressed the alarm button that had summoned him. He said that Mrs. Sand had washed her hands while he was there, and the deputy asked if he'd seen any blood on her.

"She had on dark clothing and there wasn't much light in there," Booker answered. "She did point to the blood spots on the floor and said she thought maybe the man had blood on him when he ran out..."

While Czajkowski was interviewing Booker, Betty Hawkins arrived.

At 4:45, Fred Lastar, a balding, paunchy, thirty-nine-year-old detective who would be the chief investigating officer on the case, arrived.

After being briefed, Lastar went into the second bedroom and made contact with Mrs. Sand as she sat with Betty Hawkins. She appeared quite shaken but was able to speak rationally. Lastar asked her to give a description of the suspect she'd observed inside the residence.

The man had been approximately five feet, ten inches, Andrea told Lastar, and he had dark hair and a slim build and may or may not have been wearing gloves.

She'd woken up hearing Bob calling her from the other bedroom and thought that he must have fallen out of his wheelchair. When she got to the door of her room, on her way to the master bedroom, the man ran by and pushed her.

She went into the master bedroom and found her husband lying on the floor. He was covered with blood. She went into the bathroom and got some towels and lay them under his head. Then she saw his stomach stop moving and his eyes turned black. She left the bedroom and went to the living room. She saw the sliding door was open and went to it.

Then the security guard arrived.

Lastar asked how many people she saw. She answered only one. She hadn't seen his face.

2

A marked unit, an unmarked unit, and an I.D. Tech truck from the sheriff's department were parked in front of the cul de sac at 6 Brandeis Court when David Chapman, the deputy district attorney in charge of the Palm Springs office, arrived at 7:12. When he got to the door, he was surprised to find no one on duty there. He walked in and saw several investigators and other police in the den to his immediate left.

Detective Lastar had just allowed Mrs. Sand to leave with Betty Hawkins, with the understanding that he'd be contacting her later at the Hawkins' home. Investigator Rudy Garcia, who had called Chapman, nodded as the deputy D.A. walked into the room. A video called "Andrea's First Date" was beginning on the VCR. A woman, evidently the lady of the house, wearing a tight-fitting black sweater, and an unidentified man were seen sitting in a room together, a tableau that seemed to promise, in the perennial style of porno films, a quick segue into nakedness. After a few moments the woman jumped up and said, "I know what you want!"—and took off the sweater. She was wearing a white brassiere under it, but the film abruptly ended before anything more happened.

After being briefed by Garcia, Chapman went to the master bedroom.

The deputy D.A. had been called to the scene of close to a hundred murders. Once it had been to a small room in which a motel manager's head had been blasted at point-blank range with a shotgun by a disgruntled tenant. The manager's brains were hanging from the ceiling and off the walls. This room wasn't as bad as that, but it was among the three or four worst that he'd seen.

There was a lot of blood on the carpet beside the body. But there was also blood on the embroidered room divider a few feet from the body, on the wall behind the bed, on the pillows and the bedding, and on the sliding mirror door of the closet on the other side of the room. It was clear that it had been a violent scene. The man had put up a struggle for his life. There was a part of a broken drinking glass lying near the body.

Chapman walked into the bathroom. Over the toilet was a poster of the woman in the video in a wet tee shirt, which struck him as an unlikely decoration in a home in the Springs Country Club, the most exclusive and expensive residential resort in the Palm Springs area. It was something out of a college dorm room.

Before leaving, Chapman instructed Lastar to print all the carpeting in the master bedroom for blood types. In addition to the I.D. Tech, Mike Reyes, from the Indio Sheriff's Department, the Department of Justice in Riverside had been contacted for their assistance. Criminalist Steven Secofsky from the DOJ had arrived just after seven. Once briefed, he began collecting evidence with the assistance of Reyes, who photographed the scene.

There were blood spots on the carpet in the living room and on the kitchen floor, in addition to those in the foyer and the hallway. There seemed to be an inconsistency in the bloodiness of the master bedroom and the absence of blood on the curtain in front of the sliding glass door in the living room, where the assailant had made his escape. There was a discernible track of blood to the glass door, but outside on the patio, there was only a single bloodstain. And on the grass, which had a covering of dew, there were no footprints.

Detective Lastar asked Garcia to check the perimeter of the country club for any evidence of a suspect.

The Springs was surrounded by a six-foot chain link fence, Garcia discovered, and in some places the fence had three strands of barbed wire on top. In certain areas there was also a block wall and oleanders lining the outside of the fence. Garcia couldn't find any evidence that someone had jumped the fence but noted that construction was going on in the area south of the Sands' condo. A security guard at the construction entry gate on Kensington Drive told him he'd reported to work at six that morning when the construction crew started work and hadn't seen any suspicious people or vehicles in the area.

At 9 a.m., the coroner arrived; and at 9:45 two representatives from Wiefels Mortuary removed the body. Paper bags were placed over the victim's hands so that fingernail scrapings and trace evidence lifts could be made by the criminalist later.

The victim, it was clear now, had been stabbed. Sgt. James Kennedy, who supervised the detective division at the Indio station and had arrived that morning with I.D. Tech Reyes, checked the roof of the residence for a possible weapon but didn't find anything. Investigators Manuel Mapula and Larry Pedone, who had arrived at 8:30, were assigned to check the residence and nearby area for a weapon.

Detectives Lastar and Mapula went to the Hawkins' condominium at 30 Stanford in the Springs at 11:15 that morning. Mrs. Sand had agreed to accompany Lastar to the Eisenhower Medical Center across Bob Hope Boulevard for a blood and urine test. He wanted to verify that she'd used a sleeping medication she'd said Bob had given her the night before and also get her blood type.

While they were at the Hawkins home, Lastar asked Andrea if she had any cuts. She didn't, she told him. Would she mind checking her feet? Lastar asked. When she took off the sock on her right foot, she discovered a cut under the third toe.

She was given two stitches at Eisenhower.

After the hospital, Andrea agreed to return to 6 Brandeis Court with Lastar to see if she noticed anything unusual or out of place. The detective escorted her through the living room, the second bedroom, and the kitchen. In the kitchen, she noticed that a small knife was missing and drew the detective a picture of it.

She didn't notice anything else missing but asked about her exercise boards, one-by-fours about two feet long, she used during movement exercises. Lastar said he remembered seeing one in the secured master bedroom. It would probably be taken as evidence.

Around two that afternoon, shortly after Andrea had returned to the Hawkins home after going through her house with Lastar, Investigators Garcia and Pedone were entering the living room area at 6 Brandeis Court through the sliding glass door when Pedone spotted an object under the edge of the sofa only a few feet from the door. It turned out to be a knife that resembled the one in the drawing Andrea had made only a few minutes before.

It was a small kitchen knife, with a blade a little less than four inches long and about three-quarters of an inch wide. The knife had a bent tip but appeared to be clean. However, a hemistix test Secofsky immediately performed came out positive for the presence of blood. Deputy D.A. Chapman was called and arrived back at the residence at 2:45. Locating the weapon in the house was added to the earlier questions with regard to Mrs. Sand's story.

At 7:30 that evening, the autopsy on Robert Sand was performed by Dr. F. Rene Modglin at the Wiefels & Son Mortuary in Palm Springs. Lastar attended along with Detective Skip Royer, who was assigned to take photographs. In his report Dr. Modglin noted "twenty-five incisional wounds of body; abrasions, lacerations and contusions of skin; internal scalp hemorrhage; incisional wounds of lungs; right hemothorax; two transections of right internal mamary artery;" and "incisional wound of heart." The cause of death was listed as "incisional wounds of aorta and heart, due to stab wounds of chest."

The Hawkins had two couples to dinner that night, the Simpsons, an older couple who were very religious members of Betty's evangelical church, and Peter and Elaine Shepherd, an appliance salesman and his wife who were staying over that night in the second bedroom, while Andrea would be sleeping in the den. At one point the dinner conversation touched on relationships.

"Well, my relationship with Bob was strictly genital," Andrea remarked matter-of-factly, causing a silence to fall over the table.

Peter Shepherd had a bad feeling about the woman and had no doubt at all about who had killed her husband. When he was in bed that night, he had a hard time getting to sleep and eventually pushed a chair and a bureau in front of the door.

$$3$$

The next morning Betty Hawkins found Andrea sitting on a stool at the kitchen counter looking forlorn.

"Andrea," she asked, "have you accepted Jesus Christ as your Savior?"

Andrea looked wistfully at Betty. "Is that who I've been looking for all these years?"

Betty felt a pang for her. She'd tried very hard, Betty knew, to be a good wife to Robert Sand, obviously not an easy man. The joke at the Springs, where there were so many of these May-December alliances, was that the average age was fifty. The men were seventy, and the women thirty. And now this terrible thing had happened. She invited Andrea to join the church group meeting she was having at the house later that morning; it was the same group Andrea had gotten together with when the Sands first arrived at the Springs.

The *Desert Sun* ran a story that morning that mentioned the police had found the knife. Detective Lastar didn't know if Andrea had seen it when he picked her up in the afternoon. She was being cooperative and had agreed to give a full statement at the office in Indio. Whether or not she knew she was a suspect, the detective didn't know. On the ride from Rancho Mirage on Highway 111, she admitted that, in addition to working as an actress, she'd been a call girl. Lastar appreciated the honesty. Cooperating, of course, was the best thing she could do. Then again, she'd been an actress and would obviously know how to play a role.

A little before 3:30 in the afternoon, in the small conference room, Lastar turned on the tape recorder and made sure Andrea understood her Miranda rights. The investigator knew the tone in himself he wanted and found it easily. He was a gentle, concerned human being, someone you knew was going to give you a fair shake.

She pretty much stuck to her statement of yesterday morning, with the addition that when she got to Mr. Sand in the room and turned him, blood squirted up into her eye and on her face and the little nightgown jacket she was wearing.

"I walked into the bathroom and washed my hands and face," she told Lastar.

"That's the bathroom off the master bedroom we're talking about?"

"Yeah. I think that happened. OK, wait—golly, this is crazy—I think that when I moved him, and the blood squirted in my face—that's when I went and washed my hands, and that's when I got the towels and brought the towels, and put them under his head to make him comfortable. My hands were all full of blood, and I realized that there was blood sprayed all over my little blue top, and I took it off, and I went and put my—I was real cold—I went into the closet and got my bathrobe and put that on, a heavier bathrobe, and I just started wandering around the apartment till they arrived. It took them maybe five minutes at least, it seems. It might have been shorter, it might have been longer, I don't know."

Dr. Modglin estimated Sand could have been dead from thirty minutes to two hours when the ambulance arrived. Two hours was the estimate the ambulance attendant Rode had given. In either case, there was unaccounted time there.

Lastar asked about the knife. Andrea said it had been part of a set she'd ordered and then sent back because she didn't like them. Somehow this one wasn't returned, and she found that she liked it. She cut Bob's orange with it that night and was sorry she'd sent the rest of the knives back.

"Did he appear that he was carrying anything at that time?" Lastar asked, referring to the assailant.

"One part of me says he was carrying something," Andrea said. "It seems like he didn't have his shoes on 'cause he wasn't making any noise. Of course, there's a carpet, but you still hear the walking, you know. I didn't hear him. It was like he was barefoot or had socks on."

"Could he have been wearing tennis shoes?"

"Maybe."

"Did he appear to be carrying anything in his hands?"

"The feeling I had was that he was—when I thought about it—maybe he was carrying his shoes and had them up by his face. That's why I didn't see him. That's a feeling. I don't know if that's right or wrong."

Twenty-five stab wounds, Lastar thought, and the guy's tip-toeing with his shoes in front of his face?

"Andrea, in talking to you, I'm going to ask you a question that I'd like you to answer for me," Lastar said softly, cushioning the words, when close to an hour had gone by. "Did you kill your husband?"

"No."

"No?"

"No."

They got into Sand's will for a minute. Evidently he'd just redone it favorably to her, but it still hadn't been signed. They had planned to go over it the morning Bob was killed.

"Andrea," the detective said, "Mr. Sand was sixty-nine years old, and you're thirty-nine."

"Yes, that's correct."

"Was the marriage out of love or was it out of money? Did you marry him for love, or did you marry him for money?"

"Neither."

"Why did you marry him?"

"Companionship."

"In other words, you did not love him."

"I loved him. I wasn't in love—madly in love—with him. I loved him. I respected him. I admired him. He was a very well-read, very intellectual man. I enjoyed talking to him. He had a good sense of humor. We sent cards—we got funny cards—back and forth to each other, you know, we did a lot of cute things together. We had a good relationship. I wasn't afraid of him, you know, I felt safe with him. I had just gone through a marriage that was crazy. It almost drove me insane, and I guess I was a little afraid of men, and I felt very safe with him. I felt protected for the first time in my life. I was being taken care of and being protected. And I was like his servant. And I didn't mind it. I'm used to it. I raised two boys. I did everything for them that I could, you know. And he felt he was handling his end of it, and I was handling my end of it. I never turned him down sexually."

4

On the morning they got the news, Sylvia had spent the night at her mother's big apartment on the second floor on North Mayfield in Hancock Park, where Florence had moved after selling the house. Her mother wasn't given to theatrical gestures, but that cloudy morning, Sylvia heard her scream. She ran from the kitchen to the den, where her mother was on the phone.

"Daddy's been killed!" Florence said, looking up at Sylvia in pure panic.

A few minutes later a phone call came from Jonathan, Sylvia's ex-husband, who had just gotten the news. Sylvia hadn't had much to do with him for months, but the next thing she knew, he'd moved in with Florence and her and six-year-old Alexandra at the apartment. It was as if they were huddling together on blind instinct, not knowing what to make of what had happened, whether it had to do with them or not, and what might happen next.

A few days later Nina Rhodes' sister, Suzy Summers, told Sylvia that Nina was dead sure Andrea had done it. She said Nina had seen them in Rancho Mirage, and Andrea had lost her temper with Bob in front of her. It was obvious to Nina that Andrea had married him only for his money.

On Monday morning, May 18, Sylvia was sitting with Florence and Jonathan in an anteroom at Forest Lawn, having taken personal charge of her father's burial arrangements. After some wrangling through their lawyer, Andrea had released the body to the family. They quickly ruled out any funeral ceremony. For one thing, if the word got out, probably all sorts of hookers would show up. Florence knew what Bob had wanted—a mausoleum-type crypt—and now it was just a question of picking out a casket.

"Would you like to see your father?" the Forest Lawn man asked Sylvia. "He looks just fine."

"No, thank you," she answered briskly. She didn't even have to think about it.

"Well, then," the man said, "you'll just need to step into the next room here and pick out the box you'd like..."

She stood up, took one step, buckled, and fell down. She didn't faint, she just couldn't walk.

Jonathan helped her back to the chair and then went into the
room with the man and picked out the most expensive casket
there.

5

Detective Lastar heard from Andrea around 10:30 on Monday
morning that she'd been doing some prayer work and was now
able to remember the night of the murder in more detail. Lastar
didn't want her to go into detail over the phone, so he arranged
to see her at the Hawkins home around noon. Sergeant
Kennedy, Lastar's supervisor, came with him for the interview.

The three sat around the coffee table in the living room.
After turning on the tape recorder, Lastar repeated her rights to
her.

"OK, Andrea," he said then, "what I'm going to let you do,
is just let you talk about what you were telling me on the
phone..."

"Well, I've been working trying to remember everything,"
Andrea said, "and I remembered some things that I felt I'd
blocked out. Through some prayer work, it came to me that
when I came out of the bedroom, I was pretty dazed, and I
never saw the man's face, and that there was a person in front of
him who might have been a woman. It was a smaller form.

"And I remember going into the bedroom, and—I still can't
remember if there was a light on, or I turned it on—but I just
remembered when I saw him—ah, I pushed the buttons, and he
asked me to help him, and I was, I was trying to help him—and
I just remember kind of going crazy. And I pulled a knife out of
him. There was a board under him—I pulled that out from
under him. I cleaned them up, I dried them off. I put the towels
under his head to make him comfortable. He was still breathing
at this time, and his stomach was still moving, and then his

stomach stopped moving—you know, I was holding him—and just before his stomach stopped moving, his eyes turned black.

"And that's when I got up and started carrying on around the room, trying to clean up everything. I was going to give him a bath. I thought it would make him better. I was going to wash him. And I was trying to get out through the glass. I picked up the curtain, and I was trying to get out of there. I couldn't get out. I realized I couldn't get out of the room, and I started screaming for someone to help me. And I remember washing my feet and washing my hands two or three times. And, ah, one time I found some flesh on me. I don't know where it came from. And I flushed that down the toilet."

On the one hand, Sergeant Kennedy thought, you could understand the woman being upset and not making a lot of sense, after what had happened to her husband. But you also had to wonder why the intruders would choose to just brush her aside. And why she was washing every piece of evidence.

"Was your husband lying face down on his stomach?" he asked.

"When I came in and saw him, he was just a blob, he was like this kind of, just like this..." She lay down on the floor.

"OK," Lastar said for the tape, "you're lying down now. In other words, his face was looking up."

"Yeah," she answered from the floor. "He was like this, and I kinda like, when I turned him around and saw the knife, that's when I pulled it out. And when I pulled it out, all the blood squirted up into my face, and in my eye, and was all over me. And I don't know whether it came from him breathing, or it came from somewhere else, or whether it came from the puncture wound. I don't know where it came from, or whether, moving him, it just came. I had a hard time getting the knife out. As soon as I did, that's when..."

"In other words, you moved him to take the knife out?" Kennedy asked.

"I didn't know the knife was there until I moved him."

"OK..."

"When I saw the knife, I was trying to comfort him. I was afraid of him."

"Afraid of your husband?"

"Yeah."

"Why?"

"'Cause he looked awful. It was frightening me."

Lastar pressed on. "You said you found a piece of flesh on your hand..."

But she was crying now.

"Come up and sit down here, sit down, come on, you're doing OK, Andrea."

"It's like seeing him all over again."

"I know."

Lastar turned off the tape recorder for the moment.

After he turned it on again at 2:15, Andrea agreed to take a polygraph test the next day. Later that afternoon, though, when Lastar phoned her from the Indio station to say he had a man coming down from Sacramento the next day to administer the polygraph, Andrea put him off. She said she had a lot of financial papers to put together.

"I've got a lot of things to do. And it's hard for me to do them."

"Well, yet, as I say, Andrea," Lastar temporized, "I can't force you. And I'm not going to force you. But what I was trying to do is get this thing cleared up once and for all, OK?

"Yeah, I know."

"And if, you know,..."

"But I'm so paranoid around you 'cause I keep feeling like you're trying to trip me up, and I'm gonna..."

"Andrea..."

"I feel like you're trying to get information from me and use it against me. That's what I'm feeling."

After another moment, Andrea asked Lastar if she could phone him back and they hung up. When she didn't call back after an hour, he phoned her again. She'd fallen asleep. Lastar said that because of the imminent air traffic controller's strike, he might not be able to get the police polygraph expert down from Sacramento again soon.

"I feel like I'm being accused of something I didn't do..."

"Andrea, that's not going to do any good, OK. You're not being accused, OK?"

"Well, I thought lie detector tests were for guilty people to prove themselves innocent."

"No, no, no," Lastar said. "You know a lot of businesses require people to take lie detectors before they're even hired."

"Yeah."

"OK, so why are they for guilty people?" Lastar asked.

"I don't know. That's what I always thought."

"Well, you know, a lot of people think that we're able to solve cases in ten minutes, or during an hour television show, like they do it there. We're able to get fingerprints out of, you know, nowhere—we're able to identify everybody's fingerprints, too. You know, a lot of this people have a misconception of..."

"Yeah."

"We're not infallible."

"Did you find any fingerprints?"

"I don't think they did. You also told me that the person felt like he was wearing gloves."

"Yeah. But, you know, there was, I'm pretty sure there was another person, 'cause it seems to me—I remember hair flying around the corner, you know what I mean. Like the idea of it seems to be in my mind, and it was a tiny person—it could have been a guy with long hair or a girl."

Andrea told Lastar that she'd gotten back to doing push-ups since her back had been hurting again.

"I'm strengthening my stomach muscles, which strengthens the spine," she said.

"Uh hunh."

"That would be good for you, Fred."

"Shut up," Lastar said gently. "You don't have to say something like that."

"When I broke my spine in 1968," she said, "I want you to know, my legs looked like they belonged to two different people. One leg looked like it was my father's, and the other one looked like it was my mother's. My legs were completely deformed, and my rear end was like forty-two. It's like thirty-four now or thirty-five. It was like forty-two around, and I had a potbelly on me and everything. I mean I was a mess."

"Uh hunh."

"Rolls coming down the front of me 'cause I laid in the hospital so long, and I couldn't maneuver myself. I couldn't do anything. I couldn't even drive a car, it was so painful."

"Well," Lastar offered, "I'm doing a little swimming."

6

Betty Hawkins had seen quite a bit of stuff from Andrea's previous life, before she accepted Christ as her Savior, at the Brandeis Court condo. Today she'd come back with Andrea and an old friend who was visiting, Elaine Stevens, with the specific purpose of ridding the place of these cult objects.

The three women came across a crystal ball in a drawer in the second bedroom.

"Andrea," Betty said, "this is dangerous—no, really, *dangerous*—to have this—and we have to get it out of the house. It's strong enough to hurt you."

"I don't want it, Betty. Let's throw it away." Andrea took the object with the intention of putting it into the kitchen garbage can.

"Wait," Betty said, "we shouldn't leave any of this here when we go. I want you to be free of this. There's energy here right now that's Satanic, and we've got to get it out of here."

"How?" Andrea asked, looking at Betty and Elaine.

"Let's get everything together in a pile here and then put it all in trash bags, and we'll drive it to a dumpster and get rid of it once and for all."

The pile eventually included, in addition to the crystal ball, astrology books, est portfolios and programs, numerology books....The poor woman had been duped by every charlatan that had ever crossed her path, it seemed, and Betty felt great relief getting all the material together. She knew Elaine understood exactly what she was about, but Betty wasn't certain Andrea herself really got it.

"This blocks the energy," Betty said to her, fingering a copy of *Penthouse* that had shown up on the pile.

"Oh, that's just one of Bob's magazines. He loved big breasts."

After a day or two of living with Andrea, Betty and Herb had realized that she hadn't really been educated and from time to time would innocently make a comment like this, that would embarrass everybody around her. Yet it was innocent on her part. She was a free spirit who desperately needed the comfort of her Savior. At the same time, Betty sensed something in her that wasn't 100 percent where it should have been, even while she went to church and to Bible study meetings and said her prayers. There was still this streak of the wayward child in her.

On Wednesday, May 20, Detective Lastar spoke with Tim Clark, the tennis pro at the Springs Country Club. Bob Sand had usually been there when Andrea played or practiced, Clark told Lastar over the phone, and she was able to handle her husband in his wheelchair usually without needing any assistance. In fact once Andrea told Clark that she did between two and three hundred push-ups a day, and it was clear that she was in very good physical shape.

Lastar also spoke with Dana Spengler, a Springs resident who knew Bob and Andrea. Spengler said she'd seen the two at the courts and that they appeared to be very happy together and that Andrea seemed quite concerned about Bob. Lastar asked if she'd ever seen Andrea with any other men, and Spengler said that she hadn't.

Betty Hawkins arranged for Andrea to visit with George McCready, an elder of her church, who in his youth had been everywhere and done everything. If anyone would be able to see into the poor child's soul, it was this sophisticated, worldly man, who had made Monte Carlo his home base for many years. She drove Andrea to his house one morning so that the two could discuss things in quiet. It was hoped that Andrea would deepen her commitment to Christ.

Betty waited in George's beautifully furnished living room reading the New Testament while George and Andrea went off to talk in George's den. It was early and already hot outside.

Before very long, though, the door to George's den opened, and Andrea came back out looking a little wide-eyed. George followed her, with his eyes looking right into Betty's while he shook his head. They said polite goodbyes.

Betty and Andrea got into Betty's cream Lincoln Town Car and began the trip back to the Springs.

"That was quick," Betty said after the air-conditioner made the car habitable again.

"Well, I didn't do anything wrong," Andrea said, "and he wanted me to say I was a sinner."

"But Andrea," Betty said, "everyone of us is a sinner."

"Well, I'm not."

Betty glanced at Andrea and noticed for the first time a stubborn set to her jaw.

"You know, Andrea," she said, "while you were talking with George, I was reading from 'The Book of John' and came across one of my favorite passages. It goes: 'Except a corn of wheat fall into the ground and die, it abideth alone: but if it die, it bringest forth much fruit.' That's what it's like for each of us when we come to Christ. That's what it's like to be born again. We have to surrender and admit that we've sinned before He can become our Savior. We have to let go and die to Christ to be reborn.

That's all George wanted you to do—to surrender to Christ, sweetheart!"

"Well, Betty," Andrea said, "I haven't done anything wrong, and I'm not going to say that I did."

After being told by a chiropractor that therapy might help her cope with Bob's death, Andrea made an appointment with Dr. Morton Kurland, chief psychiatrist at the Eisenhower Medical Center. On hearing her story, Kurland advised Andrea to stop talking to the police and get herself an attorney. She was most likely a suspect in a murder case, and no good was going to come out of her having conversations with the detective, a man she seemed to have a crush on and kept contacting.

"He put his hand on my leg," she said. "I think he likes me."

Kurland told her that to keep talking to him was crazy.

"But I didn't kill Bob."

"I'm not saying you did," Kurland said. "But you need an attorney. Call Gary Scherotter. He's the best criminal lawyer out here. Tell him what you told me, and let him tell you what to do. You need to protect yourself."

"But what if I can help them find the people who killed Bob?"

Over the years, Kurland had had as patients a number of beautiful women whose older husbands had died. Palm Springs was full of them. At least a few of them, he suspected, were superior criminals who had inherited large estates and gone on to live exactly as they pleased without the inconvenience of a doddering cohabitor. He *knew* this was the case with one woman. Ironically, a few years after committing the perfect crime, she killed herself.

But after a few visits with Mrs. Sand, it was clear to him that for all her physical charms, she was a different order of woman. Genuine sociopaths were clear and convincing and even stylish, and they stuck to their guns. This lady's conversation was loosely associative, all over the place, and she was probably in shock from what had happened to her or, perhaps, from what she'd done.

Talking as she was to the detective on the case would have been inconceivable to a real sociopath. By now a real sociopath would be grieving in the south of France or some such place. He even suggested to her that she consider taking a vacation somewhere.

After four sessions, Andrea discontinued seeing Dr. Kurland.

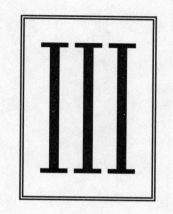

1

Responding to a call the station received through the telephone operator, a young patrol officer with the Indio Sheriff's Department, Colleen Word, arrived at 6 Brandeis Court a little after 6:30 p.m. on Thursday, July 23.

There was no car in front, and the front gate was locked. Deputy Word could see two suitcases sitting in the entryway. She climbed the fence and knocked on the front door. When there was no answer, she tried the door, discovered it was unlocked, and went inside.

The place looked like it had been ransacked. A purse was spilled open on the foyer floor, pills were scattered around, along with a broken whiskey bottle, a knife, and various articles of clothing.

In the living room directly beyond the foyer, both the television and the stereo were on loudly.

The deputy didn't see anyone.

"Mrs. Sand!" she called. "Mrs. Sand!"

She heard a response coming from the kitchen area.

In the kitchen, the deputy found Andrea naked on the floor with her hands and feet tied behind her. She was trussed up, a clothesline-type rope tightly binding her hands and feet, her legs pulled up under her. There was a blue kitchen towel tied around her head, blindfolding her, and there were several strips of blue bed sheet-like material wound snugly around her neck. The telephone receiver, off the hook, lay beside her on the floor.

There was blood over Mrs. Sand's lips and chin, and, strangest of all, Deputy Word could see about two inches of the wooden handle of a knife protruding from her rectum.

The deputy removed the blindfold, slipping it over the victim's head. When she picked up the telephone receiver, she discovered the operator was still on the line. She called the station and requested another officer, an I.D. Tech, and an investigator.

After hanging up, Word checked the kitchen drawers for scissors to cut the rope. The victim was complaining of pain and said she had no feeling in her legs. Word found a small knife, but it proved to be too dull to cut the ropes. Andrea told her there was a pair of scissors on the desk in the bedroom.

Deputy Word retrieved the scissors and cut the ropes. Then she carefully removed what turned out to be a small paring knife from the victim's rectum. She'd brought back a large blue bath towel from the laundry room by the master bedroom and covered Andrea with it. She gave her first aid, cleaning the blood from her mouth and chin, and asked her what happened.

Andrea told Word she'd arrived at the airport after a two-week trip to New Jersey where she'd visited her mother. No one knew she was returning. She took a limo from the airport and arrived at the house at around 4:30. The driver carried her two suitcases to the front gate and after being paid twenty-four dollars, left.

Andrea unlocked the gate and carried her bags to the front door. She went to the mailbox, and on her way back, locked the gate. She unlocked the front door and stepped into the foyer, carrying her purse and overnight case and looking through her mail.

She realized her television and stereo were on, glanced at the alarm in the foyer, and saw that it was turned off. She started for the kitchen to push the panic button when a man entered the foyer from the living room, grabbed her, and hit her over the head with a bottle.

The man, Andrea told Word, was a dark-skinned Indian, around nineteen to twenty-two years old. He was approximately five feet, nine inches and weighed around 140 pounds. He had dark eyes and full black wavy hair that was mid-ear length. The man wore a white tee shirt, jeans, and soft shoes, possibly moccasins.

After being hit, Andrea passed out. When she woke up, she was lying naked on the carpet in the living room with the blindfold on.

The assailant asked Andrea who she was and said he was looking for Mrs. Sand. Andrea lied and said her name was Phyllis, and that she was Mrs. Sand's sister. Mrs. Sand, she told the man, was out of town.

"How old is Mrs. Sand?" the man asked.

"About my age," she said.

Andrea became aware, she told Word, that there were two other people in the room. One was a man with a heavy Mexican accent, and the other was a woman. She couldn't describe either the second or third suspect because she was blindfolded.

She wasn't sure which of the three suspects said what and lost consciousness several times.

She couldn't be Mrs. Sand, the suspects told her, because Mrs. Sand was an old lady. "We're supposed to kill old Mrs. Sand."

They said they wanted the pictures, which Andrea thought meant the nude photographs Bob had taken of her. She told them that there were only a few pictures of her, that she'd cut up the rest.

They didn't believe her and during this discussion ran a knife point across her breasts and over the rest of her body. They threatened to cut off her breasts.

"Kill her! Kill her! Cut off her head!" the woman shouted.

"Shut up!" one of the men told the woman, who teased the man that he liked Andrea.

They banged Andrea's head on the floor and kicked her several times. She offered no resistance and again lost consciousness.

Both men, Andrea told Word, forced her to orally copulate them, and one, if not both, ejaculated in her mouth. Both suspects, Andrea said, also had vaginal and anal sex with her. She couldn't remember how many times intercourse occurred and didn't remember the knife being inserted into her rectum.

When Andrea regained consciousness, she was lying in the foyer, bound and blindfolded. Feeling around on the floor to get her bearings, she sensed that the intruders had gone. She crawled into the kitchen, found the telephone cord hanging from the counter, and pulled it with her teeth. When the phone fell to the floor, she located the digital dial and pressed "O" with her nose.

2

The following day, Chris Brown, a tall thirty-nine-year-old detective assigned by Sergeant Kennedy to the rape case (Kennedy emphasized that he wanted to keep the case separate from the murder investigation), called a Los Angeles phone number provided by the limo driver who drove Andrea home. Interviewed at the Eisenhower Medical Center, where she'd been taken after being discovered by Officer Word, Andrea told the police that after arriving in L.A. from New Jersey, she'd stayed overnight in Santa Monica with a man named Tim.

A man answered, but told Brown that no Tim lived there and said his name was Charles Livingston. After Brown explained the reason for the call, Livingston said he knew Andrea and verified that she'd stayed with him the night before last, after arriving from New Jersey. He refused to say whether or not they had had sexual intercourse.

A couple of hours later, Livingston called the detective back and said he did have sexual intercourse with Andrea but hadn't climaxed.

The next day, Brown along with Inspector Larry Pedone tape-recorded an interview with Andrea at Eisenhower Medical Center, where she was still being treated for back pain and undergoing tests.

"You say you didn't have sex with him?" Brown asked about Livingston.

"No, I didn't have sex with him," Andrea said.

"He says that you guys did, but he doesn't want to get involved, needless to say..."

"Does he know I was raped and everything?"

"I didn't go into it..."

"He made me promise not to tell. I was just going along with him."

Brown asked if Detective Lastar had told Andrea she was a suspect in her husband's murder. Pedone, who had spotted the knife at the murder scene, had told Brown he didn't know why Lastar hadn't taken her into custody that day.

"Yes, it's terrible," she said.

Brown contacted Jack Richard of Colt Security, the alarm system company for the Springs. According to Richard, a lit red warning light in the condo's alarm box and hall sensor meant the system was working. If the key is turned in the front door, the alarm is normally activated until it's turned off by the owner after entering the house. Richard said he found it unbelievable that Mrs. Sand would enter her condo, after her husband had been recently murdered there, when the alarm's warning horn failed to sound.

On Monday, July 27, home from the hospital, Andrea phoned Detective Brown and asked him to come to the condo, alone, and bring a tape recorder. She said she didn't want to talk to two detectives at once.

Brown, who had made detective rank in the department several years before in a record eleven months, thought this was probably the break they'd been waiting for: She was ready to confess.

When he arrived at the Springs condo, Andrea answered the door in a jumpsuit that wasn't buttoned up very far in front. After leading the detective to the living room sofa, she started to sit down beside him, but Brown said maybe it would be better if she took the chair across from him.

When they both were settled, Brown turned on the tape recorder. Andrea asked if the machine was on, and Brown said yes. She asked him to turn it off; she wanted to talk for a little while before taping.

Brown turned off the tape recorder.

Andrea said she had double- and triple-checked everything before leaving for New Jersey, making sure the house was neat and everything was put away, and the alarm was functioning. Fred Lastar told her to do that, she said, and she'd done it. She was smiling a lot at Brown and would get up to fix something on the coffee table, bending down and showing cleavage.

Brown wondered if anyone else was in the house. One of the scenarios he'd considered was that Mrs. Sand had a boyfriend, and they'd planned the killing of the old man. (Coincidentally, another passenger in the limousine that brought her home was named "Livingston," but he'd run a check, and it turned out it wasn't Charles Livingston.) She could yell "Rape!" and someone could pop out of nowhere and shoot him.

Andrea said she couldn't understand how anyone could have gotten inside the residence without a key to the front door and a key to the alarm. She told Brown she knew how to operate the alarm system; she'd been taught how to work it several times. She was sure the incident was related to her husband's murder. The man she saw coming from the living room was the same man she saw on the night her husband was murdered. The police report Detective Lastar did on the murder, which Brown had just gone over, said Mrs. Sand hadn't seen the man's face.

Brown asked how she could stay in the house after her husband had been killed there and after the incident that had just occurred. It was bizarre to him, he told her, that she would go on living here. She said that she felt safer now, because, if they'd wanted to kill her, they'd have done it.

"I'd already be dead," she said, "because he's had two chances to kill me."

After describing the night Bob was murdered, Andrea gave the detective a new description of the rape incident, making no mention of being hit on the head with the whiskey bottle. As soon as she entered the house, she told Brown, a man ran up to her, ripped all her clothing off, threw her down, and started pounding her head on the floor. Both of the men forced her to give them head, and she was spitting the sperm out onto her chest. The two men, she said, were sticking their small dicks in her mouth and up her rectum along with other unknown objects.

"I can tell you one thing," she said. "They had smaller dicks than Charles, and Charles can't even ejaculate because he's having sex problems."

Andrea asked Brown what he thought about this and whether he believed her.

Sometimes a suspect told you a long story, and when you said you didn't believe it, they broke down and confessed. But it was obvious to Brown that the lady was an actress, and at the same time you almost had the sense she believed every word she was saying.

Sergeant Kennedy had discussed with Brown the fact that Mrs. Sand had been found tied up partly with slipknots, so that it was conceivable that she had tied herself up. He'd also pointed out that there was no damage to her rectum from the knife, which meant it had to have been inserted very carefully, despite the rough behavior of the assailants she described.

Brown said he honestly didn't believe her. All the evidence pointed to her killing her husband, and this new incident was phony. Unless she could convince him otherwise, that was how he saw it.

"Why don't you arrest me then?" Andrea asked.

"It's still possible that you'll be arrested," Brown said. "Based on my past experience, one of three things is going to happen. You'll either kill yourself, kill someone else, or I'll have another call back here for another phony situation."

"I just tried to kill myself," Andrea said. She showed Brown her left arm, which had a lot of fine cut marks on the wrist and the elbow joint. "I tried, but it didn't work. I used a broken thermometer. If I go to jail, I'll finish the job."

At that moment, Brown could feel the hairs on the back of his neck stand up. Here was someone who would go to any extreme. He had a sense of absolute evil in the room.

The wounds were very minor and looked like they'd been done the day before. There was no blood, and they appeared to be healing. Brown decided she wasn't a danger to herself. In any case, her son was about to arrive, and Brown decided to wait and tell him what the situation was with his mother and suggest he keep an eye on her. The other possibility was to take her in on a 5150, a seventy-two-hour hold on her at Riverside Hospital for psychological observation, but she might end up using that to plead insanity.

The Riverside Regional Criminalistics Laboratory's "Physical Evidence Examination Report" on the rape, signed by Criminalist Steven Secofsky, was filed on August 13. Among the evidence considered was:

Item #1 Sexual assault evidence kit from Andrea Sand:
        A) whole blood sample
        B) chest area swab
        C) vaginal/cervical smear swab
        D) vaginal swab
        E) cervical swab
        F) rectal swab
        G) exemplar pubic hair
        H) saliva sample

I) pubic area combings

J) fingernail scrapings

K) exemplar head hair

Brown had considered that any sperm that showed up might possibly have come from Charles Livingston, and, embarrassing as it was, called him back.

"I'm sorry to have to ask you about this," he said. "You're completely cleared. But is there any possibility, at all, that there could have been an ejaculation?"

"In her mouth," Livingston said without preamble.

With that, the detective was prepared to run a DNA comparison on a blood sample from Livingston, and the semen sample from Andrea's chest, or anywhere else, but there turned out to be no sperm. The summary read: "Seminal fluid was not detected on the vaginal, cervical, rectal, or chest samples submitted from Andrea Sand."

3

For years Andrea had been corresponding with an inmate at the North Nevada State Correctional Institution named Richard Cordine, who originally wrote to her after coming across her address in an astrology magazine. Later on, she'd sent him a copy of the wet tee shirt photograph that was in the master bathroom at 6 Brandeis Court and then she sent him more copies, since Cordine was making money selling the photographs to other inmates. The two had never met. On July 31, the fifty-five-year-old Cordine, who was in prison for violating a work parole after an armed robbery conviction, wrote to her in his careful hand:

> Dear Andrea
>   I hope that you enjoyed your stay with your mom's and returned to Cal. well rested.

Andrea, I am in need of a favor. There is a good friend of mine who is in need of a parole plan in order to get out of Prison. Larry really is a decent, and extremely goodlooking young man of the age of (21)

It is most difficult to secure a suitable parole plan from within the prison. A letter from you stating that you will provide a place for Larry to stay and promise of employment will be sufficient. The letter should be directed to Larry Schweinfut c/o PO Box 100 SNCC Jean, Nev. 89019. Larry has a few dollars of his own and does not wish to pose a burden. I firmly believe that Larry is a worthy person or I would never endorse such a favor from you.

It is also important that the letter directed to Larry be here by next week as his release date is at the end of August. I have never appealed to your compassion before but please understand that I find it necessary.

I trust to hear from you soon.

Love,
Richard

On August 7, Andrea wrote Cordine that she'd been beaten and raped on July 24 and also told him that she would write a letter for his friend.

At 3:40 in the morning on Friday, September 4, a woman approached Patrol Officer Lowrey Spencer while he was parked at the corner of Highway 111 and San Clemente Circle in Palm Desert, the town just east of Rancho Mirage. She couldn't remember who she was or where she lived, she said.

All she could remember, she told the officer, who stepped out of his car, was walking out of a black metal gate and going to a mailbox. Then she returned through the gate.

The rest was a blank. She couldn't remember where she was, what the date was, what her name was, or anything else but the black gate.

She told the deputy that her forehead and the top rear area of her skull hurt, as if she'd been hit there, that her fingers were numb, and her tailbone hurt. As far as Officer Spencer could tell, there were no visible signs of wounds. He noted there were cut scars on her left arm.

The woman had no identification on her, and the long black dress and brown sandals she wore bore no identification marks.

The deputy drove her to Indio Station, where a mental health form was completed for a seventy-two-hour hold at Riverside General Hospital. A Springs ambulance was called and the woman was transported to the hospital and admitted as "Jane Doe."

Around 4:30 in the afternoon on the following Monday, Deputy Carla Gordon went to see Dr. Steven Curnow in the neurosurgery ward at Riverside General Hospital regarding the Jane Doe admitted on Friday. Dr. Curnow told her the subject had been admitted suffering from amnesia, but through pieces of information supplied by the woman, they believed they'd identified her as Andrea Sand and that she lived at the Springs Country Club in Rancho Mirage. A resident of the Springs had advised that Sand matched their description, lived there, and hadn't been seen for several days. The hospital had also been advised that Betty Hawkins was a friend of Sand's, and Hawkins would be coming to the hospital tomorrow to confirm whether or not the woman was Sand.

Dr. Curnow told Deputy Gordon that the woman had been remembering parts of an assault that he believed occurred just before she suffered amnesia.

After speaking with Dr. Curnow, Deputy Gordon went to see the woman in room 411 of the neurosurgery ward. The woman said she still didn't know who she was, or where she lived, and remembered almost nothing before being taken to the hospital.

She could recall writing out checks to pay bills on a night she thought was probably last Thursday night. She went to the mailbox to mail the bills and returned to her residence. She turned off the TV—she thought she remembered Johnny Carson was on.

She saw a security guard go by and decided to make sure everything was locked securely. Outside in the front yard, she heard the gate rattle. She thought it was the security guard because they frequently checked to see if the gate was locked.

Suddenly she was grabbed from behind around her waist and hit on the head with an unknown object. The next thing she remembered was waking up naked on the front lawn and then walking into her house, carrying her underpants and dress. She told the deputy she felt "dirty" and took a bath. Afterward, she dressed in the same clothing.

She remembered feeling she couldn't stay in the house and getting into her car. But she was shaking so badly, she couldn't get the key into the ignition. She hid the car keys and left on foot through the garage. She stopped to close the electric garage door behind her.

She wandered around the streets for a while, and then got scared because she couldn't remember who she was or where she lived, and she approached a deputy for help.

On Tuesday, September 15, Andrea wrote to Cordine:

Dear Richard,

Glad all is going well with you. I have been having my problems.

I think I was attacked again. I really blacked out & had amnesia. I am starting to remember everything, I think, except that.

Anyway, your friend Larry called me at 3:00 A.M. one morning after I got out of the hospital

and wanted to come to my home. I told him I
only wanted to help him get out of prison, I
really did not want a live-in. He said he saw my
picture and was in love & wanted to marry me. I
told him I had two sons older than he was & was
a grandmother. My grandson's name is Aaron.
I'm so happy about it.

I had a difficult time convincing Larry I
wanted nothing to do with him. He called back
at 4 A.M. & woke me again. I was being picked
up at 7 to go to Newport Beach to a bible study
with seven of my girlfriends & I never went back
to sleep.

Larry said I bet Richard said some bad things
about me & I said Richard never said anything
bad about anyone to *me*. He kept saying you're
worried I'll rip you off & I kept saying I just
don't want to be bothered with you (Larry). He
said he was stoned & was thrown out of where he
was living. That's all I need (ha ha)

Anyway he hasn't called again & if he does I'll
just keep telling him I don't want anything to do
with him. He sounded like a snake in the grass to
me.

I am going for counseling as I am not dealing
with my problems. I can't seem to deal with anything lately except church functions. So that's all
I'm doing.

I just keep reading the word & memorizing
scripture.

> Your friend,
> Andrea
> (the confused

IV

1

With the exception of a couple of weeks in August when the Riverside County sheriff's deputies went out on strike and Sergeant Kennedy filled in for him, Detective Lastar had worked continuously as the chief investigator on the Robert Sand murder case. It had seemed likely to him almost from the outset that Andrea had killed her husband, although he hadn't arrested her and forced the hand of the district attorney, he'd brought the case pretty quickly to Deputy D.A. David Chapman and asked him to file murder charges. But Chapman put him off.

This was a wealthy woman, Chapman said, with the resources to put up a very good fight against any case they brought against her. So they needed to have their ducks all in a row before they charged her and ended up spending a lot of tax-payers' money and embarrassing themselves. The case would get a lot of publicity, too, of course—the press and media would be out in force. And as it was, there just wasn't enough concrete evidence. Everything was circumstantial. If almost everybody believed she'd done it, still, the burden of proof would be on the prosecutor, and he'd have to prove beyond a reasonable doubt that she was the killer. And there might not be enough there yet to do that.

For some reason, the crime scene hadn't been dusted for prints. The Department of Justice criminalist and the Indio Sheriff's Department's I.D. Tech must have each thought the other was taking care of it, a major oversight by any standard that made them all look stupid. That also held Chapman back. The longer they waited, in any case, the more likely it was she would be caught in a lie, and they could then discredit the rest of her story.

Since Palm Springs wouldn't try the case anyway—Chapman just happened to have homicide-beeper duty the night of the murder—the deputy D.A. referred the case to the Indio office, the head desert office for Riverside County and the one with Rancho Mirage in its jurisdiction.

Kennedy and Lastar brought the case to Tom Douglass, the chief deputy D.A. there, and layed it out for him. Douglass was hesitant for the same reasons Chapman had been, but took the two officers, who came from downstairs in the sheriff's department, around the corner to run it by Deputy D.A. Jim Hawkins.

"I haven't filed this," Douglass said to Hawkins. "If these gentlemen can convince you to file it, you'll be responsible for it."

Hawkins, a good-looking thirty-six-year-old prosecutor with a wry understated manner, knew about the case and was intrigued by it but was also wary.

Douglass didn't stay very long. "You catch it, you clean it," he said to Hawkins as he left.

Dan Riter, a D.A.'s investigator whose office was next door, stopped by while Lastar and Kennedy went through the case for Hawkins. Riter suggested Lastar stake out the Brandeis Court condo until another incident occurred. Then, if Andrea called that she was being raped or assaulted, and no one was at the condo but her, they could confront her and maybe break her story of the murder night. But Fred said he didn't have time for that kind of a stakeout.

Hawkins didn't want to file immediately either. But he took the case with the idea that they would do further investigation.

Andrea continued to contact Lastar regularly—for which the detective took a lot of ribbing from others in the department and in the D.A.'s office. "Fred and Andrea..." an officer would sigh wistfully within Lastar's hearing. "How's it going, Poopsie?"

Lastar did in fact have very long telephone conversations with Andrea. But while she went on and on, he would listen patiently, waiting for her to finally step off the deep end.

On September 16, after they'd talked less than ten minutes— during which Andrea wondered how it could be that no indication of sleeping pills had showed up in her blood test the day of the murder when she knew Bob had given some to her the night before—Andrea told Lastar that on the night of the murder, when she got to the door of the master bedroom, she felt there was someone in there with Bob.

"I started to go in and there was still somebody in there..."

"You feel that there was," Lastar said.

"I can remember that."

"Okay."

"I can remember it now, but I couldn't remember it then. I don't know why, but I couldn't remember everything then."

"Hmm...Well, how did he get out?"

"What?" Andrea said.

"How did he get out?"

"How did he get out? I went back into the bedroom, 'cause I was gonna try to see who it was, but I didn't want the person to see me. I didn't want him to see me. So I went back into the guest bedroom, my bedroom, you know."

First she had told him there'd been one man who pushed her as he ran by the door to her bedroom, as she came out to go to Robert Sand.

A few days later, the one guy turned into two people, the second being a very small man or maybe a woman.

Now someone was still in the room when she got to it.

Later she got into the amnesia incident.

"They gave me a lot of tests in the hospital, and I have a pretty bad brain concussion. I just came from Riverside not too long ago. I had to go there for a checkup today."

"They said it was caused by a blow to the head?" Lastar asked.

"Yeah."

"Hmm..."

"It could have been, too. That, along with all the stress I've been under, was too much for me to handle."

"Mmm..."

"It was just a combination of too many things."

"Hmm."

"I guess I figured since no one believed me the last time, no one was gonna believe this either, and I just couldn't deal with it."

"I don't have answers, Andrea," Lastar said.

"No, but..."

"Right now, you know, the little hair I have, I'm still pulling it out, still trying to figure answers, and I don't have 'em."

"You know," Andrea said, "I used to be very, very psychic."

"Mmm..."

"And I purposely closed off my psychic part because I felt that there was too much of my mind, my own mind, my brain mind thinking, involved in it, instead of just being like a mystic or being psychic. And it was too confusing."

"Mmm..."

"I knew a lot of psychics, and I kind of went to psychics, and, you know, they were sometimes correct, but most of the time, it was pretty wrong. But anyway, I closed myself off psychically. But when I got hit, one of the things that happened to me, was, I was a little bit open psychically again. And one of the things that I got, was that Bob's death was a vengeance death. It was somebody who really had a vengeance against him."

The condition of the corpse had left no question in Lastar's mind about that.

"Well," he said, "I think both of us agreed to that a long time ago."

"I mean, it was really done purposely. It wasn't—well, I thought it was just someone that may have come along, just as a per chance kind of thing..."

"I don't think so. It just doesn't make sense, per chance, on that."

"Well, you know that book *The Second Deadly Sin*... They have a whole write-up in there about a man just killing a girl, just to see what it would be like to kill her..."

"Mmm..."

"...while he was making love to her."

"Hmm."

"I mean, you know, people can get that crazy."

Sergeant Kennedy had told Lastar that another story in the book, which they'd found in the condo, could have been a scenario for Andrea killing Robert Sand.

2

In a letter dated Monday, October 5, which she didn't address to anyone but passed on to Fred Lastar, Andrea wrote:

> I am typing this as you must be very busy since you have not returned my calls. A young woman confronted me outside my home on two occasions recently. The first time I was getting my mail. She said she was here the night my husband was murdered. I thought she was trying to upset me so I started walking toward the house when she said she had a gun, and did not want to frighten me, but she had to talk with me. She said she felt terrible about what happened and she did not know until the next day that Bob was murdered. She said she had lots of money & could she help me in any way. I told her the only way

she could help me and help herself was to turn
herself in to the police. She said she had thought
about it many times but could not disgrace her
family. She said she would rather be dead than
hurt them that way. I gave her Fred's [Lastar's] and
Jim's [Kennedy's] telephone number and told her
they would help her and I would help her if I
could; it all just seems bad now and she'd be surprised how her family would stick by her and
help her, too. She said she didn't trust or like
cops, and if I did I was crazy. I don't think I could
could convince her that Jim and Fred were different and would help her.

How do I know you are telling me the truth?
[I asked her.] Tell me something to convince me
that you were really here that night. There were
five of them drinking at a bar [she said] when one
of the men said, let's make a party and have some
fun. They parked their car and climbed over a
wall. The men had flashlights & one of them had
keys to open the door. They all went to the first
bedroom and flashed a light on a girl sleeping
alone and then to the next bedroom. She said
both doors were closed when she went out to the
livingroom with one of the men to have something to drink and eat. About a half an hour to an
hour [later] she heard the old man yelling for help
and about 30 seconds later, the other girl and one
of the men came running out, each with a pillow
case full of stuff. They said, let's get out of here
and we all started for the front door, [she said],
then decided it would be safer to go out through
the sliding glass door. We couldn't get it opened
at first but then one of the men managed to get it
opened. We all waited by the side of the house
until the other man came out, and he said, "We

woke the girl"—and we took off through the gate, across the street, and over the wall to their car. Nothing more was said about that night except the last man that came out said, "This could be the last of them."

She said she did not know that Bob was murdered until she heard it on the radio the next day, and a couple of weeks later, her male companion was murdered. I asked her if she knew why my husband was murdered. She said she wasn't sure, but one of the men was saying he was going to get even for his father: his father lost his business, had a heart attack, and soon after his mother passed away, too.

She said she has been coming back to this house whenever she could and watching what has been going on here, and she saw me many times and wanted to talk to me, but never got up the nerve. She needed to know if I was alright. I told her I really wasn't, and [about] what has happened to me since. She said she had just met the young man she was with that night, but the other three she knew to be freaky, and she wouldn't put anything past them. The girl was a watch while the two men robbed. She said she had participated in many robberies and they were all involved with drugs. She'd been hanging around alot of bad characters for a long time, and she knows alot of people in jail. She feels if she turns herself in, she hasn't got a chance. She's never been busted for anything, and she's never been involved with murder. She did not know that they used a knife from the kitchen to kill Bob. She liked stealing because it was dangerous and exciting. The other girl and her two companions have an airplane, and she did not think they lived here at the desert but that one of the men was originally from here. She said they were professionals and had keys and knew how to get into almost every lock made, and one of the men could get into almost any safe. She said they were all wearing surgical gloves that night and wore them whenever they did anything not legit. She was trained by the best.

I told her I would check out exactly what would happen to her if she turned herself in to the police, and I have not heard from her since. She did not want my telephone number. She said she'd get back back to me before Monday and today is Tuesday. She left me with the impression [that] if she did not get back to me by Monday I would never hear from her again. She said she would do something to help me out with the police, and Monday I found two letters in my mailbox. If I had not put some letters in the mailbox for the mailman to pick up the next day, the mailman would have taken those letters, and the one addressed to me did not have a stamp.

I asked her, from what she knew of the other three, did she think they would come back and hurt me anymore. She said they liked danger and doing crazy things. She switch[ed] back and forth from speaking perfect English to a Spanish accent.

Next? Lastar thought.

The detective eventually asked Andrea to make a drawing of the woman, which she did. It was a full-face portrait and—to the right of that—a profile, ending just above the waist. In the upper left corner, in Andrea's hand, was a description: "About 22 years old/5'3" 90lbs/Black hair/Dark brown eyes/Medium olive skin/Large teeth." At the bottom of the drawing, Andrea had written: "Karen—Kathy—Nancy."

That part didn't figure at all, but then what else was new?

The two letters, one of which was in a stamped envelope addressed to the Palm Springs Police Department, were word collages of printed words and phrases that came out of magazines. Both letters seemed to have to do with the murder, Lastar allowed, but it was hard to make head or tail of either of them in terms of suspects or as documents that would help Andrea. "Two men murdered...I didn't know they will attack him/the old man..." etc.—some of the pasted-on words were much larger than others, like ransom and bank holdup notes. And then there was stuff that seemed more likely to be thoughts from Andrea herself: "i now have emotional problems ... No Life won't be worth living ... I die now HELP."

Lastar sent the letters to the Department of Justice in Sacramento for a comparison to latent prints they knew belonged to Andrea, which he also enclosed. He advised them to check underneath the words that were pasted to the paper and underneath the stamp on the envelope.

On November 2, Lastar heard from Samuel R. Erwin, Jr., Latent Print Analyst II with the DOJ's Bureau of Forensic Services, by telephone. A few days later he received Erwin's written report, dated November 3. The summary read:

> Examination and processing of the submitted items resulted in the development of numerous smudged and fragmentary impressions of no value and five usable latent impressions.
>
> These five usable latent impressions were developed on the reverse side of the machine copy of a pasted on letter.
>
> Two of these impressions have been identified as being made by the right index and right middle fingers of Andrea Claire Sand. The remaining latent impressions were not made by subject SAND.

$$\boxed{3}$$

On Saturday, September 26, Andrea reported to Detective Lastar, she had received a phone call from Joey Triano, the ex-husband of a friend of hers. Triano claimed to have information about Bob Sand's murder and wanted to meet with her in Los Angeles. Andrea said she would drive there and be at her son Guy's house in two or three hours. Triano said that would be fine. He would phone her there.

But when she got to Guy's house, she waited several hours, and no one called. Since she didn't have Joey Triano's number she called Sheila, Joey's ex-wife. Sheila was a schoolteacher, Andrea told Lastar, a legitimate person. Andrea always wondered what she saw in Joey. She thought it might have been excitement since she really was so different from Joey.

In fact she'd been reluctant to give Lastar the name of the man who'd called her; Lastar talked with her for almost half an hour before she would. The reason, she said, was that Joey Triano was a person with criminal contacts, and she might get killed if Lastar tried to arrest him, for instance.

Lastar said he was investigating a specific murder case. If Triano could help him with it, that would be all he would be concerned with, unless of course Triano was making trouble in Riverside County, but that didn't seem to be the case.

After Andrea told Sheila about driving up to Los Angeles and Joey not phoning her, Sheila told her she'd contact Joey and get back to her.

In a little while, Sheila called to say that Joey had found out that Andrea had nothing to do with the murder of Robert Sand. Joey told Sheila that Bob Sand had owed a lot of money to some of his friends, and that if Andrea had had anything to do with the murder, she'd be dead right now. Sheila told Andrea that Joey was watching a football game and didn't have time to talk with her.

When Lastar reached Sheila Triano on Thursday, October 8, she confirmed talking with Andrea at the end of September, as Andrea had said. However, Sheila denied contacting her former husband or giving Andrea any of the information Andrea said she'd gotten from her.

On Wednesday, October 21, after Lastar told Andrea how Sheila responded, Andrea said Sheila had told her she would lie if the police called and questioned her. She was afraid to tell the truth, Andrea told Lastar, because she thought Joey would cut off her child support.

"It should also be noted," Lastar wrote at the end of the police report he filed on the episode on November 3, "that during my conversation with S. Triano, she advised that she did not have her former husband's phone number and did not know how to get ahold of him."

4

Dan Riter had gotten permission from the owners of a home outside the Springs, just across the street on Country Club Lane, to use the top of their garage, which they'd turned into a patio, for a stakeout. There was a table with an umbrella up there, and Riter could see across the fairway into the back of Andrea's house.

She would come outside and water her plants.

One afternoon she went to town to buy groceries and window shop.

One afternoon her sons visited.

Riter, Hawkins, and Judy Campbell, a victim witness advocate in the D.A.'s office, had been discussing how long Andrea could go without phoning in another rape or assault or whatever it might be.

The feeling was, it was getting very close to zero hour again. Hawkins and Riter enlisted Campbell, a tall, attractive blond, to lie out by the pool across the street at the Springs, so they'd have the front of the house covered.

It was a hot day, and Andrea came out to wash her white Toyota Celica.

Campbell, who'd gotten on a float in the pool to try to keep cool, was impressed by the thoroughness of the job Andrea did, washing and waxing. She even popped out the little back windows, cleaned, and replaced them.

Lunchtime had come and gone by the time Campbell got out of the pool, the only person still there in the sun. Parched, she called Riter on the Handi-Talki she had in her purse.

"Anything, Dan. A diet Coke?"

Of course, Dan had forgotten she would need to eat. Finally, J. Brown, another D.A.'s investigator who was on patrol (and would follow Andrea if she took off anywhere until Riter could catch up in his car), delivered some cafeteria food to her, a wrapped baloney sandwich and a Coke, from Eisenhower Medical Center across the street.

Andrea came out of the house and looked across the street right at Campbell. Campbell thought she was probably wondering who would be stupid enough to stay out in the sun all that time.

Then suddenly Andrea got in the car and drove away.

Campbell immediately called Riter on the Handi-Talki, but there was no answer.

The detective had already left and ended up following Andrea all the way to L.A. He had to pee so badly that he finally did it in a paper cup while driving. Then, in L.A., he lost her.

He forgot to call Judy Campbell to tell her she could go off duty. Campbell went home at the end of the day with the sunburn she knew would be inevitable.

A day later, Riter was back on the roof, and Andrea came out by the edge of the Springs property and looked across at him, sitting at the umbrella table.

She looked right at him, and then she waved.

That woman isn't afraid of *anybody*, Riter thought.

5

A week after the stakeout, on Friday evening, January 22, at around 5:30, another rape was reported. Deputies responded to a call from 6 Brandeis Court and found the garage door open with a car in it and lights on in the house. The gate was locked. Deputies Rick Kothlow and Bill DeLuna, who was on training duty, jumped the fence and went to the front door, which they discovered was open.

The house had a strong odor of gas and both the stereo and television were on loudly. Kothlow spotted Andrea's feet protruding from under a coffee table by the fireplace in the living room. She seemed to be semiconscious, lying in a full-length nightgown with red spots on it that might have been blood. A telephone was lying off the hook on the floor above her head.

While DeLuna secured the rest of the house, Kothlow, observing numerous scratches over the exposed parts of the victim's body, checked and found that she had a good pulse and was breathing regularly. The deputy immediately advised dispatch of the situation and requested a Springs ambulance.

While the deputy waited for the ambulance, Andrea regained consciousness and got up. Kothlow asked if she had any other injuries, and Andrea answered groggily that something was stuck up her rectum. The deputy helped her to the sofa.

When Paramedics Steven Stiers and Mark Barrier arrived, they partially removed the upper part of Andrea's nightgown and observed a wound in her left collarbone region. There were numerous shallow knife cuts on her left hand, arms, back, and legs. Stiers checked the buttocks area and saw that a paring knife was inserted approximately an inch into her rectum. The knife had a black handle with a small metal ring at the end of it. Careful not to smear any latent prints on the handle, Stiers removed the knife by pulling on the ring.

DeLuna was asked by Investigator Rudy Garcia, who had arrived on the scene, to accompany Andrea in the ambulance on the way to Eisenhower Medical Center. En route, Andrea was only semiconscious and spoke very softly. DeLuna had a hard time making out what she said, beyond asking several times for Fred Lastar.

In the emergency room, DeLuna tried to gather more information from her and was able to make out that a man with black hair, about five feet ten inches tall and wearing a white tee shirt, had broken into the house. She said his name was Manuel and he looked Italian.

At the hospital, Dr. Irwin Schiffman was unable to determine if Sand had had intercourse because she was having her period. He sutured the collarbone wound.

The doctor didn't find any damage to her rectum.

Detective Garcia considered the case to be complete bullshit. He'd been at the murder scene and had wanted to arrest Andrea the following day, Friday, which would have given them the weekend to write up the case for the D.A.'s office. But Sergeant Kennedy held back.

After Andrea was out of the emergency room, Garcia instructed I.D. Tech Reyes to photograph her phony wounds. Reyes reminded him it was against regulations for a male officer by himself to photograph a naked woman. Garcia sent in Colleen Word, who had arrived at the hospital, with Reyes.

When they reviewed Reyes' photographs Monday morning in Deputy D.A. Jim Hawkins' office, Judy Campbell noted that there were no significant marks on Andrea's right hand or right shoulder, or on her breasts. From her work, Campbell knew that assailants weren't normally very considerate of a woman's breasts. The right hand being unmarked indicated, of course, that maybe that hand had made the cuts. But it was almost too obvious.

"You know," Campbell mused, "this lady may actually be crazy."

As crazy as a fox, Hawkins thought.

1

Andrea had been introduced to Joe Mims, a recent widower in the water pump business, at a Christmas party at the Evangelical Free Church of Palm Desert by Herb and Betty Hawkins. It was clear to Betty that Joe, a tall well-put together man of fifty-six who was the very soul of gentleness, was smitten from the moment he took one look at Andrea.

It wasn't just that she was a lovely woman. She also knew how to dress as well as any woman Betty knew. She wore white hats with very wide brims, for instance, and they were wonderful on her.

The flip side of it was, she'd get in a certain mood, and you'd show up at the condo to pick her up for a Bible study meeting, and she'd come out wearing some long dark dress and looking for all the world like an unkempt hippie.

But Joe knew nothing about that side of her. He only saw her at her loveliest and practically fell in love in front of Betty's eyes. It was sweet to see something like that. It turned out he thought Andrea was Herb's and her daughter.

After Gary Scherotter heard Andrea's story, he was amazed she wasn't already in custody. He decided to let her know it, too, in front of Joe Mims, who had made the appointment and come to the office with Andrea. Scherotter hoped it would keep her from contacting and talking again with Detective Lastar, which was only helping the police build their case against her and had to lead to her eventual arrest. The lawyer was sure it was just a matter of time anyway, but going on talking with Detective Lastar could also hurt his defense once the charges were filed.

"Call me the next time you want to call him," he said to Andrea.

He didn't know if he was getting through to her, but maybe Mims could help him out. It was hard not to feel sorry for the man, a solid older citizen, under the spell of this siren.

A little after four in the afternoon on Friday, January 29, Joe Mims went to see Detective Fred Lastar at Indio Sheriff's Station. He told Lastar that Andrea had received two letters that day and enclosed along with the letters were a key to her home and one of her articles of jewelry, a necklace with a gold cross. He and Andrea had opened both letters with gloves, Mims said. The cross and key they kept and then put the letters back in their envelopes, and Mims was now delivering them to Lastar. They hoped that he could get some latent prints off them. Andrea hadn't come with Mims but had written a note to Lastar in which she said she recognized the handwriting in the letters.

On the back of one of the envelopes, both of which were addressed to Andrea and written in the same large and childlike scrawl, were the words: "I always/love/you/my beauty/Andrea." The letter was written on pages of five-by-five-inch notepaper, with only a few words on each page.

> Dear Andrea,
> p.s.
>   i forgot to
> give you thees
> i will always
> love you
>
> (next page)
> You are good
> I so sincerelly
> sorry. I sorry.
> I sorry.

(next page)
I sincerelly
will never
bother you
again. i wish
things will work
out. I sell your
things.
    Your friend
i don't have to return
        these

(next page)
I wish I
could have you
I no now I
    can not

On the back of the second letter were the words: "goodby/
forever/My sweet/Andrea." The letter inside, written on the
same notebook paper, read:

Dear Andrea,
I am greatly
sorry for what
happen Last
friday aftemoon.

it will never
happen again.

(next page)
Im 31 years old,
im in love with
you. I want you
to know Andrea

that i have money
of my own.

(next page)
You could use
a hand around
the house and
I would gladly
help out as much
as i can. I want
you to know Andrea

(next page)
It would be
much easeyer
to no you were
dead and no one
else Could have
you but i glad
you live.

(next page)
I sincerelly
offered for you
to me a chance
but you not even
look at me. I
did it for you

(next page)
how you feel
now Andrea?
Rich and
blond and
butiful and
     cut

(next page)
even if you no
date me even
as a friend. I
keep you money.

HA HA

On the following Monday afternoon, Detective Lastar
phoned Andrea about the note she'd sent him along with the letters. She recognized the handwriting? Lastar asked.

Yes, she said, the handwriting was similar to handwriting in
other letters she'd received in the past. Lastar asked if she knew
who the sender was. Andrea said that she didn't.

She told Lastar that the rape on January 22 had been the
sixth time she'd been raped since Bob's death. Another time, she
said, she'd been abducted from a bank parking lot. She was
forced into a tan, older model four-door sedan, held for about
two hours, and then let go about a mile from her vehicle. She
told Lastar that during the other rapes, she wasn't harmed, so she
didn't report them because no one would believe her.

No argument there, Lastar thought.

Andrea told him that when she was abducted, they tried to
force her to write a confession that she killed her husband.

She wasn't sure if she wrote one or not.

On Tuesday, March 2, Joe Mims went to see Lastar at Indio
Sheriff's Station and told him that he was in love with Andrea
and wanted to marry her. He was aware of Andrea's past, he said,
including the fact that Bob Sand had had cancer.

Lastar asked who had told him that. Mims said Andrea.

He should do what he wanted to do, Lastar said to Mims,
but he should know that Andrea was a suspect in the murder of
her husband.

$$\boxed{2}$$

When he looked at her, Joe's face brightened in the same way Bob's used to when he saw her for the first time in the morning. Like Bob, too, he was respected in the community. Andrea had a sense of being protected again, and it made her love Joe.

At the same time, there was the terrible stress that she couldn't get rid of, being the subject of a murder investigation. Sometimes she felt ready to explode with the tension, and it would make a rip right down the sky. And it wasn't something she could talk about with Joe, even though she tried.

"It's going to be all right," he'd say, having hardly heard her. "Trust in God, and be optimistic."

It was a tension that didn't seem to respond that well to prayer, either. A lot of times, when Joe told her to get down on her knees and pray, she did. But it didn't really work.

Then sometimes the twins would come back, Karen and Kathy, who were always fighting. And Nancy and Larry. Her old companions.

At night it would be almost impossible to sleep unless she took something. She missed Bob and never realized how much he had meant to her until he was gone. They talked about everything together. He knew her better than anybody ever had. Even if he made her do things she didn't like doing, he'd given her so much, and she was so proud of being his wife. He had become her God. Did he go to heaven? She hoped maybe in the final seconds of his life, he'd asked for God's mercy, because then she could look forward to seeing him in heaven.

Joe didn't try to make love to her because it was against his religious beliefs unless people were married. Dotty, his wife who had died, had been sick for twenty-five years, but hadn't been dead six months yet. But Andrea knew he was going to ask her to marry him.

When it got really heavy, there was this very strong, bad odor, and a fuzzy greyness in everything. After that, the blackness would come.

3

Just after 7:30 on the evening of Wednesday, March 17, Deputy Colleen Word came to 6 Brandeis Court to interview Andrea about another rape. Joe Mims was also there. He and Andrea were now engaged to be married, and Andrea had put the condo up for sale.

Andrea told Deputy Word that at 3:45 that afternoon, she'd returned home after shopping. Her grocery bags were in her arms as she entered her courtyard from the garage. Suddenly she was grabbed by a man, and her mouth was covered with a white rag. Three other men appeared and forced her to drink a bottle of red wine. She didn't get a look at the bottle, she told Deputy Word, but it tasted like Gallo.

"Sand first advised that the suspects forced her to drink three glasses of red wine," Word noted parenthetically in the report she filed. "Then she revised her story and said that they made her drink from the bottle."

One of the men injected something into Andrea's right upper arm with a hypodermic needle, telling her it would make her feel better. He injected her three times while the first man brandished a switchblade and threatened to cut her if she didn't follow orders. The men led Andrea to the walled-in area in her front yard and took off her clothing.

With a small manicure scissors, one of the men cut off her pants. After her panties were off, he cut holes in the crotch.

Andrea told Deputy Word she wasn't sure of the exact order of what happened next because now the drugs and wine were taking effect. She was forced onto her knees, her head shoved towards the ground, while all four suspects sodomized her. Then she was raped vaginally by the four men. And then she was forced to orally copulate two of the men, one of whom ejaculated into her mouth. She didn't know which of the four men those two were.

While she was being raped by one man, the other three were masturbating. At another time, while she was being raped, one of the suspects poured a bucket of cold water on her. The man used a yellow pail she kept in the garage. Raped repeatedly by the men, she was also struck several times across the face and cut with the switchblade knife. At some point, a knife was put in her rectum. During the acts of rape and sodomy, she couldn't distinguish one man from another, because all were wearing ski masks, and they didn't take off their clothing. All of them, she told Deputy Word, spoke "Gringo Mexican," which she defined as slang English spoken with heavy Mexican accents. She said she thought they were "gardener types."

After the men had raped Andrea on the lawn, they forced her to unlock her front door and told her to deactivate her alarm system. Two of the men then took her back outside, while two remained in the house. The two with Andrea took the money from her purse, which she'd discarded when she was attacked, and then tied her up, using an assortment of scarves she stored in the garage.

It was then that Joe Mims arrived at the front gate. Not visible to Mims, the suspects heard him calling Andrea and fled toward the rear of the house. Andrea was gagged and couldn't respond to Joe's calls.

While Deputy Word took Andrea's statement, Investigator Manuel Mapula looked around the residence and yard with Joe Mims. Mims showed him where he'd found Andrea on the front lawn, naked with her hands bound behind her back. He told the detective that Andrea had told him she'd been soaked with cold water poured from her yellow plastic pail.

Mapula asked where the pail was; Joe said he didn't know. They looked in the front yard and the garage but didn't find it.

Andrea hadn't had an opportunity to move the pail or put it any-where since Joe had arrived, and he was puzzled by its absence.

Detective Mapula later asked Andrea where the bucket was. She hesitated a moment and said it must be in the yard or the garage. Mapula told her it wasn't in either place, that they'd found the pail in the laundry room, which was inside the house. Andrea said then she must have brought it in herself.

Mapula asked her how she could do that if she was tied up, and Andrea said she had been tied up and let loose several times.

"Sand told Deputy Word that she was raped and sodomized by all four suspects," Mapula wrote in the report he filed. "Later in the interview, she also said that she thought one of the sus-pects was a female."

I.D. Tech David Pong checked the front and side lawns for any evidence of people in the area but only found one set of footprints, barefoot, leading from the backyard to the front.

$$\boxed{4}$$

On Friday, March 19, Betty Jo Crane, a resident of the Springs, telephoned Detective Lastar. He had interviewed her in January after learning from Tim Clark, the Springs tennis pro, that she knew Andrea.

Crane said she had seen Andrea at the Springs Tennis Club that day. Andrea seemed upset, so Crane started talking to her. Andrea told her she was raped by three Mexican males and a female, and that her boyfriend had heard her yelling when he arrived at her home and scared them off. Andrea said that if her boyfriend wasn't so stupid, he could have caught them, and now she wasn't sure she wanted to marry him.

Three weeks earlier, Crane told Lastar, Andrea mentioned her house wasn't selling, so she might have to paint and wall-paper it. Crane said right now real estate wasn't moving, and Andrea said she'd have to find a boyfriend to pay the bills.

"It should be noted," Lastar wrote in the report he filed, "that Sand's boyfriend is Joe Mims."

Three days after the last reported rape, just after noon on Saturday, March 20, Deputy Cynthia Sjoquist went to see Andrea at 6 Brandeis Court to take down her account of another rape. Joe Mims was also present. The report Sjoquist filed read:

> Her doorbell rang about 9:30 p.m. Friday night. She heard a couple of voices at the door and someone told her if she didn't open the door, they'd shoot it down. Sand was told nobody wanted to hurt her. She replied that they had hurt her before. One of the suspects replied that they just wanted to get her shook up. Sand also stated this same suspect told her something to the effect to not alarm anyone, or people might get killed. Sand opened the door and let suspects #1 and #2 in the house.
>
> In describing the men she could only advise that the man doing the talking appeared to be older (45-50) and gave the impression of being in charge. He spoke with authority. He wore a gold pinkie ring with a diamond and a gold watch, and had a small handgun in his possession. She believed both these men were Caucasian. Sand said that all four suspects she had contact with wore dark ski masks and gloves.
>
> Sand believed that the younger suspect, #2, had been in the house before. He went directly to the utility room, took out a piece of rope and tied her up. The rope was the same as that used to tie her on previous occasions, she said.
>
> Sand was told to sit at the desk chair in the hall outside her bedroom, while suspects #1 and #2 started searching the house. She could hear

drawers and filing cabinets being opened. She did not know what was being looked for but assumed it may have been something of her husband's. Sand told the men she had thrown a lot of her husband's things away and the attorneys had taken the rest.

Each of the men got themselves a drink from her bar. She was asked if she wanted a drink and said yes, wine. Her hands were untied and she was allowed to drink. Sand asked if she could write a letter to her husband. She was told as long as she didn't move she could write. It is unclear but it seems about this time she was told to take 7 or 8 pills provided for her by one of the suspects and [she was] injected [by him] with an unknown substance in her right arm. Sand later stated another suspect did it.

Sand also remembers suspect #1 telling her he had her jewelry and she'd get it back. This was clarified by the victim as being property stolen last Wednesday, the 17th.

Sand thinks it was about a half hour later that suspects #3 and #4 came into the house. They spoke Spanish and she believed they were Mexican. One of them tied her up again and both Mexicans then walked her out to a car parked in the cul-de-sac. Suspects #1 and #2 stayed at the house.

Sand was told to get in the back seat. Suspect #3 got in the back with her and held her down on the seat with a hand over her mouth. Suspect #4 drove. Suspect #3 slapped her on the face several times and caused her nose to bleed. While in the car her hands had been untied so she was able to wipe her nose with a tissue. Sand thought there might be some of the tissue still in the car.

This suspect also threatened her with a knife which he apparently took from his belt. He held it to her back saying if she didn't do what he wanted, the knife would go in.

Suspect #3 told her to take off her clothes, made her lie on her stomach and had anal intercourse with her. He then made her turn over and orally copulate him. He then had vaginal intercourse with her.

The suspects changed places. Suspect #4 also had anal and vaginal intercourse with her but did not threaten Sand with a knife. Both suspects, according to Sand, just pulled their pants down to assault her and wore the ski masks during the entire drive.

Sand was allowed to put her clothes back on. Her hands were re-tied and she was let out of the car in an empty lot with a few houses around. She does not know where she had been driven or where she had been let out. Sand does remember walking back to Highway 111 and passing "Nastys." She had been able to untie herself and stuck the rope in her pocket.

Sand walked east on Highway 111 to Bob Hope Drive and got a ride from there to Country Club Drive with some people. She walked the rest of the way home.

Her house was unlocked when she got back. Suspects #1 and #2 were still inside. When Sand came in, suspect #1 made a phone call and the two Mexicans returned. All four then left. Sand said suspect #1 seemed to be satisfied, as if he had located something in the residence. She was not bothered by any of the suspects during this time.

After the suspects left, Sand called her fiance, Mims. She then took a hot bath, douched, and went to bed. She also advised later that she had had a bowel movement. Sand did not know if either suspect ejaculated at all during the assault.

I checked Sand for external, visible physical injuries. Her lip was cut inside and she had several small, slight scratches on her upper chest and upper back. She does not remember feeling suspect #3 use the knife on her at all. Sand also had what appeared to be a scratch on her stomach, right side. She also had slight swelling just behind her right eye which she said happened last Wednesday.

In interviewing Mims he confirmed that Sand had called him about 3:15 a.m. Saturday morning. He said she sounded upset and said she felt paralyzed but did not tell him what had happened. He came over at about 4:00 a.m. and tried to wake her but couldn't. He stayed the night and spoke to her when she woke up about 8:30 a.m. They talked for a while, called her attorney, and then called the Sheriff's Department.

During the course of the interview, Sand stated she had been sexually assaulted seven times since her husband died and had only reported four of the assaults.

I.D. Tech Hopf took the clothes she said she had been wearing at the time of the incident. However, her underpants could not be found. Sand thought they might be in the car but did not really think so.

Detective Mapula later contacted Andrea to ask how it was possible she knew one of the suspects was wearing a pinkie ring when all the men were wearing gloves. He also didn't understand how she could determine the age of the men when they were wearing ski masks. Andrea said she was confused.

A little after 9:30 that Saturday night, Deputy Czajkowski arrived at 6 Brandeis Court in response to another call from Andrea, requesting a police officer.

When he arrived, the gate was locked. When Czajkowski rattled the gate, trying to open it, Andrea came out and unlocked it.

She told Czajkowski she'd received a telephone call from one of the suspects who had raped her. The suspect spoke with a deep, gruff voice, she said, and told her he'd returned her jewelry and jewelry box, and that it was inside the front courtyard of her house. She said she'd asked for a deputy to respond rather than a Springs security officer because the deputy would have a gun.

Czajkowski found the jewelry box on a stepping-stone about five feet from the entry walkway.

Andrea told Czajkowski that the suspect must have climbed over the courtyard wall or the gate to leave the box. Using a pen, the deputy opened it to confirm that it contained Andrea's jewelry.

The caller had told her, Andrea said, that the jewelry was being returned because of her cooperation.

"What do you mean by cooperation?" Czajkowski asked.

She said it meant that she cooperated when they tied her up and raped her.

VI

IV

1

Deputy D.A. Jim Hawkins heard on Tuesday afternoon that Joe Mims and Andrea Sand were downstairs, talking to the desk sergeant on duty in the sheriff's department. She'd certainly kept them busy at the end of last week. Given this pace, it might be hard to find time to do anything but investigate her cases. Hawkins had never met either Mims or Sand and decided to go downstairs to see what they looked like.

In the sheriff's department lobby, he sat in a chair by the wall with the sergeant's desk in front of him.

"If you investigated the way you should," Mims was saying to the desk sergeant, "you'd probably have the murderer by now. This lady isn't receiving the protection from the police that she pays for as a taxpayer. What has to happen for you to do your job? Does she need to be killed?"

"No, sir..."

Mims was tall and solid, a gentleman of the old school, a knight in shining armor, and Hawkins found it hard not to like him, a typical idiot male.

He was angry. A beautiful woman, *his* woman, kept being found with a paring knife inserted in her rectum. It occurred to Hawkins that there might be a sort of grim irony in the fact that these knives were, in size and shape, like the murder weapon. If Andrea had killed her husband, and Hawkins was about dead certain that she had, then she'd metaphorically, as it were, shoved one right up her butt. That is, if they could ever arrest her for the murder.

On the other hand, the lady was a vision of innocence. Beautifully dressed for, say, an afternoon garden party: white dress and white hat, nice figure inside the lace. It wasn't a hooker's outfit; she had a genuine flair for the idiom. And she had Mims to do her bidding: a big guy with his brains on fire because he'd found this beauty right out of some Edwardian romance. And underneath the lace and crinolines, good old American know-how. It was a winning combination. Hawkins felt an odd moment of communion with his fellow males of the species, ever vulnerable as they were to such a woman.

"You know, if you don't start doing your job, I can take this to our attorney. Maybe you people need to be sued to get serious. If that's what has to happen..."

"No, sir..."

Hawkins found himself on his feet and standing beside Mims, who obviously was in deeper shit than he knew.

"Mr. Mims," he said. Joe turned to him. "My name is Jim Hawkins, I'm a deputy district attorney here, and I've been assigned the Robert Sand murder case. "

"Yes," Joe said, and they shook hands, a nice formality to mitigate the waves of animosity in the air.

Then Hawkins also shook hands with Andrea, who looked even more young and innocent when you saw her face. It was the face of a girl, someone your natural instinct would be to protect. However, he'd been moved by a very different proprietary mission here.

"Mr. Mims," he said, "I want you to know that we take the murder investigation very seriously, and our chief suspect is, and has been all along, Mrs. Sand. I've heard you're planning to get married, and if I can, I'd like to stop you. We're very close to charging her, and if I have to, I'll charge her right away to impress on you how serious we are about this."

Once he charged her, the defense would have the right of discovery and would receive all the police reports, the taped interviews, everything. The prosecution, on the other hand, had no reciprocal discovery rights, and Gary Scherotter was a very tough defense attorney. Hawkins knew he wasn't heading up Easy Street. The only new information Hawkins would receive would come from his own ongoing investigation. On the other hand, enough was enough.

"Go ahead and charge her," Mims said. "I'm marrying her. You people haven't done your jobs. You just decided that she did it because she was there. She didn't have to call you. You haven't got anybody else, so she did it. That's not an investigation..."

"I'm sorry you feel that way, Mr. Mims," Hawkins said. "I'm going to charge her with murder, and I hope you'll give some more thought to whether you should marry Mrs. Sand. This isn't going to go away now. We think we have a pretty good case that she murdered her husband, sir."

Andrea—Hawkins realized a minute later, as she and Joe Mims walked out—hadn't said a word.

2

As a courtesy, Gary Scherotter notified the sheriff's department that he would surrender Andrea Sand at any time. Since her arrest was imminent, this gesture would be useful when it came to trying to reduce her bail amount. The call came in the afternoon on Thursday, March 25. Scherotter brought Andrea into Indio on Friday morning but asked Municipal Court Judge Philip LaRocca if he could have more time to prepare on the question of bail. LaRocca granted the request and set the arraignment for 2:45 that afternoon in Palm Springs.

Scherotter wasn't able to attend the arraignment. Instead, Rick Erwood, the other attorney in his office, was there to represent Andrea. He entered a plea of not guilty to the charges of murder and "using a deadly and dangerous weapon," an allegation that could add a year to a prison term. Deputy D.A. Chapman, representing the prosecution, requested that bail be set at $250,000. Erwood asked that Andrea be released on her own recognizance, saying Mrs. Sand would not be leaving the area. LaRocca, noting that law enforcement representatives had been in constant contact with Mrs. Sand as a suspect over the ten and a half months of the investigation, set bail at $100,000.

Andrea, wearing an off-white, wide-brimmed hat and a matching blouse and skirt, stood next to Erwood during the arraignment but didn't speak to Judge LaRocca. The preliminary hearing was set for Thursday, April 1, in Palm Springs. Andrea posted a bond for her release after she was booked into Palm Springs city jail.

The Reverend James Rehnberg of the Evangelical Free Church presided over the marriage of Joe Mack Mims and Andrea Claire Sand on the afternoon of Sunday, March 28. It was a small ceremony with members of the church attending. Betty Hawkins was a witness, along with Joe's brother, Edwin Mims. Both Andrea and Joe had lost their spouses within the past year, Andrea on May 14 to murder, and Joe on August 22 to long illness. It was his second marriage and her sixth.

On Tuesday, March 30, Detective Fred Lastar wrote his final police report on the Robert Sand murder case. He noted that on or about January 20, he had contacted Betty Jo Crane regarding information she might have about the case. Crane told him she had known Andrea from January 15, 1981, to about April 21, 1981, when Crane left the area to go to her other residence in Connecticut.

Crane told Lastar she'd observed both Robert and Andrea Sand at the Springs Tennis Club. She'd talked with Andrea, though not with Mr. Sand for any significant period of time. While she was at the courts, she observed Robert Sand yelling at Andrea while she played and thought he was a hard taskmaster. Andrea controlled her temper but appeared frustrated. Lastar asked if she'd ever seen the couple argue, and Crane said she hadn't.

Andrea had told Crane that she couldn't use a telephone in private, and couldn't have friends over, or go anywhere, without her husband. She had not known Bob Sand's first name, Crane said, until after she returned to the desert, because Andrea referred to him only as her husband. Andrea told her on one occasion that her husband was lazy and wouldn't try, and on another that he had MS and would be dying soon. When Crane told her that she knew someone with MS and he'd lived a long time with the disease, Andrea looked puzzled. Crane said she got the impression from Andrea that Robert Sand was very possessive, but she didn't feel that from seeing him.

"Crane advised," Lastar concluded, "that she also considered Andrea Sand to be a liar."

At the end of the report, Lastar typed "Status: Case Closed by Arrest."

At 5:30 in the evening on Wednesday, March 31, Deputy Darryl Czajkowski came to 6 Brandeis Court regarding a note Joe Mims had received in the mail on Tuesday at his home on Broken Arrow Trail in Palm Desert. Joe had just gotten to Andrea's when Czajkowski arrived. The note was handwritten and addressed in a bold print:

> Joe—
>
> Bet you don't wake
> up some morning
> w/ a knife in you
> gullet.
> Also, she's fairly well
> used, I know the from
> use.
>
> You dummy

Both Andrea and Joe had read and handled the letter, they told the deputy, and then contacted their attorney, Gary Scherotter. He'd advised them to call the sheriff's department.

Copies of the sheriff's department's files were turned over to Gary Scherotter. He went over the police reports, interviews, and medical records, trying to get a handle on the case, and also met with Andrea and Joe Mims in his office, sometimes along with Joe Jones, a former policeman who often did investigative work for Scherotter. Andrea asked to look over the reports, and the attorney had copies made for her. Her story wasn't an easy one because there were so many changes in it and so little supporting evidence. However, he had been hired to defend her and was obliged to take what she said on good faith, until such a time as her story might change. Every so often she would laugh in a place that didn't seem appropriate in discussing a murder case, but that wasn't anything he could do much about, either.

At the preliminary hearing on April 1, Scherotter was able to get a postponement to gather more information. He wanted an analysis of each blood spot found on the carpet the morning of the murder, which would take more time to complete. A new preliminary hearing was set for Friday, May 28.

On Wednesday evening, May 19, at 5:30, Louis DeGeus, the director of security at the Sheraton Plaza Hotel in Palm Springs, was leaving the Palm Springs Police Department on East Taquist Canyon Way, where he had picked up a burglary report. He noticed a letter on the ground outside the police station entrance and brought the envelope, which was addressed to the Palm Springs Police Department, back inside and gave it to a policeman on duty.

Inside the envelope was a handwritten note, dated May 18:

To who this may interest
    I found it by Some Garbage
I held it for as much
as I could not getting
it together to give it
to you I just no I
should. I do not want to
get involved. I am just
a nobody and old
    I donot want to
encourage any problems
I been reading my
horoscopes every day

      surely a loving
      friend citizen
      for others

The enclosed letter was written on soiled and tattered stationery from Laughlin's Riverside Resort and Casino of Laughlin, Nevada, and mailed in one of their envelopes. It was undated, written and addressed in hand to a man named Ignacio Sanchez with an address on Merle Drive in Rancho Mirage:

Iggy

    Sorry did not get to you sooner. lost your number. You get this last job done for me you wont regret. Just get the Sand girl really good this time. Don't kill her don't hurt her to much don't leave no Dam evidence just Scars.
    Drug her real good *1 thousand each man* At least 4 Do it Many times—Get it done before May 27 1 will keep tabs. I just finish here.
                regards from

The letter was signed, in a crudely executed monogram, with a capital M floating over a capital A, and under this signature were the words: "Be in town soon. Do not Goof/UP."

The next day Detective Lastar and D.A. Investigator Dan Riter picked up the letter at the Palm Springs Police Station.

At 3:30 on Thursday afternoon, Lieutenant Kennedy, who had recently been promoted, and Detective Lastar went to the address on Merle Drive to see Ignacio Sanchez. It turned out to be an expensive home in a good neighborhood. Sanchez's wife, Hilda, told the officers that her husband wasn't home but would be returning from his job at around six the following evening. After a brief interview with Mrs. Sanchez, Kennedy asked her to have her husband contact him when he got home. Kennedy would still be in the Indio office at that hour, he said.

Lastar let Deputy D.A. Hawkins know about the letter and asked him to contact Gary Scherotter about the threats against Andrea.

At 2:00 in the afternoon on Friday, May 21, Lastar got a call from Joe Mims, who told him Andrea had been kidnapped. He was going to meet Andrea for lunch between noon and three that day, Mims told Lastar, but when he arrived home and opened the garage door, he found Andrea's purse, shoes, and a broken necklace on the garage floor. On the golf cart, which was parked in the garage beside his car, he found Andrea's hat, bathing suit, and bra.

Inside the house, Joe found a note from Andrea on the refrigerator saying she had gone to the driving range. He phoned the Springs range but was told they hadn't seen her that day. Then he called Scherotter, who advised him to call the sheriff's department.

Lastar reported receiving Mims' call and was told to respond to the scene. They would also send a marked unit. Before leaving, he phoned Deputy D.A. Hawkins and requested that either he or Dan Riter go to the scene.

Lastar arrived at around 3:00, and Joe showed him what he had found in the garage and the note Andrea had written. Lastar said he'd be requesting an I.D. Tech and asked Mims to leave everything alone. When Hawkins arrived, Lastar briefed him.

Sgt. Wayne Carlson arrived and picked up the bathing suit, bra, note, necklace, shoes, and hat and dusted for latent prints on the golf cart.

Lastar told Joe an all-points bulletin would be put out on Andrea's disappearance, and all Riverside County stations would be contacted. She would be listed as a missing person under suspicious circumstances.

Lastar went to see Andrea's next-door neighbor at 3 Brandeis Court, who told him she hadn't been outside her residence that day and hadn't seen anything. The detective searched the areas around the condominium but didn't find anything.

Lastar asked Mims what Andrea had done that morning before she was supposed to go to the golf course. Joe said Andrea went to the post office to mail some things, to a printer in Rancho Mirage to have some copies made, and to a Bible study class at Betty Hawkins' home. He said that Andrea had complained to him about getting phone calls and having the other party hang up when she said hello. Mims got another of these calls that afternoon while Lastar was there.

Lastar contacted Betty Hawkins and was told Andrea had arrived at the Bible class between 10:00 and 10:30 and left at approximately 11:30. Betty also said Andrea had complained of receiving hang-up calls.

An investigator named Jim Snodgrass responded to the scene. Lastar asked him to call all the hospitals and mental health facilities in the Coachella Valley to see if Andrea was at any of them. None reported having Andrea.

At around six that evening, Lastar and Snodgrass stopped at the Sanchez home to see if Ignacio Sanchez had returned. Hilda Sanchez said her husband hadn't gotten back yet, but that she would have him call the detectives as soon as he arrived.

At ten minutes before seven, Ignacio Sanchez called Lastar, and the detective told him he wanted to see him right away at the Indio Station.

Sanchez, a quiet-spoken middle-aged Latino-American, arrived at 7:15 and was taken to the interview room by Lastar. Lastar told him why he had wanted to see him, and why it was urgent, and showed Sanchez the letter and envelope addressed to him.

Sanchez said he didn't know anything about the letter and didn't know the sender. Did he know anybody with the initials M. A.? Lastar asked. No he didn't, Sanchez said.

Did he know anyone who called him Iggy?

No one, Sanchez said.

Lastar said that, according to what Sanchez's wife had told them on Thursday, some friends of theirs in San Diego called him Iggy. Sanchez said, yes, that was true. He'd forgotten about it because he didn't have much contact with them. It was a couple, Dave and Dolly Johnson, and Dave Johnson worked for J. H. Youngsdale Construction in San Diego.

Lastar asked him where he had been that day, and Sanchez said he'd worked in San Fernando until around three. He was a painting contractor and had a contract to paint the Chatsworth High School. Sanchez's son, who was also named Ignacio, was painting the San Fernando High School. He gave Lastar the names of the plant managers at both high schools to verify that he and his son were working there.

Lastar asked Sanchez if he knew anyone at the Springs Country Club. Sanchez said he didn't. The detective asked if he knew anyone who worked at the Springs, and Sanchez said that to the best of his knowledge he didn't.

Did Sanchez know or had he ever heard of Andrea Sand? No, he hadn't, Sanchez said. Lastar told him that she had been arrested for the murder of her husband. Sanchez said he remembered once he'd gone out to breakfast and read about her in a newspaper, but he knew nothing else about her and to the best of his knowledge had never seen her.

The detective asked Sanchez to have his son call him.

Just before nine, after Sanchez had left, Lastar called Joe Mims and asked if he'd heard anything from or about Andrea. Joe said no. He'd found Andrea's house key under a box of Kleenex, where she usually left it when she went to the golf course.

Lastar told Mims to contact him right away if Andrea returned home.

4

At a quarter to one that night, Lastar got a call from the station asking him to respond to the Mims residence. Andrea had returned.

On his way over, the detective stopped at the Country Club Lane gate to the Springs and talked with a guard there named Erwin Koenig. Lastar asked if anyone had walked into the Springs within the past hour and a half and told Koenig he was specifically interested in Mrs. Mims. Koenig said he hadn't seen anyone, and they contacted the other Springs gates by phone. No one at any of the gates had seen Andrea return.

Indio Sheriff's Deputy Janet Rubien responded to 6 Brandeis Court at 1:00 a.m. She was let into the house by Joe Mims. Andrea was lying spread-eagled on the living room floor wearing a blue golf shirt with a green skirt and holding a scarf. A second scarf was tied loosely on her right wrist. She wasn't wearing shoes.

Deputy D.A. Hawkins was also there and told Rubien that Detective Lastar was on his way.

When Lastar arrived, Joe told him that Andrea had arrived home at around 12:30 a.m., having been kidnapped and raped, and she had brought home a piece of paper that belonged to one of the suspects.

He was very angry.

"None of you believe Andrea," he said, "and this keeps on happening, over and over again. And it's because you're not doing your jobs. I want some action on this, real action, immediately. This *can't* keep happening."

Lastar said Andrea should be taken to Eisenhower Medical Center for an exam. They would continue their investigation as soon as they had information from her on the incident.

Joe Mims seemed sadder than ever to Jim Hawkins, who told him the district attorney's office would also investigate the incident. Hawkins said he would personally see that his people took the case very seriously.

Dr. Harold Tarleton examined Andrea at the medical center and completed the sexual assault kit. Andrea told Deputy Rubien that she felt drugged, and the story she told the deputy was vague and out of sequence.

She was at a friend's house within the Springs Country Club that morning, Andrea told Rubien, and returned home some time between ten and noon. She parked in the garage and unlocked a small door behind which she kept her golf cart. She went into the house, changed clothes, ate, and left a note for her husband to meet her at the driving range. She expected him to be home between noon and one.

Then she went into the garage to get the golf cart. Suddenly she was grabbed from behind by an unidentified male suspect who put his hand over her mouth. Another man was also present, she told Rubien. First she said she didn't see either suspect, but later in the interview she remembered they were wearing ski masks.

The men took her to a four-door car she couldn't identify, and the suspect who had grabbed her got into the backseat with her. He blindfolded her and pushed her to the floorboard.

"Lie still and you won't be hurt," he said.

They drove for ten or fifteen minutes before arriving at an unknown residence and pulling into a garage.

Inside the house, Andrea was told to take off her clothes and was given an injection of something in her right arm.

One of what were now three suspects raped her on the carpeted floor.

Then she was taken outside and forced to give head to all three suspects.

Then one of the suspects went into the swimming pool with her.

After getting out of the pool, she lay down on the deck for about half an hour.

She was taken inside the house again. She asked for a glass of water but was given a glass of beer, which she drank.

After drinking the beer, she fell asleep on the carpet.

She was woken up by one of the suspects, who was lying beside her. He raped her and cut her with an unknown sharp object on both breasts and both outer thighs.

The cuts turned out to be minor and didn't require special medical attention.

Andrea told Deputy Rubien she was raped several times—including anally—during the period she was at the residence, but she couldn't remember specific details of any of the rapes and couldn't distinguish which suspects committed which acts.

Finally, she was told to get dressed, after which her hands were bound behind her back with a scarf.

She was taken outside and put back into the car.

They drove for about five minutes and dropped her off on a side street somewhere in the Cathedral City area.

Though Andrea was still blindfolded and her hands loosely bound, she was able to remove both the blindfold and the scarf.

She couldn't remember who she was, she told Rubien, but when she stopped at Nastys, after she had danced with a couple of men, a waiter recognized her, and her identity and address came back to her.

She walked to Highway 111 and continued home. She entered the Springs Country Club at the Country Club Drive gate. She didn't stop at the gate but went directly home.

"Mims' account of her ordeal," Deputy Rubien wrote in the police report she filed, "is disjointed and vague. She advised she was kept blindfolded throughout the captivity, including when she was in the swimming pool, and at another point when she was forced to take a shower. For that reason, she is unable to provide suspect descriptions. However, she was able to pick up a piece of paper while in the residence, and to remove some cash from a wallet. She put the items in the pocket of her golf skirt, which she was able to locate between the time she was told to undress and dress.

"Mims advised she believed the suspects were either Mexicans 'playing around,' or others pretending to be Mexicans, by their accents. The only conversation they had with her was to give her instructions. She said they kept referring to her by her former married name of Sand, and that one of the suspects told her her initials were almost like his own.

"Although Mims advised she had walked barefoot from Cathedral City to Rancho Mirage, her feet appeared unscathed on the bottoms except for one blister on the right foot.

"Mims was asked why she did not attempt to get help once she was released. She said she was anxious to get home."

In the report Dr. Tarleton wrote at Eisenhower Medical Center, under "Diagnostic Impressions of Trauma and Injuries," he noted: "There is no physical evidence of recent intercourse. I feel the wounds are self-inflicted."

The piece of paper Andrea said she found turned out to be a bill from Gloria Becker Music, a local booking agency, for an appearance by the Bob Rinard Trio at the Gene Autry Hotel in Palm Springs on April 29. Dan Riter contacted Gloria Becker at her office in Palm Desert and Robert Scholl of the Garrett Corporation in Los Angeles, which had paid for the appearance with a check for $455 written on May 10. In a letter dated June 2, Scholl wrote Riter that their bank had advised that the check was paid on May 18. Gloria Becker told Riter that the receipt may have been mistakenly put out in her trash, where someone could have picked it up.

5

A little after 2:30 in the afternoon on Thursday, May 27, Deputy Cynthia Sjoquist met with Springs security guard John Newton in front of 6 Brandeis Court. Springs security had called the sheriff's department after Andrea reported she'd been beaten up.

A few minutes before Sjoquist arrived, Newton had checked around the house and seen Andrea sunbathing in the walled-in patio at the rear. The stereo was on and a portable manual alarm was sounding. Newton shouted to Andrea, but she hadn't heard him.

Before going further, Sjoquist talked with a gardener working next door. The gardener told her he'd been going back and forth to his truck parked in the driveway since 12:30 and hadn't seen anyone or heard anything unusual at 6 Brandeis Court.

The deputy and security guard walked around to the rear of the house, where they saw Andrea lying on a lawn chair. Sjoquist shouted to her but got no response. She appeared to be asleep.

Sjoquist and Newton returned to the front of the house. When Sgt. Robert Kirby arrived from Indio Station, he and Sjoquist went back to the rear of the house and climbed over the gate.

Andrea lay on her back in the sun. There was dried blood on the right side of her chin and above her right eye. There was broken glass on the patio beside the lawn chair. The stereo was on and a transistor-sized alarm was going off.

Her eyelids were fluttering. Sergeant Kirby and Deputy Sjoquist tried to rouse her, and after a moment she opened her eyes and sat up.

She didn't remember what had happened. She only remembered lying in the sun on her stomach half-asleep when a man grabbed her right arm. He jerked her off the lawn chair, punched her in the jaw, and threw her up against the wall of the house. She didn't see him, she told Kirby and Sjoquist, so she couldn't give a description of him.

As Mims sat forward, Sjoquist noticed several scratches on her back. There was dried blood on a couple of them. The scratches were in the middle of her back, between her shoulder blades. They were straight lined—sometimes crisscrossing other straight-lined scratches.

Sjoquist asked how Andrea had gotten help.

A guard had called, she said, and she told him she had been beaten up. The guard asked if an alarm was going off, and Andrea said yes, she had set off her portable alarm before passing out.

Sergeant Kirby asked Andrea if she could remember anything at all about the assault. This time she described her assailant. He was white, she said, with a mustache, black hair, and an average build, and was "wholesome looking."

Andrea thought she was attacked around 1:00, or maybe 12:30, but couldn't be sure.

The broken glass was from a water glass she'd been using. She didn't remember how it was broken.

Sylvia, Robert and Florence Sand.

Andrea Claire with sons Guy (right) and Douglas.

Andrea and Robert Sand on their wedding day.

Andrea and Robert Sand at the Springs.

Outside and inside the
Springs condominium at 6
Brandeis Court . . .

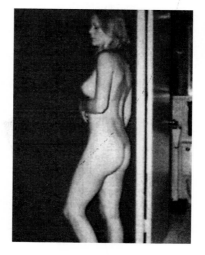

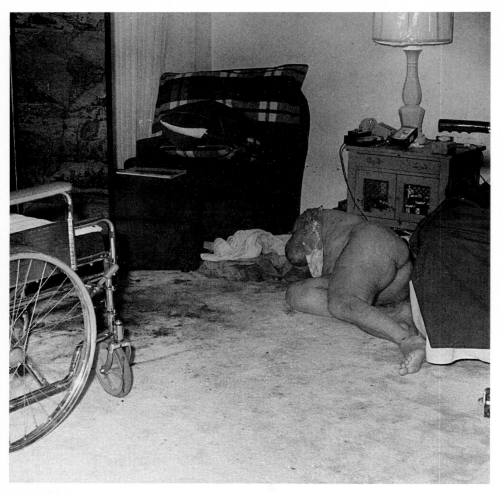

The master bedroom . . .

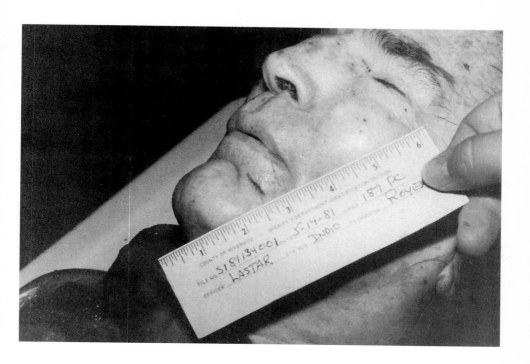

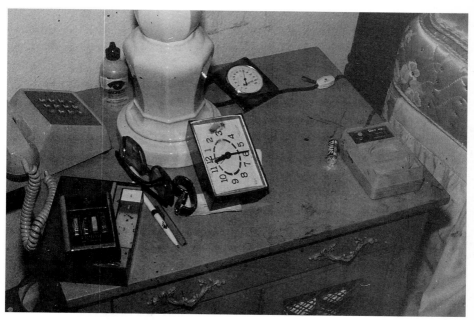

. . . at 6 Brandeis Court.

Aerial view of the Springs with 6 Brandeis Court circled.

Sheriff's Department, Indio Station. Front row: Fred Lastar (first on left), Larry Pedone (center), Colleen Word Walker (third from right).

Part of a message mailed to Joe Mims and turned over to the police by Andrea.

Sjoquist noticed what appeared to be dried blood smeared on the wall near where Andrea was sunbathing.

Sergeant Kirby and Deputy Sjoquist went through the patio doors to check the house, and Andrea came in after them. Her purse, sitting open on the kitchen counter, was missing twenty-five dollars, Andrea said. She also told the officers she had left neither the patio doors nor her purse open.

Andrea brought the officers an envelope addressed to Joe Mims, containing several sheets of notepaper with large block printing on them. It had come in the mail that day, she told them, and she had opened it. There was a threat against her in it, she said.

The envelope and pages were taken as evidence. D.A. Investigator Dan Riter arrived as Deputy Sjoquist and Sergeant Kirby were leaving.

Dan Riter hadn't seen Andrea since the day she peered over the fence and waved at him when he was on stakeout on top of the garage on Country Club Lane.

Just after he arrived, Andrea fainted on the living room floor. She was wearing a one-piece bathing suit, and Riter was the only one there, which immediately struck him as the sort of situation that could lead to trouble. He could be accused of many things, rape, fondling, who knew what. He took out his portable tape-recorder and began speaking into it.

"Mrs. Mims has fainted in her living room. This is D.A. Investigator Riter. I'm walking over to Mrs. Mims on the floor...I'm picking up her left wrist now to take her pulse...Her pulse seems steady...I'm getting up now to go to the washroom and get a washcloth and see if I can revive Mrs. Mims with a cold compress..."

After another few moments narrated by Riter, Andrea revived.

I.D. Tech David Pong arrived and photographed the victim and the scene.

Deputy Sjoquist spoke with Robert Hoffman, a security dispatcher at the Springs. He told the deputy he called 6 Brandeis Court at 2:22 that afternoon to let the owner know an Arrowhead Water truck was coming in to make a delivery. However, before Hoffman could say anything, a female said "I've been beat up." Hoffman said he would call the sheriff's department. He told Sjoquist he heard what sounded like an alarm in the background but didn't ask the woman about it.

At 3:30, Deputy Sjoquist contacted Registered Nurse Maureen Dodd and Dr. Alan Bayer at the Eisenhower Medical Center. The deputy asked whether it would be possible for a person who had been knocked unconscious by a blow to have fluttering eyelids. Both Dodd and Bayer said that if the individual were really unconscious and not faking, there shouldn't be any movement. However, if the person were having a seizure, even if unconscious, such a movement could occur. Dr. Bayer added that he would have to examine the person to be certain of anything.

The next day the D.A.'s office requested and received the letter addressed to Joe Mims that the sheriff's department had taken as evidence. Hawkins and Riter examined it. It had a Long Beach postmark. On two sheets of four-by-five-inch notepaper, in large block print, was handwritten:

> YOUR WIFE
> IS A GONN-
> ER. IF THE LAW
> DON'T GET HER
> I WILL. I WILL
> GET MY REVENGE.
>
> (new page)
> HAHA MAMA
> FROM

BOB SAND'S
★ KILLER ★
YOU WILL NEVER
GET ME. HAHA

To the right of the word "FROM" was the same monogram with M floating over A used as the signature in the letter addressed to Ignacio Sanchez. The rest of the pieces of paper were half-size, four by two and a half inches, with even fewer words printed on them.

YOU GOT
YOU PAY
FEEL GOOD
★
HE HURT
US & NOW
YOU MUST PAY

HE LIED
HE PAID
WITH HIS LIFE
★
HE DESTROY
NOW WE
DESTROY

Later that day, looking over the I.D. Tech's photographs, Riter, Campbell, and Hawkins could make out the initials M and A in the scratches on Andrea's back. If you held it in a mirror, Riter pointed out, it would look like A M, Andrea's initials. Hawkins remembered that one of the men who'd abducted her had said her initials were a lot like his. And there was the monogram on the recently received letters.

On Friday, May 28, Gary Scherotter was allowed another extension on the preliminary hearing. All the blood spots on the carpet were not yet analyzed. The longer they waited, Hawkins figured, the crazier it got.

Riter and I.D. Tech Pong drove to Phoenix, Arizona, the next day to have an expert examine the letter Joe Mims had gotten. They had a nyhindrin test machine that was able to pick up impressions left on the notepaper from pages above those on which the letter to Joe had been written. They picked up a grocery list that could have been written in Andrea's hand, but the evidence was inconclusive.

"It's getting so if he touches me, I jump," Andrea said to Gary Scherotter one afternoon in his office with Joe sitting beside her. "And I love Joe. And I hate to have this happen to us."

Scherotter knew he badly needed a psychological assessment of Andrea. When she brought up the trouble she was having in her relationship with Joe, apparently because of the effect of the rapes on her, he took the opportunity to suggest that it might be good for her to go to a therapist.

Joe helpfully concurred and had a health plan, Aetna, that would cover the costs. Andrea said she didn't want to go back to Dr. Morton Kurland, whom she found upsetting. Did Gary know of another doctor she might try? Gary suggested one he knew of in Riverside, but Andrea didn't want to drive that far. He also brought up Michael Leitman.

VII

1

As the first step in his treatment of Andrea Sand, Dr. Michael Leitman, a thirty-nine-year-old psychologist with a practice in Palm Desert, administered the following tests to her on Monday, June 7, and Wednesday, June 9: the Wechsler Adult Intelligence Scale—Revised; Minnesota Multiphasic Personality Inventory; Thematic Apperception test; Rorschach test; Bender Visual Motor Gestalt test; Sentence Completion test; Word Association test; Hand test; Clinical Interview and Behavioral Observation.

At Gary Scherotter's request, Leitman then wrote a psychological profile, noting at the beginning that "the long term effects" of the rapes and assaults Mrs. Mims had reported since her previous husband's death "have interfered with her relationship with Mr. Mims."

He described the patient's behavior during the testing:

> Mrs. Mims was cooperative and enthusiastic. She frequently commented on her own performance and often made statements about the "craziness" of her answers. In addition, whenever possible, she would interject a statement about her personal life. For the most part, the connection between her interjection and the task at hand was frequently very tangential and loosely associated. In addition, Mrs. Mims talked to herself while working on many of the testing tasks.
>
> On the whole, Mrs. Mims presented herself as a charming and adaptable woman during the

administration of highly structured psychological tests (those in which the task and expectations are clearly defined). At all times she appeared appropriately oriented to time, place, and person.

However, Mrs. Mims' performance on less structured tests vastly differed from this. While she appeared to remain appropriately oriented, her test responses became disjointed and, at times, inappropriate. Although she was aware that her performance was not comforming to what others might expect, she demonstrated neither the capacity nor the inclination to contain her deteriorating performance.

Her score in the performance phase of the intelligence test was "Very Superior," 130, but only "Average," 101, in the verbal phase, with a full-scale IQ score of 116, which was in the "High Average" range. The disparity between her performance and verbal IQ scores could be interpreted in two ways, Leitman wrote: "It could be viewed as an indication of a thought disorder. It could also be seen as a manifestation of the woman's lack of formal education," which had ended after the ninth grade.

Under the heading "Interpersonal Relationships," the doctor wrote:

When Mrs. Mims is attempting to approach another person in order to establish a relationship and to fulfill her intense needs to feel close to someone, she will either deny their negative characteristics or project those characteristics onto another person. During this period in her courtship with a new friend or lover, Mrs. Mims will typically be willing, at those times, to perform acts and participate in behavior which is not of her choosing or preference. She will allow herself to be imposed upon for the sake of her new "friend."

Ironically, the thing she needs the most is that which she cannot tolerate achieving. Mrs. Mims desperately seeks someone whom she can trust and upon whom she can lean. However, as soon as she senses she is achieving this, she feels like the relationship and the person are going to suffocate her.

Leitman noted under "Pertinent Psychodynamic Issues" that Mrs. Mims' inability to accept both "good" and "bad" or positive and negative aspects in an individual or a situation rendered her "incapable of tolerating ambivalent situations or experience and [made] her markedly vulnerable to serious deterioration in functioning at times of intense anxiety or emotional conflict." A personality structure of this type, he wrote, "is most often seen in persons diagnosed with borderline personality disorders."

This characterization, Leitman knew, would be extremely significant to Gary Scherotter. More serious than other mental disorders such as the hysteric or the histrionic personality types listed in *The Diagnostic and Statistical Manual of Mental Disorders, Edition III*, borderline personality could comprise an insanity defense.

Summarizing the results of the tests, Leitman wrote:

Mrs. Mims' test responses suggest she has a fragile personality integration which is subject to rapid deterioration under intense emotional pressure. Deterioration is manifested in a variety of areas— in the quality of her thought processes, reality testing, judgment, concentration, memory and impulse control.

In order to defend herself against intense emotional pressures, the woman creates her own reality through distortion and fantasy and then processes information filtered through her "new reality." However, this maneuver frequently fails to protect her. Mrs. Mims is constantly receiving feedback from her environment which contradicts her subjective reality. This, in turn, heightens the woman's anxiety and contributes to further deterioration of her functioning.

Mrs. Mims cannot tolerate her own negative feelings. Thus, in order to defend against these feelings, Mrs. Mims will most likely project those feelings onto the person or situation which engenders them. She then tends to deal with her projected feelings as if they emanate from outside of her and are directed at her with hostile intent. Mrs. Mims then has to defend herself against what she perceives to be an external attack.

When not under intense emotional pressure, Mrs. Mims demonstrates a "charming" personality style which masks her pathology. This strength can be seen in her ability to make new friends and to appear "normal" when she feels she is in control of her life.

Given the pervasive capacity for deterioration in Mrs. Mims' level of functioning, her erratic loss of adequate and appropriate reality testing and her inability to provide or attain appropriate corrective feedback for her hehavior, Mrs. Mims is subject to intermittent psychotic episodes. These episodes are most likely provoked by intense emotions, ambivalent situations which increase the woman's anxiety, and the experience of negative emotions in a situation in which she cannot escape, deny certain feelings or project her feelings successfully.

At the end of the report, Leitman suggested that psychotherapy might not be an adequate course of treatment:

> Although it is possible that Mrs. Mims could be able to utilize the therapeutic alliance offered in intensive psychotherapy to help contain her anxiety, certain pitfalls in the therapeutic process can be anticipated. A strong negative transference is likely and will be difficult to contain on an outpatient basis. At the height of the negative transference, Mrs. Mims may react to the therapist as if he/she has either betrayed her or is attacking her. When this happens, Mrs. Mims could either terminate treatment, deteriorate into a psychotic episode or attempt to defend herself against her negative perception of the therapist by attempting to harm him or her. Thus, the best mode of treatment would be long term hospitalization in which Mrs. Mims could be protected against her own intense feelings and other people could be protected against her actions. In this protected environment, Mrs. Mims would have a chance to work through her serious emotional conflict.

Despite these reservations, Leitman began to see Andrea regularly on an outpatient basis, with the idea of trying to contain some of her anxiety until some further determination on her case was made.

2

For Deputy D.A. Jim Hawkins, the issue continued to be how they could catch Andrea in a lie. She would stage a rape or an assault around the day of, say, a preliminary hearing, the next one being June 24. She'd just done it for the one on May 28. Unfortunately, they hadn't had her staked out. The question was whether they could come up with some way to push her buttons so that she'd do it again, and this time they'd be there.

The night he'd shown up after the last kidnapping, the guard at the Springs gate had recognized Hawkins' green Porsche 911 and waved him through saying "Again?"

And then there was Andrea, spread-eagled on the living room floor in some kind of tennis outfit with her underwear showing. It was sports underwear, so maybe it wasn't supposed to be provocative. A couple of weeks earlier, he'd gone over with Dan Riter, investigating another incident, and she'd answered the door in white pants with no underwear on. You could see her bush through the pants. Then she showed them a lock on a sliding glass door, bending over and making sure they got everything.

"If this keeps going on," she said to them, "I'm going to commit suicide. I can't stand it anymore."

She must have felt she had the two of them very well in hand.

He wanted a psychiatrist who could analyze the police reports and tell him what was actually going on. If they could catch her in a phony incident, they could break her story and go from there to discredit her testimony on the murder. Otherwise, the only evidence they had was circumstantial, pointing to her by exclusion mainly, and that might not be enough, especially with Gary Scherotter.

The Department of Justice criminalist, Steve Secofsky, had called before the last prelim and said "Hey, Jim, are they really going to make me analyze every last one of these drops?"

But in court Gary just said, "What if a third blood type shows up, and that's the assailant?" The judge went with it, which was just as well. It was the kind of issue they could use for an appeal.

Hawkins didn't have a high opinion of any of the court-appointed shrinks in the area. For one thing, they all tended to favor the defendant. He checked with the chief D.A.'s office in Riverside and asked, first, if he could have some money to pay a psychiatrist for a reading on Andrea, and second, if they could recommend someone who was decent. He got a yes on both, and the shrink's name was Dr. Anthony Oliver in Riverside. They had used him in cases up there. Hawkins had the whole file sent to him.

On Wednesday, June 9, while Dr. Leitman was administering the second day of tests to Andrea, D.A. Investigator Dan Riter talked to Dr. Oliver on the phone.

"I do have a number of opinions on the case," the forty-one-year-old psychiatrist told Riter in his crisp English accent. "And obviously one has to feel a certain reluctance about drawing them. But I think that the data leaves me very little choice...You asked me, number one, what is her problem?"

"Yes," Riter said.

"You are dealing here with an extremely hysterical personality. Number one. One of the most important clues, by the way, to this, is the episode of the amnesia. That is a psychogenic amnesia, very close to a fugue state. Interestingly enough, in a psychogenic fugue, where somebody loses memory for their own identity, they sometimes take up a new one in the fugue, and they may travel to another part of the country and take up a new identity and be totally unaware of their previous life. And that's a situation, not uncommonly, though it's a rare condition, where people have been known to act out in a very violent way. To what extent that's also associated with a psychogenic amnesia state is less certain. But that was a psychogenic amnesia, it had nothing to do with concussion, and I was amazed that the doctors who saw her at Riverside General Hospital, none of them seemed to make the diagnosis..."

"Right," Riter said. The guy would obviously make a very strong expert witness; he'd gone from zero to sixty in thirty seconds.

"It was a psychogenic amnesia, and that is a dissociative disorder, which is a form of conversion hysteria. Interestingly enough, another area of that same kind of pathology and situation—hysterical, amnestic type of syndrome—is the multiple personality..."

"Uh-hunh," Riter said.

Then Oliver went into how he'd demolished a multiple-personality defense in a recent murder trial.

"Some of the information you're giving me in this case," Oliver said, "would certainly raise in my mind a tremendous index of suspicion that we might be dealing with a similar type of dissociative disorder. Now, in the trial I felt it was unauthentic, I felt it was a malingered situation. But it would certainly be one of the considerations I would have with this individual."

So she was crazy? Riter wondered to himself

The doctor suggested that Riter might want to look up the dissociative disorders section in the *Diagnostic and Statistical Manual of Mental Disorders, Edition III.* Then he said that, as yet, there was no evidence of Andrea being psychotic, but there were clear indications of psychosexual conflict and sexual masochistic traits, not the least being her obsession with anal penetration.

"Is it serious?" Oliver went on, in his accelerated lecture-hall style. "Well, most of the time, she's likely to function in a perfectly normal manner. But the potential for seriousness, yes, is very great. If she were stressed, under various circumstances, then just about anything could happen. It's technically possible that she could have a psychotic break and become quite disturbed from reality. But in my own experience, this doesn't happen too frequently."

"Okay," Riter said. If she happened to have had a psychotic break on the night of the murder, as Oliver knew, it would render his testimony as an expert witness for the prosecution of no value.

"What will happen or could happen next?" Oliver asked rhetorically. "I would not want to go to bed with her."

Riter laughed. The guy could be entertaining, too.

"It may be that I would like to have a liaison with her," Oliver said, not acknowledging the laughter, "but I would not want to sleep and fall asleep with her. Let me make that clear. The fact that she could have done it once means that she could do it again. And if that behavior is part of a disorder, such as the type I described, where, in essence, it's not a motivated, conscious, rational approach for personal gain, but an act that comes while she's, if you like, she's deranged—maybe that's not the best word—but in an altered state of consciousness, then of course it could occur again. That's the big issue. To what extent—if she was responsible—was her killing of her husband motivated for personal gain? To what extent did she benefit from it?"

Riter told him that she was currently receiving $3,000 a month as a widow's benefit until the estate was settled and had received approximately $30,000 from an initial distribution of the $150,000 Robert Sand had left her in the codicil attached to his will.

One other thing to consider, Oliver said, was that Joe Mims might be in danger and should be warned.

"There is a chance," Oliver said, "that she may want to try to arrange for his death in a manner that might make it look as though he met his death in a similar way to her husband, to try to give herself an alibi. One possibility is if she could find somebody to actually murder him."

Riter told Oliver that they had tried to talk to Joe Mims, but he wasn't about to listen to anybody.

3

Joe Mims didn't think it was a good idea for Andrea, with the charge of murder hanging over her, to be in contact with Richard Cordine, a convict in a Nevada prison. Cordine would call collect every now and then, he knew, though it was usually when Joe wasn't around. Andrea would accept the calls and talk with him. It didn't seem right, and Joe talked about it with her, and, suggested it wasn't a good association for her, especially not right now.

The preliminary hearing was coming up on the twenty-fourth of June, although Gary would probably get another extension. Meanwhile, Joe had a big job, installing forty pumps at Camp Pendleton Marine Base, and had to be gone every day. He hated to leave Andrea every morning, never knowing what might happen.

On Tuesday, June 22, at 11:15 in the morning, Jim Hawkins tried calling Joe Mims to tell him how things were panning out in the investigation he'd promised he'd undertake with his own investigator in the D.A.'s office. He didn't have good news— every lead turned into a quick dead end. But he wanted Mims to know that he'd honored his pledge to him.

Instead of Mims, Hawkins got Andrea. The next thing he knew, or maybe it was with his own collaboration, he was in a conversation with her that went on, and on, and on. She liked to talk, and he figured he might as well listen. Maybe things would suddenly come into focus. Or maybe she'd trip up somewhere along the line and spill the beans. It was strictly against Gary Scherotter's orders, he knew, that she would talk to him at all. He was the prosecuting attorney in her murder trial. But that didn't hold her back. And on some level, he was still trying to get a handle on it—the case, and Andrea herself, both of which only seemed to get weirder. Where was she coming from, as they used to say? What was it all about?

"I'm seeing a psychologist because of things like this," she said after being told Dr. Tarleton's report stated there was no evidence of intercourse. "Because I know those men were not wearing rubbers. When I hear something like that, I feel like I'm going crazy."

They talked about the receipt she'd picked up at the place she'd been taken by her abductors. He told her it was for payment of a trio of musicians at a hotel.

"Was the trio girls?" she asked.

He told her they weren't girls.

Gary Scherotter, she told Hawkins, was worried that every time she told the police or the D.A.'s office about an incident, they thought she was only making it up.

Gary was an honorable man, Hawkins thought.

"I couldn't take a knife and cut myself," Andrea said. "I'd pass out. One report said I didn't have any cuts on my right arm. That's because my right arm was being held back. It got hurt, too. And now it's hurting my tennis game."

At the beginning of the conversation she'd talked about being run off the road in her car a week earlier by three men in the same car in which she'd been abducted. She hadn't reported the incident, she said, because no one believed her anyway. Hawkins tried to get as specific as he could about the incident, but she couldn't identify the men and hadn't gotten a license number.

When their conversation, getting on to an hour and a half, was close to the end—Hawkins wanted to get some lunch before going out to a new murder site in the mountains—Andrea told him the men had actually done more than just force her off the road. They'd abducted her, put her in the backseat of their car, and mauled her, but not raped her.

When they were stopped for a light, she punched the man with her in the backseat in the groin as hard as she could and bolted from the car, running for her life.

"I think it was the groin. It was about six inches below his belly button. I think that's where the groin is."

Had she seen any of the men? Hawkins asked.

They were all wearing ski masks, she said. They might not have been wearing them when she was in the backseat, on her stomach on the floorboards.

"The police would pull them right over," Hawkins said. "Three guys driving a car wearing ski masks..."

Ski masks again. It was as if she was some exotic species of bird with very bright plumage none of them had ever seen before.

Where had she gotten out of the car?

It was somewhere on Highway 111, but she quickly ran from there.

"I was jumping over stuff, running," she said. "I didn't know I had it in me. Whew!" she said, laughing a little.

4

On Tuesday afternoon, July 20, Investigator Rudy Garcia took a call at the Indio Sheriff's Station from a Richard Cordine in Nevada State Prison. Cordine eventually told Garcia he had information that would lead to the conviction of Andrea Mims for the murder of Robert Sand.

The next morning, Deputy D.A. Jim Hawkins and Lt. Jim Kennedy set up a conference call with Cordine. When they got him on the phone, Hawkins identified himself and said they were ready to come up to see him but wanted to be sure the information was worth a trip. He asked if the warden was in the room, and Cordine said he'd just left.

"Isn't there something you could tell me about the information," Hawkins said, "so we know we're not wasting our time."

"Yeah, well, I mean..." Cordine said. "What are you searching for, I mean? What do you want me to say?"

"Well," Hawkins said, "we're prosecuting Andrea for the murder, and we need evidence that will help us convict her."

"Well, you have it," Cordine said.

"In what form?" Hawkins said. "If you don't want to play your hand, just give us a clue so we'll know whether it's worth it."

Cordine said Andrea had told him in a telephone conversation what she intended to do to Robert Sand. Hawkins asked Cordine how long he had known Andrea. Cordine answered that they had never met, only corresponded. Hawkins established that Cordine had been paroled on a sentence of fifteen years for armed robbery and was now serving five years for getting drunk and walking away from a work-release program. He'd served two and a half years and had another eighteen months to max out that sentence.

"And you're doing concurrent time on something out of New Jersey?" Hawkins said.

"Yeah."

"And what do you want from us in exchange?" Hawkins asked.

"Well, you know..." Cordine began another verbal shuffle. "I can't tell you, you know. At this particular time, I'm at a disadvantage here. I cannot go into detail. If you want to pursue this, fine. If you don't want to pursue it, well, that's up to you..."

Hawkins said of course they wanted to pursue it, but it would be expensive to have them fly up there, and if they got up there, and...

"Well, I told you that it would be worth your while," Cordine said. "Now, if you want to put any validity to that, fine. If you don't, well, hey...I can't..."

Hawkins asked if he wanted to serve his time in California. Did he tell Investigator Garcia that?

"Well, look, I don't want to discuss that thing at any great length. The negotiations are very minute, and it's not going to cost you anything."

Lieutenant Kennedy wanted to confirm that Andrea had told Cordine what she intended to do to Robert Sand.

"Absolutely," Cordine said. "No question."

"And have you had any conversations since the homicide that had to do with the homicide?"

Mostly in letters, Cordine said. "We tried not to talk about that," he said, "because...the situation...you know, it's been about a year now."

"Has she ever actually admitted it to you?" Hawkins asked.

"Yeah."

Hawkins said that they had details about the homocide that only the killer knew and asked Cordine whether he had any information of that sort that would verify what Andrea had told him.

Cordine said he did.

$$5$$

He was tall, six feet four or five,. with a long gray beard, and very skinny. To Dan Riter, who came along on Thursday with Jim Hawkins and Jim Kennedy to interview Cordine, he was a typical con, not a really bad con, just somebody who was working the system for anything he could get out of it.

They went outside in the visiting area and sat down on the grass under a tree. It was a sunny day up in the eighties. They turned on the tape recorder a little after 3:00 in the afternoon.

"Let me really get it verbatim as to what she had said," Cordine said, only a few minutes into the interview. "She asked me, she said, 'Richard, have you ever killed anybody?' And I said, 'Of course not, no. Why, man?' And then she said, 'Can you still function if you are under sedatives?' And I said, 'It all depends on how many you take.' And she said, in a joking way— this is what confused me, she said it in a joking way—she said, 'Well, I tried to poison this old crippled bastard.'"

"Was this in a phone conversation?" Hawkins asked.

"Yeah," Cordine said. "I says, 'What?' She said, 'You don't know what it is to live with this bastard. I feel like I'm constantly a maid. I married him for luxury, not to become somebody's slave.' She says, 'I gotta think of a way to kill him.' And at that time, I didn't put any validity in this at all."

After the murder, he said, Andrea had complained to him about the police hounding her.

"'Andrea,' I said, 'did you kill your husband?' 'No,' she said. 'No, no.' But then, she said 'I might have.'"

"That's what she said? This was on a phone conversation?" Kennedy asked.

Cordine nodded. He took out a letter from Andrea and read from it:

> Sorry I haven't written but I haven't been in any shape for anything. I haven't ever felt like getting up in the morning. I am well and I am staying close to God. But I think I'm becoming a recluse. I was raped and cut up again. I didn't handle it as well as I let on I did. No one really knows what I'm feeling and I refuse to go to a shrink. You can't even know what it's like, what I'm feeling.

"Now, here's what's confusing," Cordine said. "I haven't made heads or tails out of this."

> I'm feeling like some man I smiled at got the idea he was going to do me a favor getting rid of my husband, and thought he could have me, and is angry he can't.

Cordine laughed and inhaled. "I don't know," he said, "I'm not a psychiatrist, psychologist...That really blew my mind.

"It kept on botherin' me, and botherin' me, and botherin' me," he said. "See, I've been in trouble all my life, man, but I've never killed anybody, nor could I bring myself to it. I've been drunk enough, when I was driving a car, to accidentally kill somebody, you know, on the road or something.

"I'm a chronic alcoholic, and when I walked away, I went back to to New Jersey and started working again. But I continued my pattern of drinking. And I walked into the bank that I had my son's account in—who is now deceased—and I knew everybody there, because I'd had a barber shop there for about seven years. And I knew everybody in the bank, and I even asked for the president and everything. I was almost approaching the state of comatose, but they said the bank president was at another bank now. And when they gave me the money, I didn't take the money. I just reached in the drawer, and took the rest of the money, and said that wasn't enough, and I walked out.

"They arrested me within fifteen minutes, you know. But like, everybody couldn't believe it. They didn't even know I was in prison, or on an escape status, or walked away, or anything. And when they did find out, they said, 'Whoa, this guy hasn't learned his lesson yet, so we're gonna give him additional time.' And they did."

"Can you pinpoint when you had that conversation?" Hawkins asked.

"When she said, 'I've gotta find a way to kill my husband'?" Cordine said. "Had to be early April."

"Early April. When—this year?"

"No," Cordine said. "Nineteen seventy-nine—wait, wait a minute—eighty—we're in eighty-two now. It had to be early April eighty-one. It had to be."

Cordine said there were times prior to Robert Sand's death when Andrea was so depressed that she wouldn't talk to him when he called.

"When's the last time you talked to her?" Hawkins asked.

"Yesterday," he said.

The conversation had to do with Cordine's ex-roommate, David Aldors. He had been shipped to a California prison, and Cordine might be shipped there, too. However, if Aldors was coming back to Nevada, Cordine didn't want to leave. He'd asked Andrea to try to find out what was happening by making some calls. David had robbed Citicorp and placed the money in safety deposit boxes around the country. Cordine had been in touch with Citicorp through his lawyer, and the bank was willing to drop charges against David if the money was returned. Cordine thought he might be able to persuade David to give it back.

"He's a younger guy," Cordine said. "It's the first time he's ever been to prison, and he's never experienced anything like this. You got a lot of dogs out here on the yard that are perverted, you know—over a period of years, they become perverted—and they would always, I guess, put some type of pressure on him, sexual pressures, and he didn't like that in any shape, way, or form. So, when he moved in with me, he was relieved of that..."

"Yeah," Hawkins said, cutting Cordine a little slack.

"And he didn't have to worry about that bullshit. Because as long as I've been in prison, I've never got to that shit, you know. 'Cause I can't suck dicks, and I can't fuck people in the ass, you know, I don't even advocate it. I see a lot of it happening, but usually I'm pretty sensitive to a person that has to undergo pressure of that sort.

"And he was kind of aloof, you know, when he first moved in with me. I'd never met—'cause I've been down so long—I'd never met a twenty year old with intelligence. I'd never met a twenty year old that had an extensive vocabulary. Every twenty year old I meet—they got tatoos, and they're thinkin' motorcycles and long hair."

"He's into the stock market, hunh?" Hawkins said.

"Yeah. You know, he'd enlighten me on the American Exchange and the New York Exchange, and how to buy commodities without money down, and everything. And he ripped Citicorp for $150,000, okay, and he only got four years. So I'm thinking, here I am, robbin' banks, and, you know, I get the max—fifteen years. And I was thinking, wow, this guy's a pretty smart kid."

VIII

1

From the time of his first sessions with Andrea, Dr. Leitman was aware of an ambivalence in her relationship with Joe Mims, an attitude he had more or less predicted in the psychological profile he wrote for Gary Scherotter. Leitman had written that on the basis of her test results, while it was clear that Andrea deeply wanted a relationship with a partner who cared for her, as Leitman had no doubt Joe Mims did, once she had such a relationship, she would feel uncomfortable and begin to bridle.

"I feel like I've been married to him all my life," she said during their first session on Monday, June 7. It was a double-edged comment, though she seemed to mean it to be taken positively. They hadn't been married three months.

On Friday, during their second session, Leitman recorded in his notes that Andrea "sometimes has a hard time when Joe wants to touch her as a result of having been raped." Before the rapes, she told Leitman, she had felt that she was a very sexual person, but that had changed.

During their third session, on Monday, June 14, it was as if she was quoting to him from his profile. "Feels like she is being suffocated when Joe comes toward her," Leitman recorded in his notes.

Andrea admitted to Leitman that almost every time she said she saw a vagina during the Rorschach test he had administered to her, she actually saw a rectum. She lied because she was too embarrassed to tell him she had been raped in the ass.

"I never saw their penis," she said, referring to the rapes. "They made me give them head. Now it would make me sick— it's lucky Joe doesn't believe in it—after they forced me, coming in my mouth. I used to love it."

She told Leitman about the incident she had mentioned to Jim Hawkins on the phone but did not report. Three men had held her for three hours on Monday and mauled her.

On Monday, June 21, Andrea told Leitman of a dream from which she woke up crying. "I picked up a man who was running from the police. I tried to help him. We went to bars but couldn't get anything to eat. I watched him make out with my girlfriends."

She told him that while Fred Lastar could make her laugh, Joe couldn't.

On Friday, the twenty-fifth, Andrea reported that the night before she'd felt that all men were against her because she wasn't screwing them.

"I know it isn't true," she said after telling Leitman.

Joe would sometimes cry over Andrea's situation, she told Leitman. When he did, it infuriated her. It also upset her when Joe got angry on her behalf.

Leitman attached great importance and potential danger to the way Andrea viewed Joe. Mims was, in effect, subject to becoming the person upon whom she would project her negative feelings about her own performance with him, her difficulty with him sexually, and her negative feelings about his behavior with her; and at a certain point—with this kind of "negative transference" in effect—she might lash out at him violently.

The negative transference—whereby someone outside herself would come to embody for her the source of her own negative feelings—was the most critical of the problems he faced in trying to treat her on an outpatient basis. It was clear from the tests that she might, under stress, be subject to a psychotic break and attack the person she now perceived as a threat to her. He had Joe Mims in with Andrea for part of their session on Wednesday, July 7, and talked about ways of improving Andrea's "reality testing" with Joe.

Was Joe very angry at Andrea if she couldn't respond to a sexual advance from him? Leitman asked.

Mims was very nice about it, saying he didn't mind waiting, but Leitman felt, as a doctor, that he was at best buying time.

After Joe left, Andrea brought out a Dear Abby column about the rape of a fifteen-year-old girl that had made her cry.

Detective Fred Lastar, being unavailable for a relationship, was less threatening and more attractive to Andrea. He was happily married and clearly had no interest in Andrea other than as the defendant in a murder trial, his own investigation having led to her arrest. But when she got word she had passed her GED tests, which she had taken on July 9, it was Lastar she wanted to phone with the good news.

"He laid so many head trips on me," Andrea told Leitman on Friday, July 23. "It was interesting someone could get to me."

"I need Joe," Andrea told Leitman on Tuesday, the twenty-seventh. "I'd fall apart if Joe left. And yet I don't love him the way I should. I don't love him the way Dotty, his first wife, did."

She told Leitman Joe had a violent temper. "I can't handle the emotion he puts out," she said. "It makes me cringe."

After the rapes, her sexuality changed, and she couldn't tolerate being held too tightly or close.

"When I was a kid," Andrea said, "I felt guilty for things other people did."

On Monday, August 9, Andrea told Leitman that she believed cleaning the master bedroom the night Bob Sand was killed would make everything all right.

"I'm frightened of the world," she said. "If Joe dies, I don't know what I'd do."

Leitman asked Andrea if her father had ever tried to make sexual advances to her.

She said he hadn't.

"He used to come home from work tired and dirty," she said. "Sometimes Mom would ask him to spank the kids. Dad would hit the sofa and tell us to yell."

The preliminary hearing date was extended again, to October 24, and Dr. Leitman began to think about getting Andrea to a psychiatric hospital in the interim.

On Monday, August 16, she said she feared men because of the abuse she had suffered, yet she liked men.

"Bob felt he owned me," she said. "I told him I wasn't his employee."

"First husband," Leitman wrote in his notes, "really beat A."

On Monday, August 23, she told Leitman she felt Fred Lastar had betrayed her emotionally.

"I learn the hard way," she said.

She showed Leitman a page of numbered notes she had typed up on Sunday under the heading "Things That Are Bothering Me":

1. That I have been accused of murdering Bob when I never could have done such a thing.

2. That I was deceived by the Detectives when I thought they were trying to help find Bob's murderer and all they were trying to do was set me up.

3. That there are people telling lies about me.

4. That Richard Cordine, who I was worried about and concerned for, *Deceived* and *Betrayed* me.

5. That Joe's two daughters don't want any part of me. They will see their father but not me. I told Joe he should see them and he said he would not see them until they are ready to see me too. They called today to remind him it has been a year since Dotty's death.

6. That Fred Lastar believes I murdered Bob. It makes me feel weird that people think it.

7. I am starting to feel paranoid that I am being followed or watched by someone.

8. That I just break out crying and can not control myself.

9. That there are people who don't believe I was ever *raped*.

10. That I don't love Joe as much as I should because I still am hurting over Bob.

11. That I got Joe involved in this whole mess. I didn't realize what I was getting him involved in. He says he loves me in spite of everything and will never stop loving me.

12. I never knew what it felt like to feel hate but I actually felt hatred and sorrow for Richard Cordine and David Aldors. It hurt me so much I have been praying alot. I remember feeling it for whoever killed Bob, but I did not [know] who or

why they did it and it was making me hurt so
much I had to forgive them although I feel they
still should be punished. I feel Richard Cordine
and David Aldors also should be punished for
Pergury and wasting tax payers money. How low
do the D.A. & Detective have to go to prove an
innocent person guilty? I am praying for them
too although it hasn't helped my hurt that much.
Maybe it's fear I am experiencing. I have to put it
in the Lord's hands and leave it there or I'm not
going to make it through the next two months
and that's exactly what they would like.

13. I do not feel suicidal or depressed, just angry
which is another emotion that hurts. I am going
to fight Richard Cordine to the end. I just can't
believe he is doing such a false thing. To be able
to make up such a story is shocking to me. I just
find it almost impossible to believe.

2

On Tuesday, August 24, the day after Andrea's session with Dr.
Leitman, at 9:25 in the morning, Bonnie McMillan, Gary
Scherotter's secretary, answered a call at the office from Andrea.
Since Gary wasn't there, she put the call through to Rick
Erwood.

Andrea told Erwood she had been assaulted again that
morning in her bedroom by three Mexican men. They were on
top of her when she first realized someone was in the room. She
was tied to the bedposts, hand and feet, with a white rope she'd
never seen before. She was gagged and blindfolded with a ban-
dana, and a pillow was put over her head.

She described one suspect as short, about five foot six. All of them spoke Spanish.

"This is for sure the right house," Andrea heard one of the suspects say, she told Erwood.

She had been hit on the head, and her nightgown was torn. She passed out and then faded in and out of consciousness. She thought she'd been drugged. While she was conscious, water and beer were poured over her.

Joe had gotten up about five that morning, Andrea told Erwood, and left the house at six. She could tell he had reset the burglar alarm by the light, but she was tied on the opposite side of the bed and couldn't reach it.

When she regained consciousness and found the men gone, she was able to get her left hand loose to call Gary's office.

After Erwood hung up, Bonnie McMillan realized she hadn't disconnected her own line, and Andrea hadn't hung up. The secretary heard a woman some distance from the receiver eerily singing and intermittently talking to herself.

Erwood called Scherotter, who said he would meet him at Andrea's home. Scherotter called his investigator, Joe Jones, and asked him to meet him at the Bob Hope Drive gate to the Springs Country Club.

The lawyer had been waiting to hear directly from Andrea right after another incident occurred and delayed calling the police for the moment. Maybe they were missing something. His wife, Sherry, came with him to the Springs. Both Erwood and Joe Jones were at the gate when they arrived.

They got to 6 Brandeis Court at about 10:30 and found the front gate locked. Scherotter asked Joe Jones to check the back.

Jones found that the glass of the sliding glass door to the master bedroom was broken. He stepped carefully inside. The sleep blind was drawn, and the room was very dark. He drew the curtains and blind back to let light in.

Andrea was lying naked on her back on the bed, moaning. She was positioned on one side of the bed, her left leg partially off the side. Both legs were tied to the bed frame, and both hands were tied to the headboard.

Jones went to the front of the house and let the others in by opening the garage door. He got a small paring knife in the kitchen and cut Andrea loose. Sherry Scherotter pulled a robe from the closet for Andrea. Jones found the telephone beside the bed, phoned the police, and then Springs Ambulance.

Andrea repeated to Scherotter and Jones what she had told Rick Erwood. She hadn't heard the glass in the sliding door break.

Deputy Janet Rubien arrived at 11:10. Springs Ambulance was already there. Joe Jones directed the deputy to the master bedroom, where Springs Ambulance personnel were attending to Andrea, who was sitting on the bed in a bathrobe.

Rubien took note of a thin white piece of rope around Andrea's left wrist. There was a small cut on the outer edge of each of her eyebrows. She also had what appeared to be either a cut or a cold sore in the middle of her lower lip. Since she was talking with the attendants, Rubien didn't immediately make contact with her.

The deputy observed a handwritten note taped on the bedroom door. It was on a piece of paper that looked like it had come from a pad, with the words "From the Desk of Robert Sand" printed at the top. Below that, handprinted in block letters, were the words "JOE IS GONE." The note had been stuck to the door with a strip of masking tape.

Taped to the mirror in the master bedroom bathroom was an identical piece of paper with the words "JOE IS DEAD" printed in the same block letters.

At 11:45, Investigator Gordon Hunter from the Indio Sheriff's Department arrived at the scene and began to inventory the master bedroom.

The sliding glass door leading to the patio was open about two feet and the screen door about three feet. Pieces of shattered glass lay in large piles both on the bedroom carpet and on the cement patio outside, as well as in the space between the screen and the door. It appeared that the glass had fallen to the ground from the position in which the door was found, open.

There were sections of rope hanging from the two headboard posts and from the two rear legs of the bed, as well as several sections of rope lying on the bed. In the report he filed, Hunter noted that "the knots were similar, a piece doubled back and tied in an overhand knot, leaving a loop for another piece of the rope to slide through, a slip knot."

Later that afternoon while searching the residence for evidence, Hunter found a small stepladder in the laundry room. On the ladder was a section of rope of the same type as the pieces used on Mrs. Mims, and the rope had been tied with the same slipknot.

Deputy Rubien left when Detective Hunter arrived and went to Eisenhower Medical Center, where Andrea had been taken. "Mims appeared to be very tired when I contacted her," Rubien noted in her report. "Twice I left the room to make telephone calls and both times upon returning she appeared to be sleeping. Her statement was very disjointed, and she had difficulty answering my questions."

Andrea told Rubien that as one of the suspects started to leave the bedroom, she told him that if he did, an alarm would go off and the police would respond. She told him that, she said to Rubien, with the hope of keeping him there long enough so that when she pushed a silent alarm near her bed, he would be caught. The man didn't leave the room, and said to her "I have everything I need right here," Andrea told the deputy.

Rubien asked if he said that in Spanish or English. Andrea looked confused and then said the man spoke English.

At one point, her gag was taken off, and one suspect tried to force her to take some capsules, Andrea told Rubien. She didn't know what they were, but they were similar to some that her husband had, red and yellow ones. When she refused to take the capsules, the suspect poured beer on her head. Then he tried to make her give him head, and she bit him slightly, not enough to hurt him. He hit her when she bit him, and she passed out.

Referring to the capsules at another point in the interview, Andrea told Rubien that the suspects attempted to put some of the capsules in her rectum. She didn't know if they actually had done it.

At the hospital at the time Deputy Rubien conducted the interview, but not in the room with Andrea, were Mr. and Mrs. Scherotter, Rick Erwood, Joe Jones, and Dr. Michael Leitman.

Leitman and Scherotter agreed that they needed to get Andrea into a psychiatric hospital.

3

She was admitted two days later, Thursday, August 26, to Capistrano By The Sea, a psychiatric hospital set at the top of a bluff overlooking the Pacific and surrounded by woodlands. Laurence Jackson, a thirty-two-year-old African-American psychiatrist, was her assigned doctor. He would see her for private fifty-minute sessions and was also present at group therapy.

At the time of her admission, the mental status psychiatric evaluation he conducted indicated that Andrea showed no sign of either clinical depression or psychotic thought processes. However, a significant finding of the examination was an incongruence of mood and affect, which she herself was aware of. When she felt anxious, she told Dr. Jackson, she tended to smile.

Jackson reviewed with Andrea some of the rape and abduction incidents that had occurred after Robert Sand's death—incidents that suggested she had had "dissociative reactions," blacking out and coming to with no memory of having acted out in the interim.

She didn't think she belonged at Capistrano, she told Dr. Jackson, as well as other staff members and fellow patients. Sometimes she would indicate anger about it, although for the most part the doctor thought she conducted herself as a perfectly normal and competent woman.

However, if she did become angry, she wouldn't allow herself to admit it and instead strongly denied it. Yet it would be clear that the denial itself contained anger. Sometimes too, her anxiety around a negative emotion that she wouldn't allow herself to express would lead to "a somatization of the symptom," and she would develop gastrointestinal discomfort.

Over the course of several weeks of treatment, Andrea slowly opened up more about her insecurities and in particular her fear of men.

She didn't know who she was, she said one day to Dr. Jackson, and was afraid to find out more about herself.

Why this was, specifically, wasn't clear to the doctor. Someone who had difficulty expressing negative emotion was typically the product of an unstable home environment, someone who had been neglected and perhaps abused as a child.

Even though Andrea's father, who had an air-conditioner and heating business with his brother-in-law, had deserted his family when Andrea was fourteen, she didn't express negative feelings about him. She had been in touch with him sporadically since coming to California, where he had moved after abandoning his family.

Joe Mims came to visit Andrea at Capistrano and impressed Dr. Jackson as an extremely kind and decent man, a real gentleman, who was devoted to Andrea and very concerned for her.

For her part, Andrea seemed devoted to Mims.

It was Mims' insurance carrier, Aetna, that was paying for
the hospitalization, and there was a limit of six weeks on her stay.
After conferring with Dr. Jackson on the phone, Dr. Leitman
was sorry the insurance wouldn't allow Andrea a longer stay at
the hospital. She finally seemed to be accepting the value of the
treatment, Jackson told Leitman, who had often seen treatments
inappropriately ended because of the insurance limit.

Then, on the day before her discharge, Dr. Jackson saw
Andrea change radically. In his discharge summary, he wrote:

> [She] displayed a marked difference in behavior
> and affect. She claimed that she had been drugged
> the night before, although there was no evidence
> to support it. Physically she was stable, although
> she complained of feeling dizzy and, at one point,
> feigned a faint. The issue of her leaving the hos-
> pital, and her possible anxiety about doing so, was
> brought up to her. However, she ignored this and
> continued to focus on the dizziness and nausea
> that she was experiencing.
>   She continued to make claims that she had
> been drugged and that someone had tried to
> poison or harm her, even though it was pointed
> out to her that there was no reason for anyone to
> want to do that in the hospital. She could offer
> no explanation for why anyone would want to do
> it, but continued to maintain that it had occurred.
> In her room, she presented a water cup which
> contained some water with a bluish tinge to it,
> which she claimed contained the drug that she
> had been given. This was sent off to the labora-
> tory and results revealed no evidence of any
> drugs. She continued to focus on this particular,
> and, as she did so, became increasingly agitated
> throughout the remainder of the day. It was

pointed out to her, repeatedly, that it seemed that she was experiencing difficulty in separating from the hospital. However, she would not address this issue directly. Her agitation continued and escalated to the point that when she was reviewing her chart [with me], she became acutely angry again, and tore it up.

"It was clear," Dr. Jackson concluded, "that she was experiencing more distress and psychological pain than she was willing to admit to, and she appeared to have little control over the expression of her affect. It was noted that her affect was over-controlled until it would break through her defenses, at which point there would be no modulation of it."

On Friday, October 8, Andrea, again behaving normally, was released from Capistrano By The Sea and drove back to Rancho Mirage with Joe Mims in his tan Subaru.

4

Though the stay at Capistrano By The Sea Hospital was, on balance, probably salutary for Andrea, Dr. Leitman could detect no real changes in her after the six weeks of inpatient treatment. On Monday, October, 11, at their first session together after she returned, she told Leitman that she felt the hospital staff had twisted everything she said. Her doctor, Laurence Jackson, whom she had thought was trying to help her, was the only black doctor in the place and was afraid to go to bat for her, as all the other doctors had done for their patients.

She felt like Alice in Wonderland, she said. She had no control over her life and environment.

"He still grabs me from behind," she said of Joe Mims, "even though I told him not to."

★ ★ ★

On Thursday, October 14, however, Andrea gave evidence that at least something of what they had been working on was getting through.

"Maybe I wasn't drugged at Capistrano By The Sea," she said. "Maybe it was my emotions telling me not to leave."

The situation with Joe Mims, however, wasn't going to go away.

"I feel I'm lying to myself by living with Joe," she said. "I feel like Joe would kill me. I didn't want to go home last night."

If she thought of Fred Lastar, however, she felt happy.

She married Joe, a comfortable old shoe, only because she thought she would be accepted.

There was a new element of relative self-awareness in these statements, as disheartening as the ones about Joe Mims were. Later, looking at his notes for the session, Leitman came across a paragraph written in Andrea's hand on the last page:

> I'm still in love w/Bob & the closest person after
> Bob was FRED. He held his hand on my thigh &
> talked with me. I am still trying to deal w/my
> emotional attachment towards him. How do I go
> on living w/Joe and behave normally. I love him
> & would not hurt him. Maybe I have to relearn
> love w/him. Can you help me with this?

On Monday, October 18, Andrea reported a dream she had had to Leitman: An endless corridor with no doors out, even though there were doors off the corridor.

She liked to spend time with Joe, Andrea told Leitman on Thursday, the twenty-first, but she didn't want him to touch her.

She felt tied up in knots.

"I don't like myself now," she said. "I can't do anything right. I can't even marry the right man. I don't hate Joe. I feel sorry for him, being involved with me."

Andrea was excited, she told Leitman, that a friend her age was having twins. She would have liked to have had Bob's baby, but not Joe's. Joe didn't really like kids.

On Monday, October 25, the preliminary hearing was extended for the fourth time to allow more time for all the blood samples on the carpeting to be analyzed.

At their session that day, Andrea reported to Leitman that she'd had a dream that the devil was screwing her.

She thought of all the silly things she and Bob did, she told Leitman with tears in her eyes.

Joe was not silly.

"If I'm convicted," she said, "Joe won't leave me. He'll be the martyr."

Later in the session, she mentioned that she and Joe had made a pact. If she was convicted, Joe would kill her and then himself.

During their Thursday, October 28 session, Andrea told Leitman she felt bad because Joe was working so hard, and it might be for nothing. "She avoided saying she might go to jail," Leitman wrote in his notes.

The first time she ever had sex, she said, she was raped and became pregnant.

Her mother was so involved with her own problems, having been deserted by her husband, that she couldn't help. She threatened to put Andrea, who was fifteen, into a home for unwed mothers, and Andrea married the man who had raped her, Wesley Denike.

IX

1

On Saturday evening at twilight, Joe Mims was surprised to notice the wind's movement in the curtain at the sliding glass door in the living room. He knew he'd locked the door earlier that day. He and Andrea had had many discussions about keeping the doors locked, in light of what had happened so many times to her at the house. Andrea told Joe she expected him to make sure the doors were locked, because sometimes she forgot.

Joe went over, found the door open a foot or so behind the curtain. He closed and locked it, looking out at the failing light on the grass. He wondered if Andrea was playing a game with him, checking to see whether he was really making sure the house was kept locked and she was protected. Joe knew he was taking the job very seriously, and welcomed it if she was in fact trying to check up on him. She'd find out he certainly wasn't sloughing off on the job.

She'd gone into the kitchen for a moment. He was working on a report for a client, and she was typing up a report he'd already done. She was a pretty good typist, and he appreciated the help she was giving him with his work. It was nice for both of them, to be working side by side together like this, Joe thought. It was a tough time she was going through. But then, he was too. Ever since the Richard Cordine thing, she'd seemed somehow different to him, more distant, more impatient, cutting him off in mid-sentence. But he knew she was under a lot of strain.

On the other hand, he hadn't caused the situation with Richard Cordine, as Andrea accused him of doing. He'd just told

her that if he was charged with murder, awaiting a preliminary
hearing, the last person in the world he'd want to be corresponding with, let alone talking on the phone with—and he'd
paid a telephone bill that included more than fifty dollars in
charges for Andrea's calls with Cordine—was a known, convicted felon who was in jail. And she'd agreed with him.

Then, the afternoon Joe had told Cordine not to phone
there anymore and hung up, Andrea immediately said, "Now
he's going to betray me. I know it. You see what you've done?"

"What do you mean betray you, Andrea?" he asked. "How
can he betray you?"

"I don't want to talk about it, Joe," she said.

She didn't want to talk about it. She did that more and more
often now. It turned out she was right, too. The man actually
lied to the police and the district attorney to improve his situation in jail, getting his boyfriend to move back into his cell or
something. He had lied and betrayed someone who had been
only caring toward him. Drea knew it was going to happen, too.
He'd give her that, poor thing.

"Did you hear that noise, Joe?"

Joe looked over at her, set up at her desk with the typewriter
on it. It was dark out now.

"No, Drea, I didn't hear anything."

"Joe, there's someone in the house."

"All the doors are locked, Andrea. How could anyone be in
here?"

He knew his hearing wasn't the best in the world, but how
could anyone be inside the house? Then it occurred to him that
maybe this was part of the test. Say she had unlocked the sliding
glass door earlier that afternoon, as Joe knew she must have,
because he knew he'd locked it after lunch. Now maybe they
were going to go around, checking all the locks, and she'd be in
for a little surprise. She'd discover he was looking out for her a
little better than she thought.

"Joe!" she whispered urgently, standing in front of him holding two exercise boards, her balance sticks. "Someone's in the house!"

"Here," she said, handing him one. "You go out that way," she said, pointing to the den and kitchen area, "and I'll check the bedrooms."

Joe stood up and took one of the boards. Suddenly he felt uneasy about something. It was as if she was playing some kind of game. She was excited about it; she wasn't scared, it didn't seem to him.

"Well, okay," he said. "But we'll go together. I don't want to go in different directions, Drea."

They went through the whole house and checked every single lock, switching on lights as they went. Andrea held her stick up, ready to hit someone if they jumped out at her. Joe kept his at his side. How would anyone have gotten in?

Every single entrance was locked. Last, they went over to the sliding glass door in the living room, their starting point.

He half-expected her to turn around and hug him and acknowledge how careful he was being, looking out for her. But she didn't do anything or show any indication of surprise when she discovered that the sliding glass door was locked.

$$2$$

Officially the full moon was supposed to be there on Monday, November 1. But on Sunday, Halloween night, letting in Herb and Betty Hawkins who had brought their little granddaughter over trick-or-treating, Joe glimpsed the moon just rising over the Springs. It looked like a perfect full moon to him, and so close-seeming you could practically get a ladder and climb up to it.

For some reason, Andrea had made up a very big pitcher of margaritas. Usually she'd make a big one each for both of them—the size they called a double—and that would be it. But tonight she'd made enough for much more than that and drank quite a bit while Joe just sipped his usual one. Herb and Betty seldom drank and didn't while they were visiting. The little girl was eager to get on with her trick-or-treating, of course, and the Hawkins were gone in a half hour.

Then Joe and Andrea settled down in front of the TV and watched a dumb horror movie on cable. A lot of crazy people coming out of the woodwork and making each other bleed and die. Around nine o'clock, Andrea got up from the sofa.

"That's about it for me," she said. "I'm going in and take a bath."

"Well, good," Joe said. "I'll come in and watch you."

It was something they both enjoyed doing. She liked to take baths and talk, and Joe enjoyed talking and watching her as he sat on the wide edge of the tub. Andrea was about as perfect-looking a woman as there ever was, Joe thought, and it was a nice relaxed way for them to be together.

When she'd finished her bath and had a towel wrapped around her, she looked over at him, smiled, and said "Would you like to make love?"

They hadn't made love in two, or maybe even three months. So it surprised Joe to hear her say it.

"That sounds real good to me," he said.

In the bedroom, Joe undressed and got into bed beside Andrea. Maybe it had to do with everything that had been happening lately. That was the only thing he could think of—that maybe he was more upset about things than he realized. Whatever the reason was, though, he wasn't able to get an erection. It made him feel terrible, not to be able to enjoy an opportunity like this with Andrea, after so long a time. It was what they really needed, and here she was offering it, and suddenly he couldn't go through with it.

"That's okay, honey," Andrea said. "That happens sometimes..."

Joe felt awful about it, though.

"I know," she said, like she had a bright idea. "Let's get in the car and go somewhere. It's a beautiful night, and we can find some place out in nature and make love under the stars."

"Well, that sounds wonderful to me," Joe said. Maybe the change of scene would be the solution to his problem, he thought.

They got dressed. Andrea put on a blue sweat suit and sneakers. Joe got into his denims with a tan shirt. But when they both were ready, Joe couldn't find her. It turned out she was in the laundry room with her purse slung over her shoulder.

"What are you doing in here, Drea?" he asked.

"Joe, I can't find my keys, and I thought maybe they were in here."

Joe had just seen her keys. "They're out in the kitchen, honey."

"No, they're not," she said.

They went into the kitchen, and there they were.

Before they left, Andrea got a bedspread to lay on the ground when they found a nice spot.

At first he took off toward Indio.

"Where do you want to go?" Andrea asked.

"I don't know," Joe said. He thought he might turn up to Highway 86, but then he remembered Route 74 in Rancho Mirage that led up right into the Cahuilla Hills. He turned around on Highway 111.

"I know a place," he said.

"Great," Andrea said.

They went up 74 all the way to where the pavement ended. There was a mobile home park on the right, but on the left was a road, and Joe turned on to it. It turned into a dirt road, and there was a little rough part, a ravine, but the Subaru had four-wheel drive and handled it just fine. They got to the end of the dirt road, and there in front of them was a nice place, a kind of grass clearing among the big boulders with the mountains in the background. The moon was bright out there, but not as close as it had been earlier in the evening.

Andrea was in a rush, kissing him.

"Come on, Joe," she said, taking the bedspread, her purse over her shoulder.

She seemed to want to have sexual intercourse right away. When they spread out the bedspread and lay down on it, Andrea touched him without waiting even a moment. He wasn't all the way there yet but definitely improving.

"It's not hard enough," she said.

Then she did something that Joe had never experienced before, and he had to wonder at it, and at Andrea. She took his penis right in her mouth, and in another moment or two, he ejaculated.

She spit it out into a tissue.

"Gosh," Joe said. "Well, now what do we do? I'd like to make love to you, Drea, and now I've..."

"That's all right, Joe," she said. "You roll over on your stomach, and I'll give you a nice massage and get that sciatic nerve, and you'll relax, and we can make love again, honey."

"Okay," Joe said, "sounds good to me." He rolled over on his stomach.

Joe had his pants off but not his shirt, and Andrea was out of the bottoms of her sweat suit but still had the top on. She sat on him with her legs on the ground at his side.

The massage felt good, and Joe began to relax.

Something that felt like metal touched his back, and he wondered what it was.

"Are you okay, honey?" Drea asked him right away, as though it might have hurt him.

"Oh, yeah, honey, I'm fine," he said, as she went on massaging him real well.

Something like a rock hit his head, hard. He gasped. Then he was hit hard again. A cross between a scream and a moan of pain escaped him involuntarily. He began to struggle to turn around. Somebody was attacking them, he thought. The people who had been attacking Drea had followed them. Using all his strength, he turned as he took a third blow on his head.

When he turned around, Joe saw Andrea holding a hammer in the air about to hit him again. He saw a look in her eye that he'd never seen before. It was as if she was a different person. He pushed her off, grabbed her arm, and managed to get the hammer out of her hand.

"Andrea," he said, "what in the name of God are you doing?" He could feel his head bleeding.

"Joe," she said, "I've got to knock you out." It was like she was pleading.

"What do you mean?" Joe said. "Knock me out?"

"I've gotta knock you out, Joe," she said. "I've got to knock you out, so that people'll believe me. If you're knocked out, then they'll believe me, that I've been raped."

"Well, how in the world will they believe you, that you've been raped," he said. "Here, *you'll* still be all right..."

"No," she said, "I'm going to hit myself in the head with the hammer. Maybe I'll hit myself in the head with the claw part, and I'll kill myself."

"Well, if I'm alive," Joe said, "I'll tell 'em that you weren't raped." Then he said, "How do you know that you wouldn't have killed me?"

"Oh, I wasn't going to hurt you," Andrea said.

"What do you mean, you weren't going to hurt me?" Joe said. "You've already hurt me. Blood...look here...running all down on me...on my face. Yes, you've hurt me, Andrea. I don't want to die."

"Well, *I* want to die," Andrea said. "No one believes me."

"Well, Andrea," Joe said, "I don't want to die. And I don't want you dying."

He stood up, went over to the Subaru, and put the hammer in the car. He wanted it out of the way. Then he walked back to her. He touched his bleeding head.

Andrea rolled over on the grass on her back beside the bedspread.

"Let's just lay here and rest," she said.

"No, Andrea," Joe said, "I want to go home and wash and see how bad my head is..."

"Oh, you're not that bad," she said. "Joe, I didn't hurt you."

"Andrea," Joe said, "do you really *love* me?"

"Yes, I love you," Andrea said. "Sure I love you. *I'm* sorry. I'm sorry."

It seemed to Joe that she was just throwing words out to him.

"We've got to talk about this, Andrea," he said. "But I want to go home. I want to put on my clothes."

Joe began to pull on his pants.

"Now put on your clothes..." he said.

"No," she said. "I'm going to stay here. I'm going to kill myself."

"No, you're not going to stay here and kill yourself," Joe said. "I'm not going to tell anybody about this.

He was afraid for his life but didn't want to show it. He didn't want her doing another irrational act, isolated as they were. He wanted to get her back to civilization, where at least he felt he had some support. Not that he wasn't stronger than she was, but he didn't want another surprise.

He reassured her again that he wasn't going to tell anybody and tried to calm her down. She got dressed, grabbed up everything, and they got into the car.

She had the bedspread in the front with her.

"Why don't you put that in the back?" Joe said.

"No, I'll just put it underneath my feet here," she said.

Joe knew there was blood on the bedspread she was most likely trying to hide.

3

Before he started the engine, Joe wiped some of the blood off his face with his hands. Then he put on a hat he had in the car. He knew it looked silly, but it would help stanch the flow of blood, and if someone saw him—it might be a sheriff, or it might be anyone—they'd want to know what in the world was going on with him bleeding like that. This way, they might think it was for Halloween.

The minute they pulled into the driveway, Andrea got out of the car with the bedspread, went into the house, and started the washing machine.

"Take off your shirt," she said to Joe.

It was also bloody, along with his undershirt, and Joe took them both off. Andrea put them into the machine with the bedspread and some towels.

Then Joe took a shower in the master bathroom while Andrea took another bath there. There was blood on his towel after his shower because he'd washed his head. Andrea, wearing a nightgown now, picked up the towel and took it to the washing machine.

Joe slipped a .38 revolver they had purchased out of the drawer in the bedroom and put it into the briefcase he took with him each morning. She wouldn't think to check for it there.

"Andrea," Joe said when she came back into the room, "how do you know the difference between knocking me out and killing me? Maybe one more blow, or two more blows, and I would have been dead..."

"No," she said, "I wasn't going to kill you, Joe. I just had to knock you out."

"Well," Joe said, "I don't know how many blows that would take. And I don't know how many people *do* know. It scares me, Andrea. I don't want to die. I don't want you hittin' me with a hammer..."

"I'm not going to do that, Joe," she said, impatient now. "I don't want to talk about it anymore. I want to go to sleep."

"Okay," Joe said, "let's get your medicine."

They went out to the kitchen together. Joe didn't want her getting a knife and coming back at him. Andrea took what was left of Joe's margarita from earlier in the evening, which was most of it, and drank it all right down with her vitamins. He didn't say anything because he wanted her to go to sleep. Joe knew he wasn't going to sleep. He'd be watching her like a hawk all night.

When they went back into the bedroom, Joe had to go to the bathroom. His bowels were upset.

While he was sitting on the toilet, the door opened and it scared him to death. He thought she was there with a weapon.

"I couldn't find you," Andrea said smiling. "I took three Dalmane, and three Triptolane, so I should go to sleep."

"Well, good," Joe said. "You need a good night's rest."

When Joe went into the bedroom, Andrea was in bed.

"You know, Andrea," Joe said, "I don't know why you want to kill yourself. You have a lot to live for...*I* love you..."

"Joe, don't put me under pressure," she said. "I don't want to hear you say you love me. You make me think I have to tell you, 'I love you'..."

"No," he said, "I don't need that, Andrea. I'm just telling you some facts to reassure you that you have people in life who love you. Your children love you. Your little grandson Aaron loves you. You have a lot to live for. It's foolish to talk about killing yourself."

"Well, I was a horrible mother," she said.

He pointed out that her sons seemed to love her. They had never had anything bad to say about her to him. And she knew little Aaron loved her.

"I don't want to talk about it," Andrea said. "I want to go to sleep."

She went to sleep then and slept soundly through the night. Joe stayed awake in the dark, praying. Every quarter of an hour, the chimes struck. When he heard the chimes strike 4:15, and then heard them strike 4:30, and then heard them strike 4:45, he decided he couldn't stand being in bed anymore and got up. It was ten minutes to five, ten minutes before he would get up normally. He got his clothes together and left their bedroom, closing the door. He dressed in the second bedroom and went into the bathroom there.

Joe thought he'd try to eat something in the kitchen, but he was still upset. Every time he thought about what she had done to him, just seeing that look in her eye, like a wild animal, and hearing her say that she had to knock him out, made his whole body break into a cold sweat.

He made a cup of coffee but couldn't drink it. He knew he had to get out of the house. He wrote her a short note, beginning "Dear Drea, I love you. I'll always love you..." For a while, at least, she'd assume he'd gone to work as if everything were normal.

He left the house at about 5:15, still dark. He went out the Morningside gate because he was going to drive to Palm Springs. He wanted to talk to Gary Scherotter. Gary was Andrea's lawyer, he knew, but he also knew Gary was an honest man, and that he would help him all he could. Joe knew he needed somebody to give him some answers, some direction.

He drove into Palm Springs on Highway 111 very slowly, maybe thirty miles an hour. He parked in the driveway of Denny's on North Palm Canyon. He still didn't know if he could eat and sat in the car for ten minutes, trying to figure out if he felt like eating, if he should go inside the restaurant.

He finally went in. He needed some coffee and thought he might like a waffle, but they didn't have any. He ordered pancakes instead and ate a little bit of them. He was still so apprehensive. He needed to talk to Gary.

Denny's had a phone outside, but it wasn't in a phone booth, and he didn't want to talk out in the open. He drove to the first pay telephone on Palm Canyon, stopped, phoned Gary, and got his answering service.

Joe told the service it was a matter of life and death. He had to talk to Gary. They got him on the line. It was 6:15. Gary had just gotten out of the shower.

"Gary," Joe said, "I've got to talk with you, it's a matter of life and death. You've got to see me..."

"Joe," Gary said, "I'm just so busy today..."

"Gary," Joe said, "you've *got* to see me. Believe me."

"Okay, Joe," Gary said. "Okay, I'll meet you in thirty minutes at my office."

He drove to Gary's office on South Palm Canyon and sat in his car again. It was just light outside. Gary got there in just about a half hour, and they went into the office together.

Joe had been wearing the hat from the night before because he didn't want people in the restaurant to see the caked blood on his head. Now he took off the hat and showed Gary his head.

"My God," Gary said. "What happened to you?"

Joe explained what had happened.

Poor Joe seemed like the saddest man in the world that morning to Gary. He looked crushed.

"You understand my position," Gary said after he'd heard the whole story. "I'm Andrea's counsel, and I can't advise you, Joe."

"I understand that, Gary."

"I will say this, as a human being. You've got to protect yourself. I want you to talk to Michael Leitman."

"Well, Gary, I don't know his number."

"Don't worry," Gary said, "I'm already dialing." He got Dr. Leitman on the phone.

When he hung up, Gary told Joe that Michael Leitman would be at his office at eight o'clock that morning to see him.

4

It was seven o'clock, and Gary had to leave for court in Indio. Joe thanked him, left the office, and drove over to Michael Leitman's office in Palm Desert. He parked in front on El Paseo and waited. When Dr. Leitman arrived, they went into the office, which was being remodeled and in disarray. Leitman tried to put his office into order while Joe waited. Joe had his hat back on. He hadn't shown Leitman his head yet.

"Joe," Dr. Leitman said, "I can see you're under real stress. Just let me get this last chair in here, and we'll talk."

"Okay, fine," Joe said.

Joe and Dr. Leitman went into the doctor's office. After Dr. Leitman closed the door, Joe told him everything that had happened last night, word by word, just as he had told Gary.

All of Leitman's worst fears—what he'd hoped, very foolishly he could see now, to somehow sidestep with both outpatient and inpatient treatment for Andrea—had materialized.

"Well, Joe," he said to the poor man, "you're going to have to move out of the house."

"Oh, I've already made my mind up about that, Dr. Leitman," Joe said. For one thing, he'd never be able to fall asleep there again.

"Well, good," Leitman said, "because you know your life's in danger..."

"Yes, I know my life's in danger," Joe said.

They talked for a while, and Leitman told Joe that Andrea had a two o'clock appointment with him that day, and he wanted Joe to be there for it. Andrea thought it was for twelve, Joe told Leitman. Joe had suggested to her last night, just after they got home, that she phone Dr. Leitman. Dr. Leitman had told them both that he wanted Andrea to call him at any time, day or night, that he was there for her as a friend. But she didn't want to talk to Dr. Leitman, and she told Joe she'd see him tomorrow at twelve. Dr. Leitman said he'd have his secretary make sure Andrea knew the right time for the appointment.

Joe left around nine o'clock and went to his Palm Desert house up on Broken Arrow Trail, which he'd put up for sale, to see if he could get some sleep. He phoned the gas company to see if he could get the gas turned back on, but they said not unless he could be there. Joe said he'd try again later.

He couldn't sleep and eventually went downtown to have lunch. He bought another hat that he thought looked a little less ridiculous than the one he was wearing. Then he went back to his house and tried to sleep again, but couldn't.

At about 1:30, he couldn't wait any longer and drove to Dr. Leitman's parking lot. He parked far away from the office entrance because he didn't want Andrea to see him. He waited in the car until six minutes to two. He was too nervous to wait any longer, and got out and walked to Dr. Leitman's office. Joe Jones, Gary's investigator, was there.

Dr. Leitman's secretary, Margie Hill, had known Andrea before she was Dr. Leitman's patient and had met Joe socially with her. When he stepped into the office that afternoon, Joe was actually sobbing and showed Hill a wound on his forehead.

"She did this to me," Joe said. "Why would she do this to me?"

It shocked her to see a man like Joe in such a state and to think that Andrea had done it to him. Hill had met her one evening at the bar at The Nest in Indian Wells and struck up a friendship. Hill was a manicurist who was working as Dr. Leitman's receptionist before opening her own shop, and she and Andrea had had real fun together, shopping and going to restaurants.

In another moment, Gary Scherotter arrived and the three men went into Dr. Leitman's office. Dr. Leitman told them that Andrea wasn't coming, that she was at Eisenhower Hospital.

That morning she had evidently opened up all the doors of the condominium and yelled, "Come in and rape me! Come in and kill me! I don't care!"

Betty Hawkins had been called and took her to the hospital.

Dr. Leitman was emphatic now that Joe needed to protect himself, and the only way he could see for him to do that was to call the sheriff's department and report the incident. Andrea would only be at Eisenhower on a twenty-four-hour stay, Dr. Leitman told them, and there was even a possibility that she could check herself out at any time.

"Would you want to walk into the house and meet her again?" Leitman asked Joe.

"No," he said. "I'd be afraid even if my brother was with me."

"Right," Leitman said. "How do you know she wouldn't kill your brother?"

The first free moment Leitman had had that day, he'd phoned his wife, told her what had happened, and they'd decided to change their phone number and have it unlisted. Who knew what Andrea might be capable of doing at this point? Leitman might be the next person in line.

Joe Jones told Joe that he had been an investigator for seventeen years, and it was clear to him that Joe's life was in danger.

"I wouldn't, under any circumstance," he told Joe, "want you to leave Andrea loose. My advice to you, as a friend, is to get in touch with the D.A. and the sheriff's department and have Andrea arrested and file a charge against her."

"I don't want to file a charge against her," Joe said.

"Well, you have to," Jones told him. "There's no other way."

Gary, who had remained mostly quiet, explained how charges needed to be filed in order to have someone arrested and jailed. Gary explained again that he couldn't advise Joe on what to do, being Andrea's counsel, but as a friend he could say that Joe needed to protect himself. He also said filing charges wasn't going to be pretty, everything would come out now and be made public. He didn't want to mislead Joe and tell him it was going to be fun. Finally, he said it was a decision he, Joe, had to make for himself—Gary, or Joe Jones, or Dr. Leitman, couldn't do it, Joe had to do it alone.

"Well," Joe said, "okay. I want you to call the detectives."

Before he left, Gary wished Joe the best.

That afternoon, after taking a statement from Joe Mims in Dr. Leitman's office, Detective Lastar, Investigator Riter, I.D. Tech Reyes, and Joe drove up to the spot in the Cahuilla Hills where Joe and Andrea had been the night before. Looking around, Riter saw a large kitchen knife that wasn't rusted or weathered and called the others over to look at it.

Joe reacted to the knife as if he was on the verge of fainting. Riter and Lastar sat him down in the shade of a boulder and made him put his head down and just breathe for a moment. Riter could see that maybe for the first time Joe realized then how close to death he'd been.

"This proves it, doesn't it, Joe?" Riter said when he thought Joe wasn't going to faint anymore.

"Yes," he said. "It really does. You were right and I was wrong."

"Does that mean that you'll file the charges, Joe?"

Joe told them he would tell the truth.

X

1

The moment he got the news of Andrea's assault on Joe Mims, Gary Scherotter began to consider the question of her competency to stand trial. The three-tiered standard for competency specifically related to the ability of the defendant to understand the charges against her, to help her attorney in the preparation of her defense, and hypothetically to be capable of defending herself in court. The act of assaulting Joe Mims suggested that Andrea, whom Scherotter well knew had a range of psychological problems, could not specifically meet these criteria.

Then too, the whole puzzle of bizarre incident followed by bizarre incident now had an insistent coherence. The woman had a scenario she was trying to get across—one she'd in fact repeated over and over again. However, it was as if the lurid details of each incident would eclipse an understanding of the consistent theme underlying them all.

Scherotter had now been over the police reports and other evidence, had gone through them chronologically, and perhaps seen in the sheer accretion of detail what the police, for instance, might miss, since they would send different people out on different occasions.

She was being attacked by the same people who killed Bob Sand. She was staging incident after incident to prove that they were still at large and were going to kill or hurt her. She'd most likely written all the crazy communiques, too. Not that he hadn't considered all of this before, but on the one hand, it was so outlandishly bizarre, and on the other so ineffective, that it was as if he'd suspended judgment in the interests of doing the best job that he could for his client.

But now she'd done something that made it impossible to do that any longer. Although some kind of batty rationality underlay it, in fact it made so little sense that Andrea's competency had to be the issue now. In order to prove that she had not killed her previous husband, Robert Sand, she had made an attempt on the life of her current husband, Joe Mims.

It wasn't something cleverly planned out, and it obviously hadn't been executed very cleverly. She had just done it, as if there was an inexorable logic in place that would vindicate the action.

At the moment at least, her incompetency was the best Scherotter had to go with. Taken *en toto*, in chronological order, there was just an overwhelming amount of evidence of mental derangement. If she were judged incompetent, she would be sent to Patton State Mental Hospital in San Bernadino until she was judged sufficiently mentally recovered to stand trial.

At 9:30 in the morning on Monday, November 8, Dan Riter returned a call from Joe Mims. Joe immediately told Riter that he and his brother Edwin had been unable to find the kitchen knife Joe knew he owned that was similar to the one they had found in the Cahuilla Hills. Probably, then, the knife they had found was Joe's and had been taken by Andrea on Halloween night. Joe had already realized that when he found Andrea in the laundry room that night, she'd been getting the hammer out of the tool area there. It had also occurred to him that she'd meant to use the semen she spit into the tissue to verify later that she had been raped.

Andrea was undergoing psychiatric observation by the doctors at Riverside County Hospital, Riter told Joe, so the arraignment had been delayed. Gary Scherotter said that he wouldn't represent Andrea against Joe, who had paid his bills for Andrea up to November 1, because it would comprise a conflict of interest. On the other hand, if the two charges were combined, which Dan said he thought Gary might attempt to do, Scherotter would go on representing Andrea.

Joe mentioned to Dan, whom he knew to be a Christian, that he thought that in the last several weeks before the assault, Andrea seemed to be losing her faith and going back to her old cultish ways. She'd begun to say that all the people at church thought she was guilty, and she never wanted to go back there. Joe had also come across a pyramid in the house and an old astrology book she'd put out by the phone again. Most people wouldn't give it credence, Joe knew, but he knew that Dan, being a Christian, would understand the negative power of such objects.

On Thursday, January 6, Desert Municipal Court Judge Philip LaRocca granted Scherotter's motion and suspended criminal action on the case until the defendant's mental competency could be determinded. LaRocca scheduled a superior court hearing on the following day, Friday, January 7, to appoint a psychiatrist or psychologist to examine Mrs. Mims.

On Friday, Superior Court Judge Fred Metheny ordered evaluations by Dr. Lee Spencer and added a second psychologist, Dr. Donald Tweedie, at the request of D.A. Jim Hawkins. The evaluations were to be completed by Friday, January 21.

2

Andrea had been arrested on the evening of Monday, November 1, at Eisenhower Medical Center. Almost immediately, she cut her wrist with a thermometer and was transferred to Riverside General Hospital. When, after two weeks of observation it was thought she was no longer a danger to herself, she had been taken to Indio County Jail, in the same complex as the sheriff's department and the district attorney's office. She was being held now without bail.

When Dr. Leitman, who had continued to see her throughout this period, visited her in the county jail on Monday, January 10, Andrea told him she felt "like a hair in God's eye."

She reported that the night before she felt like she had been raped. The room had spun. She was reading *I Never Promised You a Rose Garden*. She had all the symptoms of the book's mentally ill girl, she told Leitman, except the names.

"I go into darkness," she said.

The morning after Halloween, she thought she would never see Joe again and tried to kill herself.

"I became schizo," she told Leitman, explaining a schizoid person saw things other people didn't. It happened, she said, because of stress.

"I never felt like a woman," she said. "I kid myself, thinking I'm a woman. Maybe this experience will be good for me. I felt like a little girl, putting on clothes and makeup to look like a woman. I feel like I've been dead ever since Bob died. I've been slowly dying. The darkness is Bob in hell."

On Wednesday, January 12, Andrea told Leitman that Bob Sand had been like a warm mother she had never had.

"My mother made me feel like I wasn't good enough to get a new dress," she said.

Dr. Tweedie interviewed Andrea for an hour and forty-five minutes on Friday, January 14, and Dr. Spencer conducted an interview the following Monday for an hour and a half.

On Wednesday, January 26, both doctors told the court that in their judgment Mrs. Mims was not competent to stand trial. Dr. Tweedie diagnosed her as a paranoid schizophrenic who harbored delusions of being an object under attack. Dr. Spencer also emphasized her delusional mental state, a state that she would accept and make judgments inside of, as if that world were real, he said.

During the proceedings, Andrea, her hair in pigtails, handcuffed, sat quietly in a corner of the jury box.

Jim Hawkins requested that a third expert, Dr. Anthony Oliver, be allowed to interview the defendant.

Gary Scherotter objected to Hawkins' request, saying that there was no legal authority for the appointment of a psychiatrist by the prosecution in a mental competence proceeding. He asked that Judge Metheny decide on Andrea's competence based on the concurring recommendations of Drs. Tweedie and Spencer.

"My intent," Scherotter said, "is to obtain the quickest possible hospitalization for my client. My belief is that this hospitalization will be long term. Under no circumstances am I asking for outpatient treatment. It will be inpatient and long term."

Judge Metheny agreed with Scherotter that there could not be an appointment of another doctor suggested by the prosecution but said he would feel more comfortable letting a jury decide on Mrs. Mims' competence to stand trial.

"I'm not blaming the two doctors," he said, "but the law is vague on this type of situation. The fault is not on the doctors, but I'm not sure I understand their language. They don't understand legalese anymore than I understand their language.

"Have faith in juries," he concluded. "Juries are street-wise, too."

The attorneys were asked to make a brief appearance on Friday, February 18, to announce if they were ready to proceed with jury selection on the following Tuesday. Unlike other civil trials, the jury in a competency case would be required to return a unanimous verdict.

Dr. Leitman saw Andrea on Monday, January 31. She had tried to cut her left wrist with the lid from a Noxema jar on the previous Friday, two days after the competency hearing.

Bob Sand never had anything nice to say about anyone, she said. The night he was killed, Bob gave her a fur coat and made her pay for it by having two guys and a girl mess with her against her will. She remembered begging Bob not to do it. She had left L.A. to get away from that kind of treatment.

Andrea remembered her paternal grandfather playing with her genitals when she was around four years old.

Her father had suffered amnesia when he abandoned them, one family story went, and Andrea had also suffered amnesia.

In his notes, Leitman wrote: "First session in which Andrea has been able to see how she avoids experiencing/perceiving the negative about someone she cares for."

She told Leitman she had had a dream that he testified in court that she was criminally insane with no hope of treatment or recovery. She woke up from the dream screaming in a sweat.

With her competency trial approaching, Andrea told Dr. Leitman on Wednesday, February 2, that she didn't feel she would be able to survive the next three weeks. This was the way she'd felt since being put in jail.

Joe had hurt her the worst of any man in her life, she said.

On Friday, February 4, Leitman received an emergency call from the sheriff's department that Andrea was threatening suicide and "falling apart." He went to the jail to see her.

She was having "blackouts," she told him. She had talked to her mother on the phone and couldn't hear her even though she was shouting.

"It's funny," she said. "I didn't want to be touched, and I got myself into a situation so nobody can touch me.

"Why didn't I know I was reliving the past when I said I was raped in the present?" she asked.

She told Leitman she kept having the desire to smash up her head.

"Then I won't feel anything," she said. "Maybe it will make the pain go away."

She said she knew she was emotionally disturbed.

"I've known it for a long time. Bob took it away. He made me feel like a little kid. It didn't hurt anyone," she said.

Leitman got a phone call on Saturday, February 5, at 1:50 in the morning from the sheriff's department. Andrea needed to talk with someone, and the Desert Medical Center representative refused to contact her.

That morning she was taken back to Riverside General Hospital for observation and remained there until Wednesday, February 16, when she was returned to Indio County Jail. The estate of Robert Sand had filed suit to block further widow's benefits to Andrea and to recover the money she had already received. After she was returned to jail, Dr. Leitman interviewed her specifically with regard to his testifying at her competency trial.

3

"I need to be on good food and vitamins, or I will die," Andrea told Leitman when he saw her at the county jail on Wednesday. Her aorta, spleen, liver, and gall bladder were all virally infected, she said. When she ate the prison food, she could feel the poison going into her.

While she was at Riverside General Hospital, she said, a lot of rapes happened—all in her mind.

Her left wrist, Leitman noticed, was black and blue and looked as if it had been picked at. Her left breast was bruised, she said, and her right leg cut. Both happened while she was at Riverside.

Her left breast was pushed the night Bob died, she told Leitman.

In the hospital, Andrea told Leitman, she felt something warm coming out of her rear end. She put her hand there and discovered a big glob of blood.

"In my mind it was Bob's ear," she said. "When I went to put Bob's head in my lap, I thought I felt his ear in my hand."

She was hiding in the hospital room so the men who killed Bob wouldn't find her, she told Leitman. This was when she got her bruises.

"I broke the window in my house," she admitted, referring to the last rape incident.

"How did you tie yourself up?" Leitman asked.

"When you're in a real heavy," she said, "anything is possible. If you think someone else is doing it, you probably could do anything."

"I didn't murder Bob," Andrea said. "If he wasn't so jaded and perverted, he wouldn't have died."

Once while she was at Riverside General Hospital, Andrea said, she was sleeping and making guttural noises. Although she thought she had been doing it for a long time, her roommate said it was only three minutes. Andrea remembered seeing a little boy. She was trying to hide from him because she didn't want him to see her getting raped. She didn't think it was healthy for him to see it.

This reminded her of an experience she had when she was nineteen in New Jersey. She had taken an apartment with her friend Carol. Andrea was with her two little boys.

"I was in my panties," she said, "and the landlord knocked on the door. He asked for the rent. When I said we didn't have it, he started messing with me. I couldn't scream because I was afraid of scaring the boys, or that they would see him messing with me. Carol finally woke up. She had some shoes that were unpacked, and she threw all of them at him. Later she told me it took a long time to calm me down."

"Bob was a trick," she said. "He suckered me in for the security so I would stay with him...If I killed Bob, it would have been for the hurt he caused me and not for money."

"I get caught in the shadows and the pits," she told Leitman.

She said she once had a dream: "I told two friends I have two sexes—only one didn't work. I showed them my female and male organs. The male organ gets long when I think about sex. I want to have surgery to have it removed.

"When I was with my mother, her father, my aunt, and some friends, I told them and showed them the long penis and balls."

"My grandpa was very mean to me," she said.

"How?" Leitman asked.

"He was good to me in many ways," she said, "and bad to me in other ways. Grandpa used to beat me because I wasn't doing things for my mother. I was working twelve hours a day as a waitress and taking care of two little boys. I fed an Indian boy, and Grandpa beat me."

"Things I want to do in Patton [State Mental Hospital] are, I want to be able to handle death," Andrea said. "I want to look at myself when I'm thinking and feeling and be in tune with what I'm feeling. I give Gary the answers I think he wants to hear.

"I plan on getting well in six months. I will work very hard. If I don't, I will never get well.

"I'm not the typical case. I don't hear noises. I'm not insane. I think I'm more competent now than I've ever been. I don't think it's wise for me to go to trial."

Leitman told Andrea that she couldn't stick to a topic.

"I can't hear what people say to me," she said. "I want to, but I can't digest it. It could be all the poisons in my body or a blood disease. I want to be on the outside. To live like a normal person. I want to face reality. I'm starting to face reality. I don't want to go to prison."

4

On Tuesday, February 22, a jury of five men and seven women
was selected for the competency hearing in Indio Superior
Court under Judge Frank Moore. The following day, both
Donald Tweedie and Michael Leitman testified for the defense
that in their view Andrea Mims wasn't competent to stand trial.

Dr. Tweedie said that the defendant had suffered from a psychotic disorder when he saw her at the county jail on January
14. It was a "gross psychological disturbance of the thought and
mood process," Tweedie said, in which Mrs. Mims was under a
delusion of being under attack and thought self-defense necessary.

After examining photographs of the defendant in evidence,
Tweedie said, it seemed to him very possible that the wounds
were self-inflicted.

"Self-inflicted wounds," he testified, "are an important
datum of abnormality."

"In the midst of her conversation about her marriages,"
Tweedie said, "suddenly with tears she mentioned she had been
raped four times while in the Indio jail."

During his interview, she had spoken of being raped at least
thirty times, including during her time in jail, by the people she
thought had killed her fifth husband, Robert Sand.

"At one point, she asked me if it was OK for a good
Christian woman to give head," the doctor told the court to an
eruption of laughter.

He had no evidence that any of the rapes actually occurred,
but Mrs. Mims felt that she had experienced them. "She got a
knife trying to ward off the attacker," Tweedie said of one incident Mrs. Mims described. "She felt she was being thrown
down, and she was cutting herself." In his report to the court,
dated January 18, 1983, Tweedie wrote: "In confrontation
regarding the reality of these forcible sexual assaults, the subject

vacillates between insistent assertion of their facticity and a troubled musing as to the possibility of delusion," and went on to quote Andrea: "The rapes are so real—so painful...I was injured...I felt a weird darkness...I thought that there was semen all over me, but they said there wasn't any...When he came at me, I grabbed a knife to defend myself, but I just cut myself...I always felt pushed around and thrown down...A knife was pushed into my rectum."

"Were there any indications that Mrs. Mims was putting on an act?" Gary Scherotter asked.

"She is not malingering," Tweedie said.

Deputy District Attorney Jim Hawkins asked if it was possible that Mrs. Mims could have had a turnaround in her condition since the interview last month.

"I suppose all things are possible," Tweedie said.

Hawkins had talked with Dr. Anthony Oliver regarding the criteria for mental disorders in the *Diagnostic and Statistical Manual III*. The deputy D.A. asked Dr. Tweedie if his diagnosis was based on the standards of the manual, the accepted authority on the symptoms and varieties of the forms of mental disease.

"I fly by the seat of my pants," Tweedie said and elaborated that he preferred to follow his own instincts rather than particular manual guidelines.

"The way she spoke, what she said, how she behaved, and the responses she made," he said were the evidence for his judgment that Mrs. Mims neither understood what she was facing nor could assist her attorney in formulating her defense. Thirty years as a clinical psychologist, he said, had given him a sense about people.

During questioning by Gary Scherotter, Dr. Leitman told the court he had been treating Mrs. Mims since June and agreed with Dr. Tweedie that she wasn't faking mental illness. He differed with him in believing she understood the nature of the charges against her. However, Leitman didn't feel she had the ability to cooperate with her attorney in preparing her defense, pointing out she had ignored Scherotter's advice and talked about her case with others.

"This could be detrimental to her defense," Leitman said. "She also hasn't provided him with all the necessary data he needs to defend her."

He characterized Andrea as a "borderline personality" and said she had had the disorder most of her life, most likely he thought because of the lack of adequate nurturing as a child.

"When I interviewed her on February 16," Leitman told the court, "she told me that when she eats the food that is served at the County Jail, she can feel the poison coming through her body. This is a distorted way of thinking."

Hawkins began his cross-examination of Dr. Leitman by asking if, in preparation for his testimony, he had reviewed the file on Mrs. Mims which he kept as her doctor.

"Yes," Leitman said.

"May I have it then, please," Hawkins said with a slight smile.

"No," Leitman said, holding on to his briefcase. "That would be a violation of professional ethics. My patient is entitled to confidentiality..."

Judge Moore, however, ruled that since Dr. Leitman had reviewed his notes, according to law, it was the right of the prosecutor to also review them.

Sitting handcuffed at her counsel's table throughout the testimony, Andrea occasionally drank from a cup of water and from time to time wiped her eyes or nose with a tissue. A number of times she rested her head in her arms on the table.

5

After court adjourned on Wednesday, Dr. Leitman visited Andrea in the county jail.

"I had a hard time taking all that in today," she told him. Dr. Tweedie, she said, made her feel like he wanted the jury to think she didn't murder Bob.

"After Bob died," she said, "I crapped thirty times a day. I walked out of stores without paying. Or I used to leave groceries in the store. Sometimes I would mess up dinner—I cooked backwards. It was a feat to clean my house. I used to tell strangers I pulled a knife out of my husband."

She asked Dr. Leitman if he thought her mother had anything to do with this, which in fact he had just testified that he did. She talked about the actress Frances Farmer, who had gone crazy trying to please her mother.

"I'm going to die," she told Leitman. "I have herpes."

Jim Hawkins could barely make out Leitman's handwritten notes on his sessions with Andrea. The psychological profile he had typed wasn't much use to him either, since he painted Andrea as a borderline personality. But Hawkins found a drawing by Andrea that seemed to make the very point he wanted to make to the court.

It was a pencil drawing of the people in her life, each of them named and numbered. In the middle of the drawing was Andrea with her arms outstretched, crucifixion-style, being bitten and clawed by the likes of Fred Lastar, Jim Kennedy, Dan Riter, and himself, all of them portrayed as giant birds with sharp claws and/or teeth. Richard Cordine was seen as a serpent coiled around her right arm, with his snake's head at her heart.

Up in the left corner, a lot smaller, were four little birds, each with initials, including G. S. (Gary Scherotter), M. L. (Michael Leitman), and J. M. (Joe Mims). The good guys.

In essence, it seemed to Hawkins, she had portrayed the "good" and "bad" people in her life, thus making it evident that she could certainly discern between the two.

In the bottom right hand corner was a drawing of Robert Sand, with a knife stuck in him. Was he smiling?

While mulling over the case, Hawkins had glued a photograph of Andrea's face on an ad for a television news report on the insanity defense. The lead in the ad read: "Best performance by a psycho in a courtroom series." In fact, he'd begun to think of the whole case as a TV miniseries. The title would be "Sandtrap," and in the opening credits, over a desert golf links landscape, you'd have a close up of a spider web and a black widow spider killing her mate after making love.

When the trial resumed on Monday, February 28, Hawkins went over Andrea's drawing with the jury and had it submitted as evidence. Then he called the forensic psychiatrist Dr. Anthony Oliver as a witness. Although not allowed to interview the defendant, Dr. Oliver testified that he had gone over the D.A.'s complete file on the case, including police reports, tapes and photographs, and had also been in court last Wednesday to hear the testimony of Dr. Leitman and Dr. Tweedie.

Oliver said he thought both doctors had misdiagnosed Mrs. Mims, whom he believed was competent to stand trial. His own diagnosis, he told the court in his trademark English accent, was based on the criteria outlined in the *Diagnostic and Statistical Manual* or DSM-3, on the D.A.'s file, and on his observation of Mrs. Mims during the time he had spent in the courtroom.

Mrs. Mims, he said, displayed signs of having an hysterical or histrionic personality with sadistic and masochistic tendencies. He found evidence, too, of the faking of mental problems, malingering.

"People who are schizophrenic," Oliver said, with regard to Dr. Tweedie's testimony that Andrea was a paranoid schizophrenic, "deteriorate in their ability to function, have an inability to make decisions, and manifest their condition in the second or third decade of their life. To diagnose Mrs. Mims at the age of forty-one as a schizophrenic raises the highest index of suspicion that the diagnosis is inaccurate."

Mrs. Mims wasn't suffering from delusions of being raped, he told the court, but having fantasies of rape which she knew to be untrue. With regard to the paranoid aspect of Dr. Tweedie's diagnosis, Oliver pointed out that in the face of the criminal charges against her, it was appropriate and not pathological that she be concerned.

As for Dr. Leitman, Oliver said he had misdiagnosed Mrs. Mims as a "borderline personality" when she was better characterized by the "histrionic" personality type listed in DSM-3. Oliver called attention to her "intensely dramatic" seductions, sexual fantasies and manipulative behavior. Mrs. Mims clearly had the histrionic tendency of drawing attention to herself, as she had done in her claims of being raped, in posing for seductive photographs, and in showing "considerable sexual attraction for Mr. Fred Lastar." Her suicide attempts were also attention-seeking devices, Oliver said, while her alleged self-mutilations showed her to be "a highly masochistic and sadistic individual."

"I suspect Mrs. Mims derives sexual excitement from her own suffering and from the suffering of others," he said.

Dr. Oliver said he also suspected that Mrs. Mims was faking mental problems in order to avoid prosecution for the criminal charges against her.

There was a question in Scherotter's mind whether Dr. Oliver would find a competency issue or an insanity defense legitimate in *any* instance.

American juries, in any case, were known to have a difficult time with an insanity defense unless it was something very clearcut. A man heard his television giving him orders to kill his neighbor, and the like. The more subtle areas comprised by Andrea's case, where she seemed to inhabit a sort of twilight zone on the border between rationality and psychosis, were extremely difficult for juries.

Dr. Oliver was good looking, impeccably dressed (always with a fresh red handkerchief in his breast pocket), clean and clear in speech, and, worst of all, he had that English accent. It was the voice of authority, of tradition and civilization, and juries fell for it regularly like a ton of bricks. It was hard to get them to see under it to the often shaky and self-serving formulas the doctor would dish up with such panache.

In cross-examination, Scherotter got it out of Oliver that he was not a board-certified psychiatrist. He had not yet passed the test the American Psychiatric Association gave for board certification, a credential that might be considered essential to his status as an expert witness. Scherotter also made the point that Dr. Oliver had said everything he'd said without the benefit of having examined Mrs. Mims, as each of the other expert witnesses had.

The jury took the case for deliberation on Tuesday afternoon. On their first ballot, four of the twelve jurors voted for incompetence. Over the course of Wednesday morning's deliberations, three of the four changed their minds. Late Thursday morning, they returned to court deadlocked eleven to one. According to the jury foreman, Esther G. Carranco, there was no way that the holdout, Herbert Moore, would change his opinion that Mrs. Mims was mentally incompetent.

Judge Moore declared a mistrial and set a hearing for Tuesday, March 8, to determine whether Mrs. Mims would be tried on the two charges against her or undergo another competency trial.

On Friday, March 4, Superior Court Judge Noah Ned Jamin named Guy Denike conservator for his mother. Under the terms of the conservatorship, Guy and the court would represent

Andrea's rights in the lawsuit filed against her by the Robert Sand estate.

Marvin Chesebro, the attorney for the Sand estate, told the court the lawsuit was based on the legal theory that a person should not be able to benefit financially by murdering a spouse. He acknowledged that the question of Andrea's guilt in the murder of Robert Sand would delay the suit.

It was also agreed that the Springs condominium should be sold and the funds put into the conservatorship. Joe Mims would be reimbursed from the funds for at least $35,000 he had spent on Andrea's behalf, most of it for her criminal defense.

At the hearing Judge Jamin asked a handcuffed Andrea whether she understood the nature of the proceedings.

"Yes," she said, and added, "my son's going to take care of me."

On Monday, March 7, when Dr. Leitman visited her in jail, Andrea showed him a handwritten note addressed to him and dated that day:

3/7/83

Dr. Leitman
     Andrea needs help. We are leaving can't help her anymore. We wrote those letters to protect her. Michael we did all of them not the one about the cut throat.

Larry
Nancy
Kathy   Karin

Each of the signatures had a different style. When she got this note, Andrea told Leitman, she felt at peace. She felt like they had left her body. After her first husband, Wesley Denike, beat her and locked her up for more than a year and a half, she said she had developed these personalities to protect herself—Karin, Nancy, Larry, and Kathy.

Karin and Kathy, who were twins, were fighting with each other all the time. Nancy was the Mexican girl who came to the house and told her she would protect her from the police and give her money. Nancy had a boyfriend named Mark. Karin, Kathy and Nancy were the daughters of an American sailor and a Cuban woman, Alicia. They were actual people, she said, from the time that she lived with Wesley, who was in the navy, outside Guantanamo Bay Naval Base.

"When they were gone," Andrea said, "I took them into my life."

She told Leitman that Joe was getting married to a Christian woman he met at church in Escondido.

"I still love him and want to be his friend," she said.

At the hearing on Tuesday, March 8, Gary Scherotter asked for a continuance to weigh the next move in his defense of Andrea, the most immediate issue being whether to ask for a second competency trial. Hearing no objection from Deputy D.A. Jim Hawkins, Superior Court Judge Fred Metheny put the hearing date back to Tuesday, March 22.

On Monday, March 21, Dr. Leitman had his last visit with Andrea. With her assets frozen, she could no longer pay for treatment. During the session, she told him she didn't kill Robert Sand.

"I was having those rapes," she said, "because I couldn't get it out that I was raped the night Bob was killed, and he paid them to do it."

She never lied about it, she said. She always believed it had happened to her.

"How could I put a knife in my rectum?" she said.

"I think I thought Joe was going to cheat on me," she said, "because I wasn't supplying him with sex. I was feeling insecure.

"I remember swinging the hammer. I don't remember hitting him."

"The day before I left Capistrano," Andrea told Leitman, "I discovered I was angry at men."

She talked about dating a man ten or twelve years younger than she when she was in her thirties. He told her she was wonderful, and, until he was ready to fall in love and get married, she was perfect.

"Do you sometimes hate Bob for subjecting you to those people?" Leitman asked.

"I don't hate anyone," Andrea said, "unless I'm not in touch with it."

"Bob was better than my mother and father," she said a few moments later. "He was my little kid."

7

The next day, Tuesday, March 22, Superior Court Judge Fred Metheny extended the hearing date to Wednesday, April 6, saying the postponement would allow time for the possible resolution of probate matters related to the Robert Sand estate, and, in turn, to Mrs. Mims' financial situation.

Outside the court, Gary Scherotter told reporters he hadn't received payment for legal services for two months, in part because of the probate wrangle. It would also be necessary for Scherotter to reach an agreement now with Andrea's conservator, Guy Denike.

Jim Hawkins told the press that when Mrs. Mims returned to court, represented by Scherotter or someone else, depending on how the payment issue was resolved, in all likelihood, one of two things would occur.

One possibility, Hawkins said, would be a retrial on the question of Mrs. Mims' mental competence to stand trial. If the defense should choose not to ask for a second competency trial, the case would go to municipal court for a preliminary hearing.

At the hearing on Wednesday, April 6, Scherotter reported that in order to continue representing Mrs. Mims, he would need to be appointed by the court and paid by Riverside County, since Mrs. Mims, because of the probate dispute, had no money of her own to pay a lawyer.

Scherotter then made the case that the county public defender's office, which under normal circumstances would provide a lawyer for a defendant without the ability to pay for one, had a conflict of interest. One of its lawyers had represented a prosecution witness.

Jim Hawkins identified the witness as one of the Springs security guards who had gone to the condominium the night Robert Sand was killed. Hawkins said a deputy public defender had once represented the guard, whom he characterized as a "minor witness in the Sand murder trial," in a marijuana case.

Judge Metheny said that on Thursday he and two other judges would discuss a contract that Scherotter had proposed. While logic dictated that Scherotter stay with the case he knew better than any other defense lawyer, Metheny said, the financial considerations were equally important, and the contract would have to have "a lid on it."

"He's an experienced and extraordinarily good and not inexpensive lawyer," Metheny said.

The hearing was again postponed, to Wednesday, April 13.

On the thirteenth, Charles Stafford, a thirty-five-year-old lawyer who had risen quickly in the Indio office to chief deputy public defender, told the court there didn't seem to be any basis for his office to declare a conflict.

Speaking softly, Andrea told Judge Metheny she didn't want to give up Gary Scherotter as her attorney, that she trusted him.

While acknowledging that Scherotter would be the "ideal" lawyer for Mrs. Mims because he had defended her from the start, Metheny ruled that, absent a conflict, the public defender's office had to be appointed to represent an indigent client. It wouldn't be fair to the county taxpayers, he said, to assume the higher costs of a private attorney if the public defender's office was available.

"I don't feel Mrs. Mims will suffer from the appointment of a public defender," Metheny said and noted too that the county would be saving "a considerable amount of money."

Metheny scheduled the new hearing for Wednesday, April 20. Stafford thought one week to familiarize himself with the case "should be enough."

Jim Hawkins knew that no longer having to contend with Gary Scherotter was a not insignificant victory in itself.

"We've decided not to contest the issue of competency any further at this time," Public Defender Stafford told Judge Metheny on Wednesday. As was necessary in such a case, Mrs. Mims had concurred with Stafford in the decision to forego a retrial, partly, he said, based on the eleven-to-one outcome in the first trial.

It was hard for Jim Hawkins to imagine Gary Scherotter surrendering so much ground so easily, at least not while he was being paid by his client.

Judge Metheny scheduled Friday, April 22, for Andrea to appear in Indio Municipal Court to have a preliminary hearing date set.

Outside of the court, Stafford said he was having no problem communicating with Mrs. Mims, and she seemed to understand what was going on. He added, however, that he could raise the competency issue again at any time.

XI

1

On Friday, Municipal Court Judge Eugene Bishop scheduled the preliminary hearing to begin in five weeks, on Friday, May 27, to allow Charles Stafford time to prepare his defense. Stafford also requested that the hearing be held in Bishop's court in Indio in the interests of security and attorney convenience. Bishop approved the request.

The week before her preliminary hearing was to begin, Andrea was transferred from Indio County Jail to the main jail in Riverside because of "personality problems" she was having with other inmates. On Wednesday, May 18, while in the Riverside jail, she tied both hands and both feet together and fell out of her bunk bed on her head. A jail sergeant reported the incident appeared not to be an accident, and Andrea was placed in Riverside General Hospital for a seventy-two-hour mental observation. On Tuesday, May 24, Riverside doctors asked that her observation period be extended by two weeks.

On Thursday, May 26, Charles Stafford renewed competency proceedings in superior court, asking Judge Metheny to appoint two experts to examine Mrs. Mims. Because of the Riverside incident, Stafford now suspected Andrea was incompetent to stand trial.

Judge Metheny appointed two Highland psychiatrists, Dr. Robert Flanagan and Dr. Harvey Oshrin, and also allowed Deputy D.A. Jim Hawkins to have the psychiatrist of his choice, Dr. Anthony Oliver, examine Mrs. Mims.

On Thursday, June 16, Andrea was released from Riverside General Hospital and returned to Indio County Jail. On the same day, Dr. Michael D. Schultz, a staff psychiatrist at Riverside General Hospital, filed the report on her stay for observation in the hospital's security ward:

Ms. Mims has been in our care from May 19 to June 16, 1983. Since she has been here she has continually attempted to manipulate medical and nursing staff for her own gains. She continually articulated suicidal thoughts to staff. However, she was heard to say to the nursing staff that this was a game to keep her out of jail. She has not displayed any intent (actions) while she has been a patient here at Riverside General Hospital.

Ms. Mims is currently taking Deseryl and an antidepressant at bedtime. It would be in her best interests to continue with this medication.

At this time she is not articulating any suicidal thoughts. She does express anxiety regarding jail. I suspect that she will become manipulative and [this] will manifest itself by suicidal ideation or a manipulated attempt. I don't see her as a danger to herself *at this time*.

Ms. Mims is free to participate in all related activities and has no restriction from a medical standpoint.

DIAGNOSIS: Major depression with recurrent without psychotic features.

RECOMMENDATION: Return to jail on following meds:

Deseryl 200 mg at bedtime
Lithium CO3 300 mg po-bid

Dr. Anthony Oliver was scheduled to interview Andrea at the D.A.'s office on Saturday. Fred Lastar was going to escort her up to the office from the Indio jail but begged off. Dan Riter was recruited and asked Judy Campbell to accompany him. When they got up to the office with a handcuffed Andrea, Dan went downstairs to find Dr. Oliver and let him in, the building being locked on Saturdays. Rather than wait in the office, Campbell took the prisoner into the coffee room where they sat down. Andrea sighed, lifting her handcuffed hands.

"I'm used to Cartier," she said.

Campbell smiled.

"They're trying to kill me in prison with baloney sandwiches. I don't eat junk food. All I eat now is candy bars. And they won't let me dye my hair. I used to be really blond. It's awful."

It was girl talk, and Campbell, who had never seen Andrea face to face before, was surprised how much like a young girl the forty-two-year-old prisoner was.

On Tuesday, June 21, Superior Court Judge Fred Metheny declared Andrea competent to face the criminal charges against her. The three psychiatrists he had appointed, Drs. Flanagan, Oshrin and Oliver, all concurred in their reports that while Mrs. Mims had personality defects and exhibited odd behavior, she was not psychotic.

The following day a new preliminary hearing was scheduled to begin on Friday, July 22. While the preliminary hearing would normally be set for ten days after the ruling, it was delayed because both Deputy D.A. Jim Hawkins and Investigator Fred Lastar would be on vacation for much of July.

$$\boxed{2}$$

At Chief Deputy Public Defender Charles Stafford's request, the preliminary hearing, which didn't begin until Tuesday, July 26, was closed to the public. Stafford argued that the sensationalism and publicity of the case might harm Andrea's stability as well as keep her from getting a fair trial.

Before Municipal Court Justice Eugene Bishop closed the hearing, Andrea waived her right to a preliminary hearing on the charge of attempting to murder Joe Mims. Bishop set the arraignment on that charge for Friday, August 5. Hawkins figured the defense was only acknowledging the obvious. Joe Mims was present in court, and there was no way the charge could be evaded. A half-dozen spectators, mostly news reporters, left the small third-floor courtroom.

Hawkins put on eleven witnesses, most of them police officers and chemists who had examined evidence from the crime scene at the Robert Sand murder. The last, however, was Richard Cordine, who had been brought in from Nevada. He testified to the incriminating conversations he had had with Andrea both before and after Robert Sand's death.

While Hawkins knew that Gary Scherotter would have cross-examined every witness at great length, in essence scoping out the extent of the evidence before the trial, and making sure that every i was dotted and every t was crossed in the testimonies, Chuck Stafford took a more casual attitude, as if to say he already knew all of this and would have it taken care of come the trial.

It was Stafford's way, and Hawkins knew from dealings with him in the past on other cases that it didn't always serve Chuck or his client that well. You might offer him a plea bargain, a good deal, in a case where the defendant was a sitting duck, and Chuck would brush you off, as if the offer wasn't worth his serious attention. Then you would nail his client, and the sentence would come up a lot worse than the plea bargain. It was like he had tunnel vision sometimes and there was no way to derail him.

Judge Bishop ruled that Andrea would stand trial for the murder of Robert Sand, and set a new date, Tuesday, August 9, for the arraignment on both the murder and the attempted murder charges.

3

The former Deputy D.A. David Chapman had left the district attorney's office in February to work for Thomas Anderson, a personal injury attorney with a national reputation, in Indio. Once installed in his new job across the street from the D.A.'s office, enjoying the higher salary and other benefits Anderson routinely provided his attorneys, including a new Mercedes, Chapman started a campaign to get his friend Jim Hawkins to come over to the firm, too.

Hawkins had an initial meeting with Tom Anderson but wasn't really looking for a job and told Anderson that he enjoyed his work in the D.A.'s office. Anderson, for his part, wasn't about to court anybody, and Hawkins went away from the interview more shaken than he thought he would be. He'd maxed out on salary, after all, and he wondered what it was, exactly, that would keep him from a move that would have such obvious benefits.

Dave Chapman figured his friend would come around and decided not to drop the ball. He kept talking to Jim about what a great job it was and kept lobbying with Tom Anderson for another meeting with Hawkins.

The second meeting happened right after the preliminary hearing, and Hawkins made sure Anderson knew this time that he was serious about the job. Anderson wanted another smart young attorney on board, and once Hawkins made clear to him his change of heart, he offered him a job on the spot.

"Can I stay and try this murder case?" Hawkins asked, referring to the Sand-Mims case, the biggest case of his career.

"If you're going to work for me, I need you right away," Anderson said.

Charles Stafford's problem was there was virtually no evidence of intruders on the night of Robert Sand's murder. Yet Andrea steadfastly stuck to her story. Hawkins hadn't exactly offered a second degree murder plea bargain, but it was a possibility, Stafford knew, except that his client wouldn't budge on her innocence.

There was also the diminished capacity-insanity plea, which probably made the most sense, but Stafford knew that wasn't something Andrea was going to appreciate hearing either, although he figured he might be able to talk some sense to her.

What Stafford was certain about was that it was going to be tough to get the jury to believe that intruders had murdered Bob Sand when there wasn't a single hair of concrete evidence that anybody but the Sands had been there.

Stafford and Lorrie Wright, an investigator for the public defender's office, met with Andrea in prison, and this was one shook-up lady. Following a session, it was like your brain had to settle back into its normal contours after getting whirled around and around.

It was a grim irony, Stafford knew, but if you said to someone, "Hey, your only *real* chance to get out of jail is the fact that you're insane"—and that person looked at you as if *you* were crazy, didn't that prove that the poor lady wasn't firing on all cylinders?

With Proposition 8, the "Victims' Bill of Rights," going into effect on June 9, 1982, between the murder of Robert Sand on May 14, 1981, and the attempted murder of Joe Mims on October 31, 1982, the standards on evidence and an insanity plea in the two cases were different, and that provided one line of defense for Stafford against the prosecution's effort to consolidate the cases and try them together.

When Hawkins requested a consolidation at the arraignment on Friday, August 12, arguing that the two cases were "the same class of crimes and basically the same crimes," Stafford argued both the different laws in effect between the two crimes and the fact that the hard evidence in the attempted murder could prejudice the jury with regard to the Robert Sand murder, where there was mostly circumstantial evidence.

In a procedural move, Superior Court Judge Frank Moore disallowed Stafford's demurrer to Hawkins' request for consolidation, treated Stafford's argument as a motion for separate trials, and then granted the motion, which tentatively required that the two charges be tried before different juries. However, he gave the D.A.'s office until September 23 to enter further written or oral arguments.

Moore said he was primarily concerned with the potential for prejudicing one case by combining it with the other.

"There should be something more substantive before the court to base a ruling that [it] would not be prejudicial," Moore said.

Hawkins, acknowledging he would be leaving the district attorney's office and taking a job as a private attorney as of August 31, said another deputy prosecutor would take the case and argue for consolidation.

After the ruling, Andrea entered pleas of not guilty to both charges against her. Stafford said he wasn't prepared at the time to enter an "insanity plea" on behalf of his client, but it would "probably be entered at a later date."

Judge Moore scheduled the murder trial to begin on Friday, October 7. Hawkins and Stafford thought the trial would take from three to four weeks.

XII

1

While there was little doubt in Stafford's mind that Andrea had killed Robert Sand, it occurred to him that she genuinely might not remember what had happened that night and was covering the fact with a series of improvisations regarding the intruders. His investigator, Lorrie Wright, had been tracking Andrea's life before meeting Sand, and it involved both an intermittent acting career—she had bit parts in *Everything You Always Wanted to Know About Sex, M.A.S.H.*, and *Return of the Valley of the Dolls*— and a high-rolling one as an international call girl, with clients like the international financier Bernie Cornfeld and the department store mogul and founder of the Diners Club Alfred Bloomingdale. Wright had been astonished at the luxury of a high-rise apartment in Beverly Hills where a call-girl girlfriend of Andrea's named Casey Storrs lived. The woman herself, Wright reported to Stafford, had been elegant and charming, as well as, of course, the perfect size six.

"Andrea must have really been one of the standouts in that scene," Wright said to Stafford.

The problem remained that all Stafford had was what Andrea gave him, this goobledegook about one, two, three, four, five, or six people being in the house the night Bob Sand got killed— only there were no tracks, prints, blood spots, or anything else to prove it. That she didn't seem to be lying, or not simply, made him think of a man in the Redlands Police Department, Sgt. Richard Hannebaum, a forensic hypnotist, whom Stafford phoned. What might happen, Hannebaum told him, was that her memory might be jogged, and they could take it from there.

Andrea agreed to the hypnotism, eventually, when Stafford told
her for the umpteenth time that they didn't stand a chance with
the case they had.

Sergeant Hannebaum was in his fifties, easy natured, with a
nice voice. Lorrie Wright sat on one side of Andrea in the interview room at Redlands Police Station with Hannebaum on the
other. Stafford was in the adjoining room behind a one-way
mirror so he could watch what happened. Hannebaum and
Andrea chatted for a while, and Andrea confessed she was upset
with herself for smoking ten cigarettes a day in prison.
Hannebaum said he might be able to help her with that.

"When were you born?" Hannebaum asked her.

"May 31, 1941," Andrea said.

"So that would make you..."

"Twenty-four," she said in a little voice, and they all laughed.

"Forty-one ... forty-two," Hannebaum said.

Among other things, Wright had found out Andrea had two
boob jobs over the years, which accounted for the fact that her
breasts seemed to have a permanently buoyed life of their own.

Hannebaum told Andrea that the subconscious mind takes
care of each of us, screens our memories, shuts out stuff that
could hurt us, whereas in fact everything that has ever happened
to each of us is stored there. He'd hypnotized a seventeen-year-
old boy the week before who had been traumatized by seeing his
mother killed by a car, and the boy could remember being born.
At the same time, the conscious mind, in this session they were
embarking on, could go anywhere it wanted to go, anywhere
Andrea chose to go—to the beach, to the mountains, her
favorite place.

He wasn't going to swing things in front of her eyes,
Hannebaum said. *She* was going to do whatever would be done.
He was just going to talk to her, and she would decide what was
going to go on. Hannebaum started by asking her to close her
eyes, to breathe deeply, and to relax all her muscles. He had a

nice calm, strong but gentle voice. He went from the feet up...and Stafford sat back in his chair in the other room and eavesdropped.

"...Calves...thighs, which are the biggest muscles in the body...small of the back...large muscle in the back...breathing becoming slower and deeper...relax shoulders...upper arms...forearms...wrists...hands and arms totally relaxed...back of the neck...scalp...every single hair of your head...relax your hair...A lot of people don't realize you can do it, but you can...the muscles of your eyes, the tiniest muscles of the whole body..." Hannebaum kept it up in an easy, relaxing way. Stafford could see how someone could go under.

"...Very, very relaxed...eyelids become so heavy you couldn't lift them if you wanted to...lips...jaw..."

Stafford saw Hannebaum put his hand gently over Andrea's face and then take it away.

"...Sinking deeper and deeper into relaxation...The deeper you go, the better you feel...All the little aches and pains and discomforts pass from your body...Any little emotional troubles...Sinking down deeper...so contented...As you relax, continue to be aware of anything, but only the sound of my voice is important. Nothing else matters. All the little distractions fade away..."

"Now," Hannebaum said, "form a picture in your mind. An elevator on the tenth floor going down to the first floor, and each floor it goes down, you become more and more relaxed...tenth floor down to the ninth...down, down to the eighth...to the seventh...sixth...five...four...each floor more and more relaxed...three...two...one...

"The elevator door opens. You walk out and sink into a very comfortable chair...really sink into it...every pore, every cell. Relax into it..."

He counted backwards from twenty, each number inducing greater relaxation.

"Now," Hannebaum said, "you are going to a place with your body, a special place with trees and flowers. No one else can go into this place. No one can upset you.

"When I touch you on the right shoulder," Hannebaum said, and leaned over and touched Andrea there, "it's a signal to relax. On the left shoulder, 'Come wide awake...'"

From the special place they were going to go to another special place...While Stafford watched, Hannebaum went on drawing soothing word pictures of mountains, flowers, and friendly wild animals.

Then he took her back to the first special place...three... two...one...

"Your right hand is very, very light," Hannebaum said. "It's so light, it can almost rise by itself. It can rise up all by itself."

Stafford saw Andrea's right arm rise about half a foot over the armrest of the chair and stay there, in the air, relaxed.

"When I count to three," Hannebaum said, "the arm will return to where it was."

One, two, three—the arm went down again.

"How you feeling? Okay?" Hannebaum asked. "Are you relaxed?"

"Yeah," Andrea answered softly.

"In this special place where you are, is it all right if I cause something to be there?"

Andrea nodded, and Hannebaum told her it was a television set, one on which you could turn the volume way up, you could zoom in on things, and you could stop the image. In her imagination, he said, he'd like her to turn on this television. She was going to be watching a documentary on the night in May when the event had happened. She was going to see people she knew. Bob would be there. Even a girl who looked like her.

While she was watching, she wouldn't be emotionally involved, Hannebaum said. It would be all right to feel sorry for the girl, or Bob, but actually she would feel no emotion.

Stafford watched Andrea sitting back in the chair with her eyes closed.

"That afternoon in May," Hannebaum said, "around noon-time. The person named Bob, the girl who looks very much like you...Tell me what you see."

"Hot turkey sandwiches, Bob's favorite," Andrea said.

"Are they discussing anything?" Hannebaum asked. "Turn the volume up."

They were discussing the cruise they were going to take to Hawaii.

At 3:30, she was washing the car while he watched.

At 4:00, they went out for a drive and, when she came back outside from the grocery store, she saw Bob sitting in the car talking to two men on the sidewalk beside his window, two men she didn't like the looks of...

Andrea had begun to breathe more rapidly, and her voice sounded upset and strained.

Hannebaum touched her right shoulder.

"Remember what you're seeing is on television," he said.

They had dinner, Andrea said. There were no arguments before sleep.

There was a long pause now.

Bob woke her up, she said. There was a phone call. Her son needed a root canal. She didn't want to talk and would call him later. She couldn't go back to sleep and decided to watch "The Newlywed Game" with Bob in bed. Then he fell asleep, and she couldn't sleep with his snoring. She had to get up and play tennis in the morning and wanted to get her sleep.

Another long pause. Hannebaum touched her right shoulder.

She got a glass of water. Then she went into the other room to sleep. She didn't want to wake him up in the morning, anyway.

She called Bob, who had woken up, on his line to thank him for letting her get some sleep. She went to sleep.

Another pause. Hannebaum touched her on her right shoulder.

The longest pause so far. Andrea was moving her head from side to side, breathing quickly.

Hannebaum touched her again on her right shoulder.

Bob is calling her, Andrea said. She thinks he may have fallen out of bed. People are running past her in the hallway.

"The people," Hannebaum interrupted, "stop the screen and zoom in."

It's a man and a woman, Andrea said. The woman's white with blond hair, about five feet tall. Both are wearing tee shirts and jeans. The man has black hair, might be Mexican.

"Can you see his ears?" Hannebaum asked.

"No, 'cause his hair is on them."

"What are they doing here?" Hannebaum asked.

Andrea was almost crying.

"I don't want you to become emotionally involved," Hannebaum said. "I just want you to watch."

She began to cry.

Hannebaum took her deeper into relaxation. "Relaxing more and more now..." he said.

There is another Mexican man, Andrea said. He has a gun, and a great big smile.

Christ, Charles Stafford thought in the adjoining room. A gun.

One of the Mexican men is hitting Bob with the paddle board. There's blood all over. Andrea gives the girl the combination to their safe, and the girl opens it and hands the Mexican an envelope with money.

The girl has big breasts and is going to cut Bob's penis off.

"I keep blacking out," Andrea said, no longer referring to herself in the third person.

The short Mexican man is hitting Bob with the paddle.

The blond girl is stabbing Bob.

When they leave, Andrea pushes the alarm, pulls the knife out of Bob, washes the dishes. There's blood on her face, and she washes it off. Pushes the alarm again. She has Bob's head in her lap and is crying.

"Please don't die!" she says. "Please don't die!"

"How long before the paramedics arrive?" Hannebaum asked.

"I don't know."

The security officer thought she was having a heart attack. She took off her bloody top and threw it in the washer.

"Reach up now and turn the set off," Hannebaum said. "You're still in your special spot. Everything you've just seen— you can remember as much, or as little, as you choose to. In just a moment, you're going to become more and more alert. You enjoyed this time. You'll find it very very easy to go into this state. You've developed a habit of smoking cigarettes. You'll find you have a great deal of willpower now to stop smoking."

Sergeant Hannebaum guided her back, out of the chair and into the elevator. "You're going up to the tenth floor...One... Two...Three...You feel good about yourself...Four... Five...Six...Seven...Eight...Nine...Ten...You get out of the elevator, you're completely alert," Hannebaum said and touched her on her left arm. She opened her eyes.

"How do you feel?" Hannebaum asked.

"Feel weird," Andrea said.

"You did good," he said.

2

On Tuesday, September 13, Stafford was granted a delay on the date the trial would begin. The new prosecuting attorney, a tall, handsome, quiet-spoken, thirty-two-year-old former Monrovia policeman named Robert Dunn, had been jamming night and day to get through the mountain of police reports, interviews, and other materials in the file since taking the case. Relieved to have some extra time himself, he had made no objection to Stafford's request.

Superior Court Judge Noah Ned Jamin set back the trial date to January 6, 1984.

Although the hypnosis session seemed largely to repeat the intruders scenario, Stafford saw two promising elements in it. For the first time, the woman was noted to be blond, as Andrea had been, though she was now entirely brunette after almost a year in prison, and it was the woman who was seen stabbing Sand. Had she obliquely acknowledged herself here as the killer?

The other development was Andrea referring to "a paddle board." Exactly what was that item? Stafford and Lorrie Wright spent the next three days interviewing Andrea intensively about her relations with Robert Sand and began to make some headway. The man wasn't exactly Mr. Rogers. For the first time, too, they began to really talk about Andrea's early life and young adulthood.

After mulling it for a while, Stafford, knowing he didn't have much else to go on, decided another session with Hannebaum might bring out the whole story of the night of May 14, 1981. Hannebaum told Stafford that a hypnotic state might be triggered just by Andrea seeing him again.

On Thursday, September 15, three weeks after the first session, Stafford and Wright took Andrea back to Redlands Police Station. Wright again sat beside Andrea in the interview room while Stafford went into the next room with the one-way mirror. As he did during the first session, Hannebaum, sitting on Andrea's right, started with conversation.

Almost immediately Andrea started to discuss Bob Sand's increasingly violent sexual demands and how they began to affect her mentally. The fantasies had started to become real to her. One night on the trip to Oregon, when they were staying in a cottage that was set back and isolated from the main building of the motel, he had pulled out a stick in their bedroom and beaten her six times with it before she ran outside into the night.

"Come back in," he called out to her a minute later. "I already came. Everything's fine."

"Why didn't you leave him?" Hannebaum asked.

After a long pause, Andrea, on the verge of tears, said, "I had all my money invested in the house."

After another moment, she began to talk about the night of the murder, essentially telling the story as she had always told it, until she woke up in her bedroom hearing Bob calling her. This time there were no people in the house when she went into his bedroom, where she found him lying on the floor. Thinking he'd fallen out of bed, she went to help him, noticing two knives on the carpet beside him.

"*Are you all right?*" she asked him. "*Are you all right?*"

Andrea paused for a long time.

She was going to press the alarm button, she said finally, but he reached out suddenly and pulled her down, wanting to engage her in a game. The next thing she knew, she was under the bed to get away from him, and he was taunting her by sticking her with one of the knives.

"Did he break the skin?" Hannebaum asked.

She didn't think so. He wanted her to play one of his games and eventually let her out from under the bed.

"The game was pretty sick that he wanted me to play," Andrea said and then paused again.

"What was that?" Hannebaum asked.

It was embarrassing, Andrea said. Hannebaum reassured her that she could tell him.

Andrea said that a woman named Karen, who worked at the local car wash and had big breasts, and the two guys she had seen Bob talking with earlier that day, whose names were Monko and Jose, were outside their bedroom, and were, Bob told her, going to come into the room. If she didn't do what they wanted her to do, there were two more people out there who were going to come in and cut her.

Karen was going to come in and suck Andrea's breasts. The two guys were going to have intercourse with her at the same time.

"*This is no game, Andrea*," Bob told her, "*this is for real.*"

When he let her stand up, Bob started hitting her on the head with an exercise board, the board he used to paddle her with when she'd been naughty.

She paused again.

"He said he was going to take tennis away from me."

Andrea's voice cracked as she said this, and the force of her emotion at that moment seemed to Lorrie Wright for the first time to be unquestionable.

"I was angry," she said. "'*You're not going to take that away from from me.*'"

Bob said he was going to cut her hair and grabbed at it. She started stabbing him in the back with a toenail scissors she had found on the bed. She was infuriated. She stabbed him three or four times before she realized what she was doing and threw the scissors across the room.

"*You see what you made me do,*" she said to Bob and immediately began to clean up a broken glass that had been knocked from the bedtable onto the floor.

Bob grabbed her again and was sticking her again with the knife. She bumped into his wheelchair. She picked up an exercise board and swung it, knocking the paring knife out of his hand, and with the backswing hit him in the head.

"*You're a lying, stealing whore,*" Bob said.

"*I asked you for money,*" Andrea said. "*I'm not taking it.*"

She stood on a knife on the floor and dropped the board.

"*Let's get you into bed,*" she said to Bob. "*Or I'll draw some bath water.*"

Bob, sitting on the floor, reached for the telephone. "*I'm calling the police,*" he said.

"*Bob, you hit me first,*" Andrea said.

"*You're nothing but a whore,*" he said. "*No one's gonna believe you.*"

He picked up another knife. Trying to get away, Andrea grabbed a board and swung it at him.

"*You're using me,*" she said. "*You're mean and cruel.*"

She fell down on her knees in exhaustion.

"*We need help, Bob,*" she said. "*We need help. Push the alarm.*"

"My head is going—Arrrrr!" Andrea said to Hannebaum.

Bob lunged at her again, and she hit him in the head with the board.

"Everything's going black," Andrea said to Hannebaum. "I was trying to get over to the alarm. '*Bob, help me. I can't see.*'"

She was walking along the edge of the bed, stepped on a knife, and picked it up.

"*You're dead,*" Bob said and grabbed her leg.

Crying now, Andrea told Hannebaum she started stabbing Bob, and when his body moved, she went on stabbing him.

She said she blacked out then, and when she woke up, she couldn't remember anything. "I remember him calling me," she said. "I remember people being in the house—the story Bob told me. Because I *couldn't* have done..."

She pushed the alarm and pulled the knife out of him. In the mirror over the bathroom sink, she saw blood all over herself.

"I didn't even realize he was dead," she said to Hannebaum.

After looking in the mirror and washing herself in the sink, she went over and held him.

"*Don't die, Bob,*" she said. "*We're gonna share my grandchild...*"

He wasn't breathing. She found a piece of flesh in her hand. His eyes were black. The top of his head was red. The piece of flesh was from his ear, and she flushed it down the toilet. She drew a bath. She would give him a bath. She would wash all the sheets and the down comforter that was bloody. She washed and dried the knives and scissors. She washed the board in the bathtub, then got in the bathtub and washed the blood off her legs and feet, face, and hair. Her body felt numb.

When she took the board out of the bathtub, something freaked her out. She started hitting the board on the carpet.

"I'm going to kill him," she thought, thinking of the one who had killed Bob. She tried to get outside through the sliding glass door in the bedroom but couldn't get it open.

When she told Bob about how her first husband, Wesley Denike, had beaten her, it turned him on, Andrea told Hannebaum.

Her second husband, Philip Green, who was probably the best lover she had ever had, was a gambler who wanted to turn her out as a prostitute three days after they got married.

Her third husband, Isaac Dajani, was a Jordanian she married so he could get a green card. Their relationship was platonic except for one time.

She almost married a nice Jewish man in New York, Elliot, to whom she loaned $20,000 over the course of eight months because he was about to start a million-dollar business. He was supposed to have taken out a $100,000 life insurance policy, naming Andrea as beneficiary.

But instead of marrying Elliot, in April of 1980, she married a man in Los Angeles who had swept her off her feet in ten days, Derek—or Derelict—Conte.

Her real name was Phyllis Corneillise. Her father was Belgian, and her mother Dutch-French-Scotch-Irish-English.

She married Derek on a Friday. He hit her right after the wedding and was never the same again. Saturday, Derek asked her to have sex with another woman. And on Sunday she got a call from New York. Elliot, the man she should have married, had died of a heart attack. It turned out he hadn't paid even the first premium on the life insurance policy.

She scared Derek after they'd been together about ten days by telling him she was thinking of stabbing him with a butcher knife. He left that night, taking with him her 1971 Fiat, along with the pink slip.

A friend of Andrea's, Sandra Ferris, told her about Robert Sand. Ferris, a madam, said there was a rich old man in a wheel-chair, living by himself, who was ready to marry. In the trade that meant Sand was a regular customer who was getting tired of paying different girls and wanted someone there for him around the clock. Ferris told Andrea that Sand sometimes liked "rough stuff" but that he had always been good to all the girls.

After Andrea started seeing Bob, it was two weeks before she could get the courage to tell him about Derek.

At first he had been so loving and so caring with her. Gradually he got into wanting her to be naked more and more of the time. Photographing her naked and putting the photographs into a scrapbook. She would do cartwheels outside naked for him. Once he urinated on her when she was sunbathing.

Hannebaum excused himself from the room for a moment, and Andrea turned to Lorrie Wright.

"Is he going to hypnotize me?" she asked.

Bob and Diana Dunn gave a going-away party at their house for Jim Hawkins. For the party, Mrs. Dunn decorated a sheet cake as a *Press Enterprise* front page. The headline for the day, Saturday, September 17, 1983, read:

JIM HAWKINS AFRAID TO TRY MIMS CASE
LEAVES D.A.'S OFFICE IN DISGRACE
NEWSMEN MOURN LOSS OF INSIDE SOURCE

Dunn had been struck by the contrast in styles between his predecessor and himself. An elder in the local Mormon church who didn't drink or smoke, Dunn was at the other end of the spectrum from the flamboyant Hawkins, who sought out and relished the media limelight. It was like moving from the playboy to Mr. Clean.

At the same time, Dunn knew he had his own mystique. He'd been told by a friend in the D.A.'s office that, after mixing it up with Dunn in the courtroom, a lawyer had reported being cut so quickly and so badly by the prosecutor that "I didn't even know I'd been cut." Thereafter, his friend told him, Dunn's nickname in local legal circles was "the surgeon."

$$3$$

On Thursday, November 17, Superior Court Judge Frank Moore ordered that Richard Cordine be transferred from the Broom Readjustment Center in Trenton, New Jersey, where he was now serving time for his bank robbery conviction, to Indio County Jail, so he would be available to testify at Andrea Mims' trial.

D.A. Investigator Dan Riter was sent to New Jersey to pick up the prisoner. While driving to the airport for the flight to California, Cordine told Riter that he couldn't fly and insisted that they drive or take a train. As far as Riter was concerned, this was typical con bullshit, and he told Cordine they were flying. The convict insisted that he couldn't go through with it, that he might not physically survive the flight.

"Fine," Riter said to the handcuffed Cordine. "We'll throw your sorry ass in the trunk of the car, and we'll drive across the country."

"Yeah, okay," Cordine said. "We'll fly."

In the air, Cordine told Riter, who was studying for his law degree, that he was going to make a hell of a prosecutor.

On Monday, December 5, Charles Stafford amended Andrea's not guilty plea by adding not guilty by reason of insanity pleas on both charges. Judge Moore appointed two psychologists, Ernest Proud and Donald Tweedie, to examine her and file their conclusions with the court by Friday, December 23.

Dr. Ernest Proud conducted interviews with Andrea and administered a battery of psychological tests to her at Indio County Jail on December 9, December 16, December 23—all

Fridays—and Tuesday, December 27. The psychological evaluation he filed, approximately seven thousand words, detailed his interviews with Andrea, summarized the extensive material on her case he received from the court, and provided a psychological profile based on her test results.

Andrea told Dr. Proud that her life was like her childhood: "I wanted dancing lessons but got piano lessons instead."

Describing to Proud her life with Robert Sand, she spoke of the escalating violence and frequency of the fantasies he required her to act out. "Whenever Andrea would sunbathe in their yard," Proud wrote in the evaluation, "Mr. Sand would roll up in his wheelchair, stand up for a moment, pull down his pants and urinate on her. This, of course, would inhibit Andrea from sunbathing...She also states that 'He was always obsessed with my rectum.'"

> At one point during this interview [Proud continued], Andrea said that she felt like a mechanical doll. She would often tell Mr. Sand—with this she stood up and became rigid in her movements—"I am an Andrea doll. All I do is suck and fuck."...
>
> She states that she started to develop a fear for her life...perhaps the fantasies were not unreal, that "they were a part of life and they were as real as anything." He would have her put knives in her arm as if she had been stabbed and, using ketchup for blood or her menstrual blood, would smear it on her body and [he would] take pictures of this. It was at this time, she stated, that she started to feel very strange and thought that she had lost control of her eyes. She felt that she was looking at people from the corners of her eyes. Sometimes, as she would be walking through the house, as always in the nude, he would throw

himself from his wheelchair on to her, often knocking her down.

"On the night of the incident," Proud wrote, "[Robert Sand] had been his angriest self, threatening that their finances were in bad shape, [and] that there were rapists coming to rape her. She was having her menstrual cycle, she states, and she usually didn't feel very well with this. She told him she wasn't interested in this and, because he persisted, she had to leave the room."

After she described the murder to Dr. Proud—detailing her own actions in hitting Bob with the board and stabbing him with the scissors and knife (at one point during the assault noting that Bob had started masturbating), and at the same time speaking of intruders being present—she told him that the next thing she remembered was that Bob "was laying on the floor and she reached over and pushed the alarm." Proud wrote: "As she could not remember what happened, she started to confabulate the situation. This means that when a person's memory is lost, we [sic] start filling in with things we believe might have happened."

The rape incidents that followed, Dr. Proud noted, "happened over and over again, much like what Bob had predicted would happen if she left the house."

With regard to her relationship with Joe Mims, Andrea told Dr. Proud that "when she refused to have sex with him because of the physical and emotional pain...he would hit his fists on the table, really hard, and yell." She said her attack on Joe had been motivated by a comment of Dr. Leitman's. The doctor had instructed Joe to call him right away if Andrea started acting strange or got violent. Dr. Leitman promised to help her, maybe hospitalize her. She was not intending to kill Joe.

She hadn't wanted to leave Capistrano, Andrea told Dr. Proud, and it had only been at Joe's insistence that she did. Given this explanation, the doctor saw the assault incident as a cry for help specifically to her therapist.

"At least twenty times since she has been in jail," Proud wrote, "she has thought she has been raped. Each time it was the same, a feeling of suffocation and an ugly odor."

He noted that she was presently taking Triavil three times a day and Motrin two times a day.

In the next part of the report, Proud summarized Andrea's scores on various tests he had administred to her. Her intellectual functioning had been measured with the Weschler Revised Intelligence test. The results were a verbal IQ of 119 and a performance IQ of 130, with a full-scale IQ score of 127, which placed her in the ninety-sixth percentile, the superior range of intellectual functioning. The doctor found no signs of central nervous system damage or brain dysfunction. "Personality factors," Proud wrote, "indicate that Andrea is an individual who tends to be passive-dependent, demanding a great deal from others but resenting any requests made of her by others." Proud continued:

> She indicates that she has feelings of depression, that she is often irritable, withdrawn and nervous. There is also indication that she has significant repressed hostility, that she is self-centered, immature and unable to form deep emotional involvements. Consequently, people like Andrea have little that can be done to make them happy, and as a result, they often have marital problems and problems in their work. They have problems within themselves but tend to project it on to others. She is highly suspicious of others and has the feeling that she is being persecuted and mistreated. She sees herself as being warm-hearted, easy-going and out-going and as being brighter than most people, as being humble and accommodating...She also has an exact, controlling

willpower. There is indication of depression
which brings on suicide ideations.

Proud compared the approach that Robert Sand had taken
with Andrea to brainwashing.

> The first requirement for a person to go through
> it is that they be vulnerable, that is, that a person
> not have a strong belief system...They tend to
> have feelings of guilt that what they have gotten,
> they got through ill-will or wrong-
> doing...Secondly, the environment must be con-
> trolled, that is, the person's movements restricted,
> and everywhere that they go, the trainer is in
> control...The captor—or, in this case, Bob
> Sand—has to be committed, strong. They must
> be persuasive, thus they quickly become aware of
> where to give approval...Confusion is very impor-
> tant. It is most effective if the victim retains the
> illusion that they have free will, that the person
> believes they are remaining with this captor under
> their own free will.
>
> Bob Sand, kept a woman who had much guilt
> about her past, who wanted desperately to help
> others, who was looking to feel attached or con-
> nected with someone, to feel loved. He knew all
> of these things and took advantage of this oppor-
> tunity...

Proud—noting parenthetically that Andrea had always been a
borderline psychotic, not knowing where reality and fantasy
begin and end—went on to say that when Robert Sand threatened "to remove her one final refuge, her tennis, by cutting her
hair so that she would be embarrassed to leave the house...she
lost control."

He concluded: "Andrea was incapable of knowing or understanding the nature and quality of her act or of distinguishing right from wrong at the time of the commission of the offense."

Dr. Tweedie, who had interviewed Andrea for the competency trial in February, was surprised that she now confessed to the murder of Robert Sand. At the same time, she spoke of intruders being present that night, and the next moment they would be gone. It was hard to figure out exactly how the narrative line of her murder confession went.

In his report—far briefer than Dr. Proud's—to Judge Moore, Tweedie wrote:

> During the examination, the subject admitted causing the death of her husband Robert Sand. She narrated a long series of sadomasochistic and "bondage and discipline" episodes during her cohabitation and subsequent marriage to him that included...hiring a male to perform oral copulation with her. [Sand] induced her to play "games" that had violent rapine, torture, and bodily assault themes with knives, scissors, and cudgels. This also included hiring of others to participate in game roles. Ms. Mims reports that this seemed very "weird" to her but that she agreed to participate sometimes with reference to obsequious wheedling and sometimes after threats of deprivation, or the showing of the pictures to others.
>
> The cumulative stress of this existence, coupled with her generally unhappy experience historically of sex as rape, precipitated a psychotic break. It was in this mental state that the homicide was carried out.

Dr. Tweedie's interview with Andrea and his review of the background and information related to the assault on Joe Mims led him, he reported to Judge Moore, "to the same professional conclusion" he had with regard to the murder of Robert Sand. This incident appeared to have been precipitated, Tweedie said, when, on October 28, 1982, three days before the assault, Joe Mims and Gary Scherotter "confronted [Andrea] with their concerted opinion that she was insane and the fact that they were determined to continue her legal defense on that basis as well as to insist that psychological treatment for her be continued."

Dr. Tweedie concluded that Andrea "at the time of the commission of the offense[s], as a result of mental disease or defect, lacked substantial capacity either to appreciate the criminality of her conduct or to conform her conduct to the requirements of the law."

On Friday, December 30, Judge Moore accepted the not guilty by reason of insanity pleas and denied the prosecution's motion to have the two trials consolidated. The murder of Robert Sand happened before Proposition 8, the Victims' Bill of Rights, had been passed and while a broader standard of criminal insanity was in effect. The test, proposed by the American Law Institute, specified that "A person is not responsible for criminal conduct if at the time of such conduct as a result of mental disease or defect he lacks substantial capacity either to appreciate the criminality [wrongfulness] of his conduct or to conform his conduct to the requirements of the law."

XIII

1

The murder trial began on Tuesday, January 17, 1984. Chief Deputy Public Defender Stafford suggested, and Superior Court Judge Frank Moore agreed, that potential jurors should be questioned one at a time in the judge's chambers about any news stories on the case they had seen or heard. Otherwise the voire dire proceeded as usual, with twelve potential jurors sitting together, each responding to the opposing attorneys' questions before the group. In order to keep the trial clear of the attempted murder charge, the defendant was referred to as Andrea Sand or Andrea Claire.

Andrea had arrived sedately dressed in a tailored suit and blouse, but, it seemed to Deputy D.A. Robert Dunn, with an unmistakable charisma, exuding a kind of survivor's confidence along with that combination of physical attractiveness and a certain vulnerability she projected. It was as if she was a movie star to the spectators who lined up to fill Indio Courtroom A, the largest courtroom in the complex.

Dunn had envisioned himself going into the trial, looking at Andrea and having her smile, and finding himself melting and losing his edge. As an antidote, that first day, he mad-dogged her, locking eyeballs as if to say, "It's been fun and games up to now, but we're not fuckin' around anymore."

The jury selection was completed and the twelve jurors and alternates sworn in on Thursday, January 26, having absorbed four days in court. Stafford told the court that he wouldn't be contesting the identity of Sand's killer but suggested in questioning prospective jurors that there could be evidence with regard to Andrea's mental state.

Ten women, most of them older women, and two men made up the jury, which Dunn considered very favorable to his case. Many women, he knew, would tend to see Andrea as a threat to their own marriages or relationships.

That afternoon, with jury selection completed and the trial scheduled to begin on the following Monday, January 30, the prosecutor was surprised to find Stafford outside the courtroom crowing that he'd gotten exactly the jury he wanted.

On Monday morning, Dunn requested that D.A. Investigator Dan Riter be allowed to sit at his table as chief investigating officer. Normally, the chief investigating officer from the sheriff's department would sit at the prosecutor's table, but Dunn had decided to rule out Detective Lastar, who he felt projected too soft an image both physically and in his demeanor. There was also some question in Dunn's mind about whether Lastar, although not co-opted by Andrea, hadn't fallen under her spell. Riter, on the other hand, he knew to be both a superb investigator and completely free of any ambivalence on the case.

Judge Moore allowed the request, and Dunn made his opening statement to the jury.

Judy Campbell from the D.A.'s office was in court that day, and the minute she saw Bob Dunn go into action she knew Chuck Stafford was going to have a tough row to hoe. Everybody in the D.A.'s office knew how meticulous and well-organized Dunn was, and how he'd really had to jam to get up to speed on the case, but what Campbell hadn't seen was how good he was with a jury. Attractive and physically imposing, he had a quiet, polite but authoritative manner, and he knew how to address the jury directly. He was exactly the sort of man you wanted between you and a criminal.

"You're going to be hearing an amazing story," Dunn told the jury, "an unbelievable story totally contrary to the physical facts, which will show that Andrea Sand did murder her husband, Robert Sand."

Her motive, Dunn said, was financial gain, as well as unhappiness at a stifling marriage to an invalid. Dunn then went on to summarize his case, touching on the many changes in Mrs. Sand's saga of the circumstances of Robert Sand's death, which, he said, was in itself an indication of her guilt. Her latest story was that she had in fact killed her husband, but in self-defense.

But the self-defense explanation didn't work, Dunn said, because "Robert Sand was incapable of attacking her." At the time of his death, he was confined to a wheelchair.

Chief Deputy Public Defender Stafford conceded in his opening statement that Andrea had killed her husband, but stated that the act did not constitute murder, because Robert Sand was far from being a helpless victim. A big man with great upper body strength, he was also capable of taking a few steps on his own. Mr. Sand was also a domineering, sometimes hot-tempered man who indulged in a wide range of sexually odd habits.

Stafford cited examples of Sand's extreme possessiveness and obsessive interest in Andrea's daily activities, how he demanded she walk around the house nude and would follow her even into the bathroom. Stafford talked of the hundreds of Polaroids Sand took of his wife naked and the "golden showers."

And he told the court of the sex games.

"Mrs. Sand would play-act she was being assaulted and raped. As the games progressed, Robert Sand became more violent. In the week prior to the homocide, there were two to three of these sessions," Stafford said. "You're going to hear how violent they were."

On the night of May 14, 1981, pretending that he was unconscious on the floor of the master bedroom, Robert Sand tried to lure Andrea into still another of his sexual fantasies. When she refused, he grabbed her and tried to spank her. In the struggle that ensued, Mrs. Sand killed Robert Sand "in a frenzy, out of control. We're dealing with a woman who is very disturbed," Stafford said.

As the defendant sat at her counsel's table with Lorrie Wright, Stafford recounted Andrea's early history, beginning with her being raped at fifteen, and her marriage to the man who had raped her.

"All the relationships that Andrea has had have been with men who are authoritarian, posssessive, abusive, and, in some respects, violent," he said. "In most cases, they are older, quite a bit older."

Abandoned by her father as a young teenager, Andrea had emerged from this trauma and the ones that followed with her first husband, as a pliant person, always trying to please others.

"She had surgery on her breasts," Stafford said, "simply because somebody told her she was too small when she was young. She changed her hair color to blond because somebody said it looked better."

Stafford rejected the prosecution's contention that Andrea had killed Robert Sand for financial gain. The Springs condominium had a big mortgage, and her cash from the estate went for the most part to making that payment.

As a victim witness advocate, Judy Campbell found the revelations about Andrea's early life and her marriage to Robert Sand very relevant to the case, and Stafford, she thought, was doing a decent job. The fact that he wasn't the prepossessing man that Bob Dunn was, and that he didn't have Dunn's rapport with the jury, wasn't, after all, Chuck's fault.

2

In the days that he'd spent jamming to get through the voluminous quantity of material on the case, Robert Dunn had come to see that his challenge as a prosecutor would be to tell the jury a story it could make sense of, and about which it could eventually make a clear judgment. The fact that Chuck Stafford had admitted that Andrea killed Robert Sand didn't change the fact that she had continuously lied, and this was going to be the cornerstone of Dunn's case.

If the chief investigating officer had been focused and strong, someone who could synthesize the material on the case and present it with an overview, he might have relied on the officer's testimony to do that for the jury. But having made the decision not to rely on Fred Lastar for his case in chief, Dunn had to go the more laborious route of orchestrating a narrative beginning with the night of the murder and a series of witnesses who had been at the crime scene.

The witnesses were called in the order in which they had arrived at 6 Brandeis Court, starting with Springs security guard Raul Cortez—Stanley Booker had since died of a heart attack—and sheriff's Patrolman Darryl Czajkowski.

After establishing when the Springs Security System had received the initial alarm, Dunn called two witnesses to establish a time lag between the death of Robert Sand, as Mrs. Sand had reported it to the police, and the condition of the body on the arrival of the security, police, and medical personnel at the condo. Peter Rode, the Springs Ambulance attendant, had been the first to examine the victim. Dunn wanted to make sure the jury understood each point he made and interrogated each witness with an unhurried thoroughness.

DUNN: What is rigor mortis?

RODE: That's the fixed position that the body lies in after it's started to decompose its gases. The muscles start to tighten and everything.

DUNN: Prior to that night, on how many occasions had you seen rigor mortis?

RODE: I've seen a total of two to three hundred dead bodies, and a lot of those—say half at least—where some signs of rigor mortis had set in.

DUNN: Are you familiar with how long after death it takes before rigor mortis is present?

RODE: It can start developing one hour afterwards.

Terry Burdo, a sergeant with the sheriff's department who had reported at 4:20 to the crime scene, also testified on the condition of the body when he observed it that morning:

DUNN: When you looked at the body in the master bedroom of the condominium, did you observe any postmortem lividity?

BURDO: Yes.

DUNN: Would you explain.

BURDO: A period of time after death, the blood will seek the lowest point of the body as it lays, causing a purplish pigmentation to the skin in the lower portions of the body.

DUNN: Had you had experience previously with seeing bodies where postmortem lividity is present?

BURDO: Yes, sir.

DUNN: On how many occasions?

BURDO: Fifty to seventy-five.

DUNN: And based upon your experience, did you have any opinion of how long the body had been in the position that you observed it when you first went into the bedroom?

BURDO: My own personal opinion was more than an hour.

Burdo also testified that he didn't see any footprints in the dew-laden grass off the back patio, where Mrs. Sand had reported the assailant escaped.

Dunn called as his next witness Investigator Rudy Garcia, whose testimony would continue into the following morning, Tuesday, January 31. The prosecutor, employing a large swatch of the cream-colored carpet, the oriental screen, and the wheelchair arranged as they had been on the morning of the murder, recreated the part of the master bedroom where Robert Sand's body was found.

Dunn first established that Mrs. Sand herself didn't appear to have sustained any injuries when Garcia saw her that morning lying on the bed in the second bedroom. The investigator went on to testify about the broken glass on the carpet in the master bedroom, the large amount of blood and blood splattering in that room, and the small drops of blood on the hallway carpeting, the foyer, the kitchen area, the two bathrooms, and the living room.

Having established the bloodiness of the murder scene and the likelihood that the assailant would have been bloodied, Dunn asked Garcia if there was blood on the drapery in front of the sliding glass door in the living room, through which Mrs. Sand said the intruder had made his escape. Garcia said there wasn't and that drapery would have had to have been moved for someone to exit onto the patio. If an intruder had rushed out "he would have left blood on that drape."

In his cross-examination, Stafford returned to the murder scene.

STAFFORD: Was there anything that indicated to you that Mr. Sand would have had to have been in other areas of the bedroom other than where his body was found?

GARCIA: Yes.

STAFFORD: And what indicated that to you?

GARCIA: The blood on the wheelchair, and on the partition or room divider.

STAFFORD: So assuming that all those stains and all that blood belonged to Mr. Sand, that would indicate to you that Mr. Sand did, in fact, move around that room?

GARCIA: Yes.

STAFFORD: Injured?

GARCIA: Yes.

Dunn took a redirect.

DUNN: You said there was blood on the ceiling?

GARCIA: Yes.

DUNN: That wouldn't indicate that Mr. Sand was walking on the ceiling?

Laughter broke out in the courtroom.

GARCIA: No, it certainly did not. I said there were blood splatters on the ceiling as well as on the wall.

DUNN: And it's possible during the beating or stabbing of Mr. Sand, blood was being thrown off the weapon, or off hands, or whatever in various parts of the room?

GARCIA: Yes. It could have been done by the victim. It could have been done by the assailants. And it could have been done by the weapon as it was striking.

DUNN: So there's many explanations of how blood would have been found in different parts of the room?

GARCIA: That's correct.

DUNN: Was there one predominant part of that room where a large quantity of blood occurred?

GARCIA: Yes.

DUNN: Where was that?

GARCIA: That was where the body was lying.

In recross-examination, Stafford brought in as an exhibit a forensic photograph of a handprint on the carpet in the master bedroom, making the case that such a handprint comprised another indication of movement.

Before breaking for lunch, Dunn called Deputy Larry Pedone, who testified to finding the murder weapon under a corner of a living room sofa on the afternoon of May 14.

Stafford had no questions.

After lunch, Dunn called Steven Secofsky as his next witness. The Department of Justice criminalist testified that, after exhaustive analysis, there were only two types of blood found in the house, and those matched the blood types of Robert and Andrea Sand. Stafford, in cross-examination, asked if the bloody handprint would be consistent with someone "pulling" himself across the floor.

"Pulling or being dragged," Secofsky said.

In his redirect, Dunn asked, "Is there anything inconsistent [in the handprint] with someone bending down to wipe blood off their hand?"

"Nothing inconsistent," Secofsky said.

Secofsky also identified a light blue, lace-trimmed pajama top found in the washing machine at the condominium, and testified that blood stains on it matched Robert Sand's blood type.

Though both the knife found under the couch in the living room, and the exercise board in the living room were, Secofsky said, "consistent with being wiped down," after hemistix tests, they both showed indications of human blood.

$\boxed{3}$

F. Rene Modglin, the forensic pathologist who had performed the autopsy on Robert Sand, was Deputy D.A. Dunn's first witness on the morning of Wednesday, February 1, and his testimony absorbed all of that day and part of the following morning. Modglin was a very large man with very long, straight and somewhat unkempt-looking hair. Defense attorneys always wanted to question his expertise.

Dunn loved to get this man, who looked like someone out of a horror movie, up on the witness stand and ask about his credentials. Since 1963 he had been a Riverside County Coroner's Office pathologist, before that a pathologist for the San Bernadino County Coroner's Office, and, on a request or referral basis, he had been a pathologist for the Mono County and Inyo County Coroner's Offices. Dunn asked how many autopsies had he performed.

"About fourteen thousand," Modglin said.

The prosecutor had an easel set up in the courtroom with a large drawing of the victim's body, both front and back sides. Then, having made sure that Modglin was supplied with a *red* marker pen, Dunn went over every one of the fifty-one inci-

Joe Mims with Andrea. They were married the weekend after her arraignment for the murder of Robert Sand.

The wet T-shirt poster of Andrea, this one inscribed to Joe Mims, "I just want to be loved for my mind."

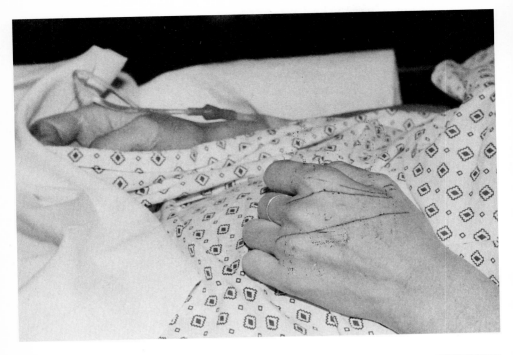

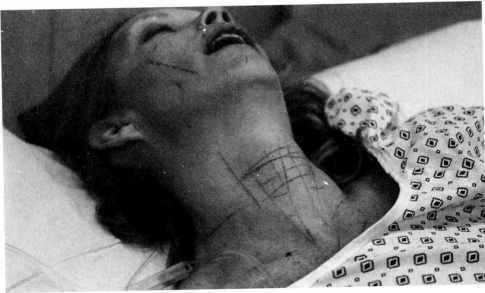

Andrea at Eisenhower Medical Center after another assault incident at 6 Brandeis Court.

Andrea's drawing of the woman who approached her outside the Springs condominium. Note the three names—"Karen-Kathy-Nancy"—at the bottom of the drawing.

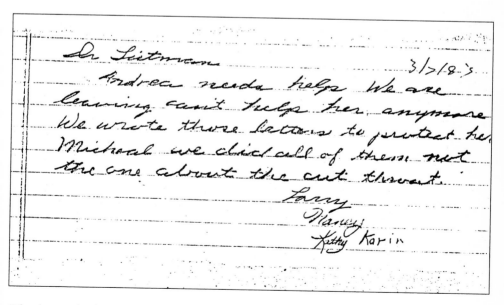

The letter Andrea gave to Dr. Michael Leitman while she was at the county jail. [The letter reads: "Dr. Leitman / Andrea needs help. We are leaving can't help her anymore. We wrote those letters to protect her. Michael we did all of them not the one about the cut throat." It is signed by Larry, Nancy, Kathy, Karin, each signature in a different style.]

First letter (left):

(P)

Dear Andrea: July ~~22~~ 23 1982

    Thanks, your gonna be a big help with my problems. (SORRY) But that's the way it is. You were right Andrea, I am bad. I don't blame you for not viseting me. (I don't care the hurt that you are going through) (I hate myself) when I get so badly drunk.. I cant write this.... I proberly wont rememba that I write this. I am depressed. I am (rotten person) Your a beautiful person. I may get to meet you now. (I want to end my life) if I don't see you. I not (I want to end my life) your problems. (I ugly.) I (very unhealthy). (Thank you for your pictures and letters) You are person - I not gonna pay for all the collect calls. I gonna use you to get out and I have hear rumers up hear that you cant of pilloff him. I care. You's hear (becomes ugly.) (I hate myself) drunk. (Andrea) thats when I do bad. I cant control myself. I don't to change, really. I so drunk.

    (for Gods sake)   (Love always)

(I lol you and (cant (Crazy)) (your friend) Richard
have you. I tried.)   (SORRY)

I'm a sinner. I gonna lie to hurt you

Second letter (right, above):

See new adress

February 9, 1982   R. E Cordine
PO Box 7000 NNCC
Carson City, Nev. 89701

US

(Dear Andrea)   (Thank you for your picture and letter.) Aaron is beautiful and so are you. Are you gaining weight? Are is it just the house coat?

    Andrea, I must tell you, that you totally confuse me, why? I'll tell you why... Just when I get to the point when I think that you have forgotten me because you havn't written and reject my occasional phone call — up pops your letter written as if you had just finished talking to me yesterday. Do you realize that we have been corresponding for nearly four 4 years? and yet I feel like a distant, distant, cousin instead of the friend I consider myself to be. I feel quite honored that a person such as yourself should even lift your pen to write to me and my only request is that you write alittle more often. I don't care if you are in your deepest hour of depression, you would be suprised how much better you could feel after writting your problems

    I

Envelope:

HARD CORDINE
(600 7000
ISON CITY, NEV.

Andrea Sand, Claire
6 Brandeis Ct
Rancho Mariage, Ca
922 70

(P1)

Deputy District Attorney
James Hawkins and his wife.

Dan Riter (right) with District Attorney Grover Trask II.

Robert Dunn, in front of the county administration center in Indio.

Dr. Anthony Oliver, the Riverside psychiatrist who testified for the prosecution.

Dr. Morton Kurland, the chief psychiatrist at Eisenhower Hospital who testified for the defense.

Gary C. Scherotter, Andrea's first attorney.

Charles Stafford, the public defender who took over Andrea's case.

The drawing Andrea made and gave to Dr. Michael Leitman before the competenc
hearing.

sions, bruises, and abrasions on the victim's body, having Modglin locate and number each of them. In effect, for the whole morning and another hour after lunch, Dunn had the jury going over the bloody details of the crime, which the coroner believed had probably occurred in a period of several minutes. If the procedure annoyed Stafford, it also gave him time to prepare for the witness.

In cross-examination, Stafford drew attention to wounds on the victim's forearms, and under his arms, and the bruises on his hands, all of which suggested a struggle during which the victim was mobile. Further, if Sand had been knocked unconscious with an initial or early blow, the number of wounds he had sustained both to the front and back of his body in so brief a time frame, and the fact that he was a man who weighed 220 pounds and was six feet two inches tall, would indicate that there was more than one attacker.

At the same time, one of the blows Sand had sustained had broken his sternum. Had the paring knife with the bent tip found under the sofa been the weapon used? Modglin said he thought it could have been, but that greater than moderate force would have been required. Stafford pressed the point.

STAFFORD: Isn't it true, Dr. Modglin, that the force that would have been needed to cause those types of injuries—assuming that Mrs. Sand was the one that actually had the knife—that it is more consistent with Mr. Sand moving towards her when she is thrusting the knife prior to the injuries being received.

MODGLIN: I think that would make it easier for them to be inflicted, yes.

STAFFORD: Dr. Modglin, taking the wounds to Mr. Sand's back just below his neck, assuming that those were caused from a hand going over the shoulder, and assuming that Mr. Sand when he received the injuries under his arms had his arms out, and assuming the scratch marks on the back of his thighs were caused by fingernails, what would you assume is occurring?

MODGLIN: Well, I would assume that some sort of combat or struggle was occurring.

A few moments later, Stafford asked Modglin if the variety and scope of the injuries to Mr. Sand would characterize "an overkill situation."

MODGLIN: Yes, to a certain—yes, definitely.

STAFFORD: As a forensic pathologist, what do you mean when you characterize a series or variety of injuries as indicating overkill?

MODGLIN: Usually means something done in a fit of passion or in a frenzy or overwhelming madness or anger of trying to get even with someone, trying to inflict multiple serious injuries on them.

STAFFORD: Dr. Modglin, when we talk about defensive wounds, we basically are talking about a person putting his body or parts of his body in a position to protect himself; is that correct?

MODGLIN: Yes, sir.

STAFFORD: In no way when we characterize wounds as defensive can we eliminate the possibility that the person who has those types of wounds may very well have been the attacker himself?

MODGLIN: Certainly they could easily have started a fight, right.

On the following morning, in his redirect, Dunn asked Modglin if he would expect the other party to have received some wounds in such a struggle as Stafford had depicted. Modglin said he would.

4

The People's next witness on Thursday, February 2, was the real estate agent, Nina Rhodes Krasner. Krasner testified that Bob Sand was confined to a wheelchair, dependent on Andrea to get him in and out of his car when they went somewhere. When receiving Andrea's help, Krasner said, Mr. Sand "lowered his head. He was embarrassed."

Krasner said that two days after the murder, she received a call from Andrea, who spoke about the intruders, in essence following the story she told the police.

"At any time during the conversation," Dunn asked Krasner, "did she state anything about her relationship with Mr. Sand up to that time?"

KRASNER: Yes. She said that she loved him very much and they had a wonderful life together and how much she would miss him.

She said they had a wonderful sex life together in the same conversation, that it was the most exciting sexual experience that she'd had and that she would pose in the nude for him and he would photograph her, that he and she both enjoyed that very much.

As a matter of fact, she said when the detective came in, he said, "You and your husband must have some exciting sex life because of all this apparatus here."

She said, "Yes, we do" or "Yes, we did."

Dunn knew he didn't have to discredit the specific story the defense planned to tell in its case in chief. If he could establish that Andrea was a liar, it would cast a shadow over any story.

His next witness was the seventy-one-year-old Florence Sand. Delicately beautiful, dressed in a green Adolfo dress, Mrs. Sand provided, under Dunn's questioning, a history of her relationship with her ex-husband. Married in 1939, Florence and Robert Sand got divorced in 1947 and then remarried in 1952. In 1973, Mrs. Sand learned that her husband was involved with prostitutes, and at that time their own sexual relationship ended. However, they remained together.

"I was concerned about him," she said quietly. "He needed to be taken care of. I didn't want a divorce and he didn't either."

It was after their remarriage in 1952 that her husband's health began to deteriorate, Mrs. Sand said. It stemmed from an ulcer operation and an addiction to sleeping pills. A reaction to sleeping pills gradually limited his ability to use his legs. Then, after breaking his leg in 1975, he never walked again.

After Florence Sand's discovery of her husband's other life with prostitutes, Bob Sand didn't stop that life, and sometimes spent as much as $800 a week pursuing it. However, it was only when he decided to marry Andrea that Sand asked Florence to put through a divorce that had been pending for years, in part so that Sand couldn't spend all of the money the couple had.

"I wished him well," Mrs. Sand testified. "I hoped it would be happiness for him."

After Sand married Andrea, Florence Sand never saw or spoke to him again.

In his cross-examination, Stafford took his own tack.

"Did he ever do anything physically violent to you in anger?" he asked Mrs. Sand of her former husband.

"No."

"Did he ever take a swing at you?"

"No."

"For no reason?"

"No."

"Are you sure?"

"Positive," she said.

Dunn knew Stafford had to have something. But he would cross that bridge when and if Chuck put it in front of him.

Dunn called as his next witness Betty Jo Crane, the Springs resident who had seen Bob and Andrea Sand at the tennis courts together, and to whom Andrea had once complained that her marriage to Bob Sand was a "mistake," a story diametrically opposed to the one she had told Nina Rhodes Krasner.

"Other than that occasion," Dunn asked Crane, "did she ever say anything to you regarding her relationship with Robert Sand?"

Andrea had complained to Crane of being unable to have phone conversations with a girlfriend in Los Angeles because of Bob's possessiveness, and she mentioned the friend wanted to visit Palm Springs.

DUNN: Did she say anything else about this girlfriend that was coming from Los Angeles?

CRANE: She wanted to know if the girlfriend came, if I knew where there would be available men that they could meet.

I told her, no, that I did not. That I didn't think it was a nice area to meet men.

And she said, well, she didn't have any trouble when she was out riding her bicycle, and I said but those are not the kind of men—you know, if they're whistling at you as you're riding by, that's one thing. But going some place to meet nice men is another thing.

Following Crane's testimony, Judge Moore adjourned court until Monday, February 6, at 9:30 in the morning.

$$\boxed{5}$$

On Monday morning, Prosecutor Dunn called Fred Kopplin, who had gone to work for Robert Sand in 1946 and was now part owner of The Sand Door and Plywood Company, as his first witness. From a photograph Dunn provided from those submitted in evidence, Kopplin identified Sand as the man who had been murdered—as a courtesy in a murder trial Dunn tried to find a non-family member to do this—and also identified Andrea at the defense table as his wife.

In his direct examination, Dunn established that during the last couple of years of his life, Robert Sand wasn't able to walk without the assistance of a walker or a cane or somebody to help him. Kopplin also said that during all the years he'd known Sand he had never seen him lose his temper.

In his cross-examination, Stafford picked up the thread of Robert Sand's ability to stand and move. Kopplin testified that Mr. Sand could stand of his own accord if he could hold onto a firm object and that he could walk with difficulty with the aid of a walker or a cane.

"And he was," Stafford said, "until his disability with his legs started, in pretty good shape, wasn't he?"

"He had his ups and downs in health," Kopplin said. "And while he appeared to be a good physical specimen, I know from all my experience that he wasn't athletically inclined although he certainly appeared to be."

Kopplin wouldn't testify that Sand had particular upper body strength.

Dunn called Fred Lastar as his next witness. The prosecutor had established the crime scene and called into question the truth of what Andrea Sand might say from day to day about her marriage or the killing of her husband. He wanted to use

Detective Lastar primarily to reinforce what had already been shown.

In the more than one hundred conversations he had had with Andrea, and with all the variations in her story of the murder night, she had never suggested to him that she killed her husband in self-defense, the detective testified.

"Did you ask Mrs. Sand if she was injured in any way?" Dunn asked, speaking of the morning of the murder.

"During the initial investigation," Lastar said, "I saw this little droplet of blood going all the way through the house, and it indicated, you know, possibly where she was walking.

"So when we were at Mrs. Hawkins' house, I asked her to check the bottoms of her feet. We looked at the bottom of her foot. One of the socks was caked with dirt and blood, and she removed the sock, and she did have blood on it. She had a small cut."

"Did you observe any other cuts on Mrs. Sand's body?" Dunn asked.

"No, I did not."

Neither had he noticed bruises on her face or carpet burns on her hands, and Mrs. Sand had not complained of bruises or soreness.

In his cross-examination, Stafford went to the fact that Andrea hadn't called attention to the cut on her foot, although it had required stitches when it was treated at Eisenhower, the implication being that she was in shock and didn't know she was hurt. It was a reasonable argument, Dunn thought, but he doubted Chuck had underlined it clearly enough for the jury.

The People's next witness was Richard Cordine. After establishing that Cordine's primarily pen-pal relationship with Andrea also included sporadic telephone conversations, Dunn asked whether in any of the telephone conversations Cordine had with her after December 1980, Andrea had described her marriage to Robert Sand.

"Yes, she did," Cordine said.

"And how did she describe that relationship?"

"There was a great deal of turbulence," Cordine said. "She felt captured—she didn't feel that she was recognized as a wife, but as perhaps a servant. There was a lot of demands placed on Andrea. She was constantly waiting on, taking care of Mr. Sand, beyond what she felt was reasonable."

Then Dunn took Cordine through the damning testimony of Andrea talking about poisoning her husband, questioning Cordine about the effects of Seconal, and asking him if he had ever killed someone.

Dunn asked if Cordine had had a conversation with Andrea when she told him her husband had been murdered.

CORDINE: Yes, she did.

DUNN: Did she tell you how her husband had been killed?

CORDINE: She indicated he had been stabbed.

DUNN: When she said that he had been stabbed, did you ask her anything further regarding the death of her husband?

CORDINE: Yeah. Because I had said, "Andrea, you didn't kill the old guy, did you?"

DUNN: What did she say when you asked her that question?

CORDINE: She said, "Yeah. I stabbed the bastard."

DUNN: After she stated that she stabbed the bastard, did she give you any further information regarding what she had done in relationship to the murder of her husband?

CORDINE: I think she told me that she went back to the couch and laid down and went to sleep.

At first, Cordine said, he'd thought she was joking. But the conversation had preyed on his mind, and about a year later, he called the Riverside Sheriff's Department in Indio, more to find out what the status of the case was than anything else.

"In spite of the fact that I've been a criminal a long time," Cordine said, "I don't advocate murder to any degree. It just got me thinking of the guy in a wheelchair, not able to defend himself."

It was, Dunn knew, priceless testimony. Cordine was a known criminal, a convict, who was repulsed by the crime.

In cross-examination, Stafford asked about Cordine's relationship with Andrea after she married Joe Mims.

"Isn't it true in June or July of 1982," Stafford said, "you had a conversation with Mr. Mims on the telephone, and Mr. Mims told you not to call anymore?"

"Absolutely."

"Didn't that conversation take place before you called the Riverside County Sheriff's Department and the district attorney's office?"

"It may have," Cordine said. "I'm not sure. It may have."

"It did, didn't it?" Stafford said.

"You can't put words in my mouth," Cordine said. "I said it may have, and I'm not certain whether it did or not."

Stafford established that Cordine had exacted a favor from the district attorney's office when he told them his story. His former prison roommate was returned to his cell a month after Jim Hawkins and Dan Riter had interviewed him in prison.

It was close to four in the afternoon. Judge Moore asked if he had much more cross-examination, and Stafford said he thought it would be a good place to stop. Court was adjourned until the following morning, Tuesday, February 7, at 9:30.

6

The next morning, Stafford picked up where he left off.

"What was your feeling," he asked Cordine, "when Mr. Mims had the conversation with you and told you not to call anymore?"

"I understood his feelings."

"You understood his feelings. You weren't angry or upset?"

"No, I wasn't."

"But you had been corresponding with her since 1978 and this was now 1982."

"Uh-huh."

"And you didn't feel upset that Mr. Mims now was telling you no more?"

"No. I didn't feel upset about that at all."

"Mr. Cordine, did you ever tell Andrea Claire that you loved her?"

"No."

"Did you ever tell Andrea Claire that you thought often about what it would be like being with her?"

Dunn wondered if a whole other side of the story that Cordine hadn't mentioned was now going to explode in the courtroom and destroy his testimony.

"Absolutely not," Cordine said.

"Did you ever convey to Andrea Claire that you had an intention of hurting her?" Stafford asked.

"No. No, I didn't."

"Did you ever tell Andrea Claire that you were going to lie to hurt her?"

"Absolutely not."

"Did you write a letter to Andrea Claire on July the 23, 1982, in which you conveyed to her your intention to lie to hurt her?"

"Absolutely not."

"Your Honor," Stafford said to Judge Moore, "I have a letter dated July the 23, 1982. After Mr. Dunn has had an opportunity to read it, I would ask it be marked as defense exhibit next in order."

The judge said it would be marked P for identification.

Dunn was given the letter, which was dated July 22, 1982, but the 22 had been crossed out and replaced with a 23, and quickly read it at the prosecution table.

> Dear Andrea:
>
> Thanks, your gonna be big help with my problems. (SORRY.) But that's the way it is. You were right Andrea, I am bad. I don't blame you for not visiting me. (I don't care the hurt that you are going through.) (I hate myself) when I get so badly drunk...I can't write this...I proberly won't remember that I write this. I am depressed. I am (rotten person.) Your a beautiful person. I have never you—But I may get to meet you now. (I want to end my life) if I don't see you. I not sorry that I make your problems. I ugly. I (very unhealthy.) Thank you for your pictures and letters. You are person—I not gonna pay for all the collect calls. I gonna use you to get out and have hear rumers up hear that you can't of killed him. I care. Years hear becomes ugly—I hate myself drunk. Andrea, that's when I do bad. I can't control myself. I don't to change, really. I so drunk.
>
> (for *God's sake*)   (Love Always)
> I love you and I can't   (Your friend)
> have *you*. I tried.   crazy—Richard
>   (SORRY)
> I'm a sinner. I gonna *lie* to hurt you

Dunn had just examined two other letters Cordine admitted writing to Andrea, which Stafford had placed in evidence, and on the basis of those letters, this new one immediately appeared to him to be a forgery. Cordine's handwriting had a very neat, regimented quality, the lines extremely straight, and he tended to write small. The handwriting in the new letter, while broadly resembling Cordine's, had been put down on the page in a far less controlled manner, the space between the lines varying widely, as well as the size of individual words. Drunkenly confessing to being drunk seemed an obvious ploy to cover this. In addition the envelope the letter came in looked tampered with.

In preparing his case in chief, Dunn had determined not to bring up any of the rapes and abductions Andrea had reported or any of the letters she may have forged, because as evidence they might play to the insanity defense. If the defense wanted to bring it up, they would deal with it then. Now Stafford had dropped this bomb, which immediately opened that side of the case.

Under Dunn's redirect examination, Cordine testified the letter was not in his handwriting. The preprinted return address label was also brought into question. Cordine always attached the labels by their gummed backing. This one was held in place by tape.

Dan Riter examined the letter after Dunn looked at it, and it struck him immediately as a forgery, Andrea's latest ploy. He wondered if Chuck Stafford had now fallen under the lady's spell.

7

Dunn used the rest of the morning finishing his case in chief. His next witness was Joe Mims. Dan Riter had heard from Joe that Andrea had called him in November and confessed to murdering Robert Sand. She had told Joe that she hadn't remembered what had happened until she'd been hypnotized. Again, the prosecutor emphasized the discrepancy between the story—with its smaller variations—that Andrea had told Mims, approximately twenty-five times Joe estimated, up to the phone call on November 10, and the story she told him then. Although she remembered killing Sand, Andrea told Joe that there were also intruders there that night, and she had been raped before she killed Bob Sand. According to Andrea, the intruders left when she told one of them, a lady, that Bob was dead.

Intruders again. It was the sort of thing that helplessly frustrated Chuck Stafford more than he wanted to show.

In cross-examination, Stafford established that Andrea had told Mims in the November telephone conversation that Bob Sand had come after her with a knife.

STAFFORD: And it is a true statement as to what she recounted to you that she told you that Bob Sand was calling out names of other individuals that were supposedly going to rape her while he watched?

MIMS: Yes. Yes. She told me this.

If Stafford could suggest that Andrea mixed reality and fantasy on that evening, it would, of course, give credence to the insanity plea. It was a balancing act between the two pleas he had filed. On the one hand, he was trying to neutralize Dunn's game plan of depicting Andrea as a common garden-variety sociopath. On the other, he needed to try to capitalize on Andrea's unpredictable statements as they came up in testimony.

At the mid-morning break, Dunn looked carefully at the alleged Cordine letter of July 23, 1982 and noticed that the postmark date looked like it had been tampered with, too. They would want J. Brown, who was the handwriting expert in the office, to take a look at it and possibly solicit other expert testimony.

Dunn called Lieutenant Kennedy. The detective testified that, when he accompanied Jim Hawkins and Dan Riter to Nevada State Prison to interview Richard Cordine, Cordine had told them about the poisoning and stabbing conversations he had had with Andrea. This testimony threw into question the "breakthrough" nature of Andrea's telephone conversation with Joe Mims in November. In effect, she had admitted to Cordine two years earlier what she told Mims in November.

Dunn's final witness was Marvin Chesebro, the attorney who had filed suit against Andrea on behalf of the estate of Robert Sand. Chesebro testified that Andrea, up to the time of the legal action, had been receiving $3,000 a month out of the estate, and another $3,000 a month as an advance out of the $150,000 Robert Sand had left her in the codicil attached to his will.

Before the marriage, Chesebro testified, Bob Sand "said that he was crazy about this girl, that they got along very well, that she didn't want anything from him. She said she'd move out anytime."

But after the marriage, there were problems.

"He would call me from his place in Palm Springs, generally in the morning," Chesebro said, "and he would complain that Andrea was off at the tennis club. And that he was left alone, and that she had a terrible temper, and that he was thinking of getting a dissolution of the marriage. And he wanted to know how much it would cost him. What benefit—what alimony he would have to pay.

"And he discussed their relationship, and he said on one occasion, 'I have been going over both sides of the ledger, the good and the bad,' and then he would itemize for me the good aspects of the relationship with Andrea and the bad aspects of the relationship, and whether the marriage would last," Chesebro said.

In his cross-examination, Stafford drew out of Chesebro that the mortgage payment on the Springs condominium was approximately $3,000 a month, and that Andrea paid it out of her allowance. Stafford also brought up a final will. Cheseboro had never seen the other will but had heard that Garthe Brown, Bob Sand's attorney, had prepared one.

Making no more of it, Stafford questioned Chesebro on Robert Sand's feelings about Andrea as a wife, specifically with regard to the ledger Sand had drawn up.

CHESEBRO: Well, he had [the sexual relationship] on both sides of the ledger. He had it on the good side, in which he said sex was excellent.

On the bad side of the ledger, he said that she had the most beautiful body he had ever seen, that she had been a prostitute, that she had had sex with Hugh Hefner of *Playboy* magazine, Bernie Cornfeld, the international financier, and some man that she had lived with for three years and had sex with three times a day, and he said now she goes into the closet to undress.

And this really bothered him.

Robert Sand didn't have a temper, Chesebro testified. He had never heard him get angry with anyone.

"Would you say he was a demanding person?" Stafford asked.

"I wouldn't. No, he wasn't demanding, but he was a selfish person," Chesebro said.

At 12:03, Judge Moore adjourned court until 9:30 Thursday morning, February 9, when the defense would begin its case in chief.

XIV

1

Judy Campbell heard that Chuck Stafford's first witness for the defense was going to be Andrea and made a point of getting to Courtroom A early enough on Thursday morning to get a seat. They ended up turning people away. Having heard Chuck's opening statement, with its references to the brutality of Andrea's early life, Campbell wanted to hear more about that background and to see what kind of weight it might have with the jury.

It turned out to be the kind of story she had heard variations on many times before in her work as a victim witness advocate. The story of Andrea being raped at fifteen, finding herself pregnant, and then being forced by her mother to marry the rapist, could be understood, if not exactly condoned, in terms of the mores of the 1950s, when there were no such things as rape crisis centers. If a girl had sex, she was promiscuous; if she got pregnant, she was incorrigible. Marriage, in turn, might be forced on her so that the family could save face. The fifteen-year-old Andrea, who had scarcely been kissed, was raped by Herbert Wesley Denike, the twenty-two-year-old brother of her older sister's boyfriend.

Denike was in the navy and after the marriage, Andrea moved to Guantanamo Bay, where she set up housekeeping with her husband. Soon their first son, Guy, was born.

Andrea was again dressed sedately in a dark blouse and skirt and made, Campbell thought, a decent impression on the witness stand.

STAFFORD: During the time that you were in Cuba, how would you characterize your relationship with Mr. Denike?

ANDREA: He beat me up regularly.

STAFFORD: And how often would that happen?

ANDREA: Whenever he was home.

STAFFORD: What was his attitude toward the baby.

ANDREA: He was jealous of the baby.

STAFFORD: While you were in Cuba, did he drink?

ANDREA: Yes.

STAFFORD: And how would you characterize his drinking?

ANDREA: He only needed one beer, and he would get violent.

STAFFORD: How would you characterize the sexual relations that you had with Mr. Denike?

ANDREA: He only enjoyed it if he had to force me.

STAFFORD: Did he ever hit you?

ANDREA: Yes.

STAFFORD: Can you recall a time when you ever had sexual relations with Mr. Denike where he didn't hit you?

ANDREA: No.

She lost a second baby to a miscarriage after Denike had beaten her up badly. One night, in a rage, the sailor punched his one-year-old son Guy in the face. Andrea took the baby, who was rigid with fear, and went back to New Jersey where her second son with Denike, Douglas, was born. Living with her mother, she got a job as a waitress. She was raped in the parking lot after leaving the restaurant early one morning. She became pregnant from the rape, carrying the baby to term. At her mother's insistence, she gave it up for adoption.

The father who had abandoned the family when Andrea was fourteen, returned, and, Andrea testified, didn't remember her as his daughter—she was now twenty-one—but he encouraged her to move to California, where he now lived. Soon after her father returned west, Andrea followed him with her two little boys. She stayed for six weeks with her father and stepmother before moving to her own apartment in Atwater.

For two years, she worked as an assistant escrow officer at L.A. Federal. After a car accident in which her neck was fractured, she couldn't return to work for six months and was eventually let go by the bank.

She took her two boys and moved to Catalina for the summer of 1965, where she worked as a cashier and had her first actual love affair, with a male model named Luke Anthony. Anthony thought she was at most fifteen or sixteen years old and broke up with her when he discovered she was twenty-four.

When she returned to Los Angeles, she couldn't get her boys into a day care center. She took a night job as a go-go dancer at the Boom Boom Room in Gardena. Riding the tide of the 1960s, the place went topless, and after having breast implants, so did Andrea. She began to pick up modeling work, and under the name Samantha Scott acted in four nudie films, as well as having bit parts in several mainstream movies.

In 1968, while making a nudie film called *Brand of Shame*, she got thrown by a horse, which then fell on her and broke her spine. She was periodically hospitalized over the next three and a

half years and wasn't able to work at any job at which she would
have to be on her feet. Stafford asked her what she did now.

ANDREA: When I ran out of money, I tried to get welfare.
They wouldn't give me welfare.

STAFFORD: Why wouldn't they give you welfare?

ANDREA: They said, "A pretty girl like you can't figure out
what to do?"

STAFFORD: When did that happen?

ANDREA: In '69.

STAFFORD: So after that occurred, what did you do?

ANDREA: Became a call girl.

A doctor in his late seventies named Jim Houston set her up
for the first time. She was picked out of eleven women to go out
with a senator and was paid $500 for it. As a call girl, she testi-
fied, she made anywhere from $100 to $6,000, and it made her
feel better about herself.

STAFFORD: The time when you were paid $6,000, what did
you have to do?

ANDREA: Had to be with another woman.

STAFFORD: And how long a period of time was involved?

ANDREA: A weekend.

There were a lot of women on the jury, and Campbell didn't
get the impression that this testimony was eliciting a lot of sym-

pathy from them. Six thousand dollars was a lot of money for one weekend, after all, especially if you happened to earn your money as a waitress, or in sales, or as a secretary, as some of these women looked like they might.

Andrea ran through her marriages after Denike. Philip Green, the gambler, who wanted her to send her boys to their father so that she could work as a prostitute. The Jordanian Isaac Dajani who needed a green card. Derek Conte, who swept her off her feet and then, immediately after marrying her, became wildly abusive.

In the early seventies when Andrea was married to the Jordanian, she bought a house in the Hollywood Hills, using as down payment the $13,000 settlement she got from the insurance company for her back injury. She continued to work as a call girl or was kept by individual men for periods of time. After two and a half years, the marriage ended when Dajani received his green card.

Suzy Summers was Sylvia's best friend and would observe the trial and then drive over and meet Sylvia and Florence—who, because they were called as trial witnesses, weren't allowed to watch the proceedings—for lunch in Palm Desert and tell them everything that was going on.

Suzy had stayed overnight many times at the Sand house in Hancock Park and been out with Sylvia on her father's yacht. Her sister Nina Rhodes Krasner had told her something about Andrea, but she hadn't been prepared for Andrea's testimony on Bob Sand's sexual kinkiness.

He wasn't a man Summers had ever really felt comfortable around—very formal, an ultraconservative politically, always in a suit and tie, always *Mr.* Sand—but he just *wasn't* a mean man. He loved his little granddaughter, would read to her by the hour, and had also been very sweet and patient with Suzy's infant daughter, Jolie, at a Christmas party one year.

And the idea that Florence Sand was some kind of religious fanatic who would lock herself in the bathroom with the Bible every night while Mr. Sand was waiting for her was absurd. Foy was a Christian Scientist, and she was devout, but she also adored her husband, and in his own way he adored her. That he would have Andrea smear her menstrual blood all over her body and act out killing Florence with a knife was completely unbelievable. Period.

2

The story she was telling didn't make sense. Dunn guessed Stafford was being pushed around by his client and was being forced to play both ends against the middle.

On the one hand, she was confessing to killing Bob Sand and gave a tearful blow-by-blow account of a knockdown, drag-out fight in the bedroom between the two of them. And on the other, there were intruders in the house; she passed them on the way to the master bedroom. Her house was suddenly Grand Central Station in the middle of the night, and she went in and killed her husband?

But Chuck's idea seemed to be that part, the intruder part, proved that she was insane; and the other part, the fight part, where Robert Sand had lured Andrea into the bedroom on the pretext that he had fallen out of bed or needed help, and then grabbed her and wanted her to act out a fantasy—that part proved that she killed him in self-defense.

But if Andrea was a liar—a manipulative, money-hungry sociopath, which Dunn knew, in fact, she was—all he had to do was keep showing where she lied. Every single instance, however small it might seem, drove his case home. After the weekend recess, he began his cross-examination of Andrea after Chuck ended his direct an hour into Monday morning.

DUNN: Do you recall testifying on Thursday that after your father left and other men took over the discipline in the home that the discipline remained the same?

ANDREA: Well, I was really hit.

DUNN: Well, what I asked you was do you recall testifying last Thursday that after your father left, the discipline in the home remained the same?

ANDREA: Yeah.

DUNN: Now you testified that before your father left, he used to pretend that he hit you but never did hit you?

ANDREA: Well, he did a little bit. He wouldn't really hurt us.

DUNN: Then you testify today that after your father left and the grandfather or uncles took over that they actually did hit?

ANDREA: Yes.

DUNN: So then wouldn't the discipline be different than it was before your father left?

Judy Campbell could see that Bob Dunn had the jury with him. It was hard *not* to be with him. He was a pillar of society, speaking for all the traditions and institutions that any citizen would value. But Andrea was telling a story that now went back into being brutalized by her husband when she was still a teenager, and that reality, Campbell knew, cancelled all bets. When a woman was locked up with a man who was beating her, she didn't think of the range of social options she had as a citizen. She was just in a state of terror. And during the fifties, of course, those options were pretty limited anyway.

DUNN: Where did you live when you were in Cuba?

ANDREA: Thirty miles off the base.

DUNN: Did you live alone?

ANDREA: Yes.

DUNN: Did you ever have contact with any other military personnel?

ANDREA: Yes.

DUNN: Who?

ANDREA: We lived with another couple for one month. We moved every month. So we didn't have to pay the rent.

DUNN: You moved every month so you wouldn't have to pay the rent.

Andrea had this habit of answering some of Dunn's questions by nodding her head up and down, like a little girl it seemed to Campbell.

DUNN: Was this other couple that you lived with in the navy also?

ANDREA: Yes.

DUNN: And you were being beaten by your husband at this time?

ANDREA: Yes. And the man we were living with, he was also beating his pregnant wife.

DUNN: Did you ever report that to the police?

ANDREA: I reported it to the pastor on the base.

DUNN: When?

ANDREA: When I was about six months pregnant.

DUNN: Did anything occur after you reported that?

ANDREA: Yeah. He got fresh with me, and I walked out of the office.

DUNN: The pastor got fresh with you?

ANDREA: Yes. But the pastor did something for me later that I found out. He must have checked it out and realized I was telling the truth.

DUNN: Well, let me go back here a second. You were six months pregnant, your husband's beating you up, and you go to the pastor to report that?

ANDREA: Yes.

DUNN: And the pastor gets fresh with you?

ANDREA: He put his hand on my leg.

DUNN: What did you do when he put his hand on your leg?

ANDREA: I just got up and left.

DUNN: Where in the conversation did he put his hand on your leg? Was it as soon as you walked in and sat down?

Laughter. Campbell knew these women on the jury were getting very impatient with the fact that every time Andrea turned around, she was raped or come on to by some man, even a priest.

ANDREA: No. I was telling him what was going on in my marriage. And what I should do about it—what should I do. I didn't know what to do.

DUNN: That was offensive to you, that he put his hand on your leg?

ANDREA: Yes.

DUNN: Did you report him?

Dunn, representing the coherent, working model of society, was asking this woman whether she was calling for help from the proper authorities. But the woman was completely outside the accepted societal loop. He asked her why she didn't report the priest.

ANDREA: I don't know. I was only sixteen years old. I was a kid. I didn't know what to do.

DUNN: Okay. Well, you were on a military base. You know there is such a thing as military police.

ANDREA: Yeah.

DUNN: You knew that?

ANDREA: I was afraid of the police.

DUNN: Why were you afraid of the police?

ANDREA: Because my husband was having me buy cigarettes, and we were transporting them off the base illegally.

And I was terrified because if we got caught, we'd be in a lot of trouble. But if I didn't do it, my husband would beat me.

DUNN: So you're working with your husband in illegally transporting cigarettes off the base?

ANDREA: So he could sell them, so he could go see hookers.

DUNN: And you participated in that because you were afraid of your husband?

ANDREA: Yeah. He would beat me if I didn't.

DUNN: And for that reason you were afraid to tell the police on the base, because you were afraid they would find out about your illegal activities with your husband?

ANDREA: I don't know why I was afraid.

DUNN: Well, didn't you just testify that you did it because you were afraid of the police?

Were you afraid of the police at the time?

ANDREA: Yes.

DUNN: Why?

ANDREA: I don't know exactly why. I mean I was afraid—well, my husband was stealing groceries out of the commissary and having me put them in the trunk of the car, which was upsetting me, and it was upsetting me buying the cigarettes, and all that.

DUNN: So in addition to taking cigarettes off the base illegally, your husband was also stealing food from the base?

ANDREA: Yeah. He didn't buy any food. He didn't pay the rent. He spent all his money on prostitutes.

DUNN: Did you ever report that to the authorities? That he was stealing food out of the commissary?

ANDREA: No. He said he would kill me if I told.

DUNN: Did you believe him?

ANDREA: Yes.

She seemed small and frail on the stand, and you even had to wonder, if only for a moment, whether such a woman could really kill somebody. Most of all, it made Judy Campbell sad. The system really wasn't set up to identify and intervene with such a person until it was much too late, and then the system had to literally surround her.

$$3$$

On Wednesday morning, Bob Dunn took up his cross-examination of Andrea where he had left off on the murder night, tracking the scene moment by moment.

"Now at that time," he said, "Mr. Sand struck you twice in the head with the board. You struggled with him under the bed. He struck you on the shoulder with the board. You had jabbed him with the scissors. You had struck him in the head with the board, struck him on the hand with the board, and knocked the knife out of his hand.

"And you asked him if he wanted a drink?"

Suzy Summers and the rest of courtroom, including members of the jury, started laughing.

"He wasn't saying anything," Andrea said.

"Was he conscious?" Dunn asked.

"Yes."

"Was he looking at you?"

"Yes."

"But he wasn't saying anything?"

"Right."

"What did he say to you, if he did say anything, when you suggested that you make drinks?"

"He wasn't saying anything."

"Didn't he say, 'I don't want a drink'—?"

"No."

"Or 'Fix me a highball or a White Russian'?"

The courtroom rocked with laughter again. As grim as it was, at least Suzy could tell Foy and Sylvia that Andrea wasn't fooling anyone.

Stafford knew he could control a trial only so far, and after that it was in the hands of the jury. His task was to get the information before the court, let them hear everything that was relevant to Andrea's case, and then let them make their decision. In a case like Andrea's, the defendant was in essence the subject of an extended autobiography. Having covered her life both before and with Robert Sand in her own testimony, Stafford now went forward with his case in chief. With the remainder of the afternoon left after Andrea stepped down, he called three witnesses for the defense.

Herbert Hawkins testified that he and his wife Betty had been seated at the same table with Bob and Andrea Sand at a tennis dinner at the Springs probably in late January of 1981, not long after the Sands had moved to the Springs. After that he would see them primarily at tennis.

STAFFORD: Did [Robert Sand] ever give you the sense that he was jealous or possessive?

HAWKINS: Well, that's a rather subjective question. I would say—have to say that as a man he was very aware of how attractive his wife was and seemed to be—oh, I don't know if I want to use the word "concerned" about it—but I presume that's fairly accurate.

STAFFORD: Did he give the impression that he was comfortable when other people were around his wife?

HAWKINS: No. I would say that from what I observed personally, and some of the remarks that were made, he was—you use the word comfortable. I guess the opposite, that perhaps he was a little uncomfortable when there were many people around her.

Hawkins said that at a dinner party he and Betty gave for Bob and Andrea and Andrea's mother and stepfather, Sand had stood up in his wheelchair and then walked, haltingly, three or four steps to a chair in the living room and fell into it.
"It was kind of an accomplishment that he made that evening," Hawkins said, "that was kind of a topic of conversation there for a while. He was able to negotiate by himself getting out of his wheelchair and got into one of our swivel chairs..."

Stafford called Richard Cordine back to the witness stand and established that the convict had been visited last Sunday at Indio County Jail by his former cellmate, David Aldors.
Dunn didn't question the witness.

Stafford asked Betty Hawkins how she would characterize Andrea's relationship with Robert Sand.

HAWKINS: Well, I really admired her. Because I had absolutely no impression at all in our contacts before he was killed that she was anything but an absolutely fantastic wife.

She was very much into nutrition. I learned a lot from her. And she had cleared up a bad skin condition he'd had with his diet and different things that she knew to do for him.

And she enjoyed cooking wonderful meals for him and making a nice home. She was thrilled to be there at the Springs with him and was trying everything she knew how as far as I could see to be a very good wife.

Stafford asked if, before Robert Sand's death, Andrea had ever confided to her that anything was wrong.

HAWKINS: There was only one time, and again I admired her because lots of women who had tiffs with their husbands come and spill everything out.

We were playing tennis, and she seemed to be very low, and afterwards another friend and I—the three of us were sitting in a pergola—and I said, "What's the matter? You seemed kind of depressed today."

She just gave the impression that she had a little hard time in the morning, that Bob really didn't want her to play tennis, they'd had a few words over it, and that things...she had a few tears in her eyes and that type of thing, and we talked and prayed with her about it, but that was the only time.

Other than that possessiveness that I began to see as he didn't want her to be with anybody else.

In his cross-examination, Dunn returned to the question of whether Andrea had sustained any injuries on the night of the murder. She had stayed with the Hawkins for six weeks following it. Did Mrs. Hawkins recall her pointing out any injuries on any specific part of her body during that time?

HAWKINS: I think this is a vital question, and you're going to throw it out.

Seemed like she did, but I can't remember. I remember one time she was bruised in a tennis game, and the next day it was gone. She heals so quickly it was amazing.

So I remember seeing things, but then they were gone right away.

DUNN: Did you see any injuries to her head during that six week period of time that she lived with you?

HAWKINS: I don't remember.

DUNN: Did she say, "Look at the cuts on top of my head or look at the bumps I've got?"

HAWKINS: Now that sounds familiar.

DUNN: Do you recall anything like that?

HAWKINS: It's been so long. And so much has happened through all that time.

I remember when you mentioned bumps, there seemed like something there, but I can't give you any date or time.

After Betty Hawkins stepped down, Judge Moore dismissed the jury until the next morning. With the jury gone, Dunn asked for possession of the alleged Richard Cordine letter of July 23, 1982 and its envelope so that they could be taken to the United States Postal Service Laboratory in San Francisco for examination.

Judge Moore wanted to know if the expert Dunn intended to employ could be brought to Indio. The problem, the prosecutor explained, was the sophisticated equipment that would be used was in place at the laboratory and couldn't be transported. He told Judge Moore that if court was to reconvene on Monday or Tuesday of next week, the documents would be available at all times when court was in session.

Moore allowed it.

Outside the courtroom after her testimony, Betty Hawkins encountered Fred Lastar, whom she hadn't seen in a while.

"You know," he said, "everybody needs someone in their corner the way you've been there all along for Andrea."

It touched her to hear that from Detective Lastar.

$$4$$

Stafford's witnesses on Thursday, February 16, included Indio Sheriff's Department Officers Colleen Walker (formerly Colleen Word, the deputy had married in the meantime) and Janet Rubien, who both testified to the details of the rape and abduction reports they had responded to at 6 Brandeis Court, and Officers Lowrey Spencer and Carla Gordon, who had been involved in the amnesia incident, when Andrea was taken to Riverside County Hospital and registered as Jane Doe.

During her testimony, Andrea had stated that the reported rapes and assaults hadn't really happened, that she was in essence still acting out Bob's fantasies, although she thought they were real at the time. Stafford, now working the other side of his defense, was in effect laying out the details of Andrea's hallucinations and amnesia before the jury.

After the lunch break, he called the real estate agent, Sally Ann Lanivich, who had handled the sale of Andrea's Tarzana townhome and established that Andrea received almost $75,000 from the sale.

The witness after Lanivich was David F. Warner, who had worked as Robert Sand's private duty nurse after he broke his leg in 1975. Warner, a witness Lorrie Wright had found, told Stafford there were times when Sand "was rather stern verbally" with him.

STAFFORD: What type of things would he do that you would characterize as Mr. Sand being stern?

WARNER: Oh, for instance, in the care I gave him, there were times that no matter what you did for him, he was not pleased.

STAFFORD: During the times that you worked for him and was in his presence, did you ever see Mr. Sand show any signs of temper?

WARNER: Okay. There was one time that stands out in my mind very vividly. We were getting ready to go to work. We were about to descend the stairs from the second floor onto the first floor. And Florence is walking by, and all of a sudden, he took a swat at her, was going to hit her.

She ducked and he missed her, and she went to her bedroom. She was a little shook up and, I believe, embarrassed about it because I hadn't seen anything of that sort.

STAFFORD: What did he actually swing at Mrs. Sand?

WARNER: His hand.

STAFFORD: Was the hand open or was it a fist?

WARNER: It was clenched.

In his cross-examination, Dunn asked Warner, obviously the witness Chuck had in mind during his questioning of Florence Sand, if there had been any other incidents. There were times when he had heard them quarreling, Warner testified.

On Friday morning, Dunn flew with J. Brown, the D.A.'s in-house handwriting expert, to San Francisco and brought the Cordine letter and envelope to the Postal Inspectors of Western

Region Crime Laboratory in San Bruno, conveniently the site of the San Francisco airport. They had arranged to meet with Inspector George Lewis, who would analyze the documents. Dunn took a plane back to Riverside that afternoon while J. Brown remained overnight. By the time he left, the prosecutor had been told by Lewis that the postmark on the envelope was doctored. Lewis had identified the month of the original postmark as February, as opposed to the July date of the letter.

It was, Dunn felt, the kind of evidence that could drive home a first degree murder conviction. It showed Andrea knew and understood exactly what was going on. At the same time, it was clearly a premeditated attempt on her part to deflect attention from her own guilt. Now, instead of undermining Richard Cordine's testimony, the letter would enforce it. The word on Chuck Stafford was that he was a competent attorney, but that he would usually make one big mistake in each trial. It looked to Dunn like this time around, this was it.

Dunn returned early in order to attend the Riverside County District Attorney's Awards Dinner. That night he would receive the award for Prosecutor of the Year. Coming into the banquet room at the Riverside Hilton, he spotted Dan Riter sitting at a table and walked over to him and leaned down.

"I think we just got it," he said in Dan's ear.

5

When court resumed on Tuesday, February 21, Stafford called as his first witness Lorraine Jackson, the Sands' maid at the Springs. She testified that Bob Sand had spoken very proudly to her of Andrea's beauty and the fact that she had been an actress. Jackson also said that one day Andrea told her Mr. Sand had wanted her to take a bath when Jackson was about to clean the bathroom. They had been in the kitchen at the time, Jackson said, while Mr. Sand was in another part of the house. The witness thought it was a little odd that Andrea would just come to her and tell her that.

Stafford put on more deputies of the Indio Sheriff's Department—Rick Kothlow, Bill DeLuna, and Cynthia Sjoquist—who had responded to 6 Brandeis Court, continuing to lay out the bizarre details of the incidents that followed the death of Robert Sand. Dunn cross-examined Sjoquist about the time Andrea reported being beaten up while sunbathing on her patio and had appeared to be asleep or unconscious when the deputy responded to the scene, but then had woken up.

DUNN: You stated she appeared to be disoriented. How did she appear to be disoriented?

SJOQUIST: When I tried to ask her what had happened after she was able to speak to me, she would start saying something and stop. Nothing specific.
    She didn't get up and walk around. She stayed in the lounge chair. Just as if she couldn't concentrate on what was being said or what was being asked at the time.

DUNN: Have you observed people that have been under the influence of either alcohol or drugs on prior occasions?

SJOQUIST: Yes, I have.

DUNN: How did her behavior compare with a person or people that you have observed in the past that have been under the influence of alcohol or drugs?

SJOQUIST: I don't believe that they would compare from my experiences that I've had.

DUNN: Which way would they be different?

SJOQUIST: Well, when she did get up and walk around, she was not staggering as I have experienced people under the influence of alcohol to do. I don't recall detecting an odor of an alcoholic beverage on her breath. Given a few minutes, she was able to talk coherently and answer questions.

DUNN: Did you have any questions in your own mind whether or not she was actually unconscious or whether she was feigning unconsciousness?

Stafford objected that the question was "irrelevant as to her personal feelings." Judge Moore asked Dunn to reframe the question.

DUNN: Did you have any evidence at the time that you conducted that interview that Mrs. Sand was feigning unconsciousness?

Stafford objected that the question called for hearsay. Judge Moore overruled the objection and told Sjoquist that she could answer.

SJOQUIST: Yes, I did.

DUNN: And what evidence did you have at that time through your visual observations that made you feel she was feigning unconsciousness?

SJOQUIST: When I came up to her while she was still in the lounge chair, I noted that her eyelids were fluttering. I also tried to open an eye to check the pupil response and was unable to raise the eyelid.

DUNN: Was the eyelid being forcibly closed?

SJOQUIST: It felt that way to me, yes.

Sjoquist also testified that, considering their location on her body, Andrea's injuries could have been self-inflicted.

Stafford's next witness was a woman named Linda Schrick, whom Lieutenant Kennedy had interviewed in August of 1981 in Los Angeles while Investigator Lastar was on strike. Schrick had been a friend of Andrea's in Hollywood from 1968 on, when the two had been neighbors and young mothers. Stafford asked if Schrick could characterize Andrea during the time she knew her.

"She was a different person in a lot of different ways," the witness said. "She was unrealistic in a lot of ways. She seemed to live in certain fantasy worlds...We never really opened up to each other about some things. She was always good to me. She was good with children. She was good with her own children and my children. I've never seen her lose her temper."

Schrick also said that before Andrea married Robert Sand, she had talked about Bob making her wear a dog collar while she scrubbed the floor nude and he took pictures.

Under cross-examination, Schrick, who was a writer, testified that several months after the murder, Andrea had asked if she wanted to collaborate on a screenplay. Dunn asked about the plot.

SCHRICK: It was about a young beautiful woman who has been accused of murdering her millionaire husband, and it had a subplot that the detective or the police officer that was investigating the murder fell in love with her and wanted to leave his wife for her.

DUNN: Did you question her about any coincidence between her idea for a screenplay and the factual situation surrounding the discussion that she had with you?

SCHRICK: No. I didn't question it because I felt that it was quite obvious that that's what—if we collaborated on a screen-play—she would want to write about. Just like Norman Mailer has done with a couple of murders in recent history.

Dunn brought up to Schrick a statement she had made to Sergeant Kennedy about Andrea claiming to have dated members of royal families, including princes.

"Did you believe her when she said that?" he asked.

"It went in one ear and out the other."

"I asked if you believed her."

"I didn't know," Schrick said. "It went in one ear and out the other."

"That's not what I asked you," Dunn said. "When she told you she was kidnapped by Arabs and raped because of her beauty and men could not resist her, did you believe her when she said that?"

"Partly."

"Did you think she was telling the whole truth when she told you that?"

"Probably not."

"Wasn't that what's commonly called lying?" Dunn asked.

"I'd object, your Honor," Stafford said. "Argumentative."

Judge Moore asked Dunn to reframe the question.

"If somebody is not telling the whole truth, doesn't that necessarily mean that they're lying to a certain extent?"

Stafford objected again that the question was argumentative.

Judge Moore overruled it and told Schrick she could answer.

"No," she said. "I don't think it's lying. I consider it living in a fantasy world. There's a difference."

"What's the difference between living in a fantasy world and lying?" Dunn asked.

"Well," Schrick said, "living in a fantasy world is to me like being a storyteller and lying is doing something for personal gain. I don't think that by her telling me she was kidnapped by

Arabs or dating princes that she was doing it for personal gain with me."

"Do you feel that Andrea Sand is a storyteller?"

"I don't know. Because I've seen too many changes in her, or I have felt that perhaps some of it was due to things that were mental."

"You're not a psychiatrist, are you?" Dunn asked.

"I think we all are," Schrick said.

5

As if to answer Dunn's challenge to Linda Schrick, Stafford's next witness, who absorbed the hour remaining of the afternoon, was Dr. Morton Kurland, the chief of psychiatry at Eisenhower Hospital. Kurland had been the first psychiatrist in the area to see Andrea after Robert Sand's death, he had seen her at Eisenhower Hospital after the first reported rape, and had seen her for several sessions at the hospital the day after she assaulted Joe Mims. He had another interview with her in February 1983 at the Indio County Jail in preparation for testifying at her competency hearing. Kurland had also reviewed Stafford's voluminous file on Andrea and consulted with Dr. Leitman. After having Kurland review his credentials and his association with Andrea's case, Stafford asked him if he had formulated any conclusions or opinions on her mental state.

KURLAND: It's my conclusion that this lady suffers at the present time and has for some time from a borderline personality disorder, from borderline state actually. It's called a borderline state in *The Diagnostic and Statistical Manual.*

STAFFORD: When we talk about a borderline personality or borderline state, what specifically are we talking about?

KURLAND: We're talking about a disorder of the mind which is such that the individual alternates on the borderline as it were between a neurotic disorder or a personality structure disorder, and a psychosis.

That is, they go in and out of psychosis according to the stress to which they are subjected either internally or externally.

Kurland thought Andrea had probably been suffering from this condition since her adolescence. Stafford asked him what kind of behavior was actually involved with the condition

KURLAND: Essentially the real test of someone going in and out of psychosis is whether or not they're able to test reality. That is, to understand the world around them. To understand it in the sense that everyone else understands it. And then to behave according to that reality and in consistency with the reality that the rest of us perceive, or, in the absence of that, if they're psychotic.

STAFFORD: Dr. Kurland, what is there in the things that Mrs. Sand told you and also the information that you were provided that you would be able to relate to this type of disorder or diagnosis?

KURLAND: Well, most of her behavior as she related it to me from time to time, but even more importantly, in the advanced bulk of material which I have now had an opportunity to digest, suggests that she has really had difficulty in dealing with reality for all of her adult life.

She has in effect not been able to understand the motives of other people, how she has been in effect used by other people for their gain without perceiving that she was being used, and how she has in effect distorted reality to the point where her productions are in fact unbelievable to everyone but herself.

Stafford probed Andrea's relationship with Robert Sand. In her initial sessions with Kurland, not long after Sand's death, Andrea had told him about the paddling and spankings.

KURLAND: She minimized the sadistic or masochistic activity and in effect said they were just preludes to sex, and tried to make it appear as if it were a game and that it was a harmless play activity, and that they were then able to have sexual intercourse in the ordinary way after indulging in this game playing. And the implication that I drew was it was a daily activity.

STAFFORD: Dr. Kurland, how would you relate that type of sexual relationship with someone suffering from the mental disease or defect or disorder that you characterize Mrs. Sand as having?

KURLAND: My own experience is that it's not an unusual kind of activity in someone with this kind of diagnosis.

STAFFORD: When you talk about the sexual game aspect of their relationship and what she basically told you was involved, would that create the type of stress or environment that would cause Mrs. Sand to go in and out of the psychosis that you describe as a part of her borderline personality?

KURLAND: It certainly could if the game playing got to be intense, or if it appeared that it was getting to be too close to reality.

The escalating violence of the sexual games with Robert Sand did have the intensity, Kurland believed, to cause her to cross over into psychosis.

KURLAND: I would assume that a person with this kind of disorder, that is, a borderline personality state that slips in and out, would begin to become more and more sucked into the game playing and have less and less ability to know what was real and what wasn't real, and would lose distinction eventually between reality and fantasy and either act out the fantasy as if it were in fact reality or even continue to live in that fantasy world after the episodes were played out, or after the other side thought the game was over.

STAFFORD: Have you ever heard the term psychotic break?

KURLAND: Certainly.

STAFFORD: And what does that mean?

KURLAND: That means an individual who has actually broken with reality, that is, has lost the ability to distinguish what's real from what's imagined, and acts as if the unreal were real.

STAFFORD: The question, the hypothetical question that I posed to you as to what would occur in an individual like Andrea who possesses this borderline personality disorder—as the games become more intense and more violent, would there be a possibility of a psychotic break?

KURLAND: Yes. I think it's certainly a likelihood, more than a possibility.

Kurland went on to testify that Andrea's feeling her eyes were not under control, a symptom common to people losing control of reality and not able "to see what is real and what's not real," was one indication she may have suffered a psychotic break at the time of the murder. The rapes that followed the murder were, in his opinion, a continuation of the fantasy life and "at the moment that she reported these rapes, [she] actually believed that they had been occurring and that she was the victim of them."

"My opinion," Kurland said, "is that the stories that she told are so incredible and so bizarre that they are not the kinds of stories that a good liar would tell. A good liar would make up a much more tight, reasonable, and logical story. One could understand these variety of rape stories and kidnap stories and intruder stories and so forth as an alibi if she were stupid, if she were of low intellectual capacity. But given her superior intellect, the quality of the stories is so incredible, so bizarre, and that she stuck to them even when confronted by me and other people telling her that they couldn't believe it—I believe that she had to be living on another plane of reality for it to be understandable in any way to me."

STAFFORD: During the rape incidences that you were consulted on involving Mrs. Sand, were you aware of any physical injuries that she had in relationship to those incidences?

KURLAND: Those particular injuries certainly were the kinds of things that people could inflict upon themselves and not feel if they were deeply involved in a loss of touch with reality. They would be so disturbed that they actually wouldn't feel themselves cutting themselves and bruising themselves.

Responding to a series of questions from Stafford, Kurland characterized histrionic personality disorder as not inconsistent but in fact continuous with a borderline personality diagnosis.

"They can oscillate," Kurland said, "between being histrionic—dramatic and exaggerated and strange—and slipping into a paranoid psychosis or just a complete loss of touch with reality."

Stafford asked Kurland if, based on all his knowledge of the defendant, he had "an opinion as to whether or not she was capable of premeditating the death of her husband?"

KURLAND: Yes. I have formed such an opinion.

STAFFORD: And what's your opinion?

KURLAND: My opinion is that she was not capable at that time at all of any kind of premeditation or planning or prior thoughts.

STAFFORD: Assuming that she did in fact kill her husband on May 14, 1981, have you formulated an opinion as to what in fact caused the defendant to do that act?

KURLAND: Yes, I have.

STAFFORD: And what's your opinion?

KURLAND: My opinion is that at that particular point of her life, she and her husband were engaged in rapidly escalating and more and more frequent sadomasochistic game playing in which the two of them were playing victim and aggressor and which got to the point of being more and more real in her mind; and probably in his mind—he was acting out more and more of his fantasies which he probably had had for many years.

That the fantasies grew in intensity, that she put up with them for an incredibly long period of time relatively speaking until they were so overwhelming that she slipped out of reality and exploded with rage and acted out the fantasy and killed him.

STAFFORD: I have nothing further, your Honor.

As he walked back to his table, it was as if Stafford could feel the floor solidly beneath his feet for the first time since the trial began.

Dunn only had time to ask Dr. Kurland if he could see his notes in order to review them. After a conference at the bench, Judge Moore asked Dr. Kurland if he would be available tomorrow afternoon, and when he said yes, the judge recessed court at 3:40 that afternoon until the next morning at 9:30.

$$\boxed{6}$$

When court reconvened on Wednesday, one of the jurors, Mrs. McIntosh was out ill but had reported that she thought she would be able to come to court the following day, and both counsels agreed to adjourn until the following morning.

On Thursday, Stafford called as his first witness Ellen Scott, Andrea's mother, who had flown out from New Jersey with her husband. Watching Andrea's short and plump mother on the stand, sometimes struggling with her own memory for the facts, and at the same time trying not to allow the circumstance of the trial to bring any more disgrace on her family than it already had, Judy Campbell could almost see the tension playing itself out in the poor lady's nervous system.

Mrs. Scott was a study in unrelenting denial. As Stafford probed the family tragedy of the father, Cornelius Corneillisse, deserting them, the lady seemed to take a business-as-usual perspective:

"Was there anything out of the ordinary that happened on that particular day [he disappeared] prior to him saying he was going to work?" Stafford asked.

"No," Mrs. Scott answered. "It was a normal day."

She didn't hear from her husband until the FBI contacted her after seven years and said they had found him. At which time, having changed his name to Steve Gilbert and remarried, he returned to New Jersey to get a divorce. In his cross-examination, Dunn went back to the desertion day.

DUNN: Were you having marital problems prior to the   time he left?

MRS. SCOTT: Pardon?

DUNN: Were you having marital problems prior to the time he left?

MRS. SCOTT: Everything was wonderful.

DUNN: Everything was wonderful?

MRS. SCOTT: Yes.

Dunn questioned Mrs. Scott about an incident he remembered from one of the psychiatrists' reports. She hadn't allowed her daughter to join a school club.

"What was the reason why you refused to let her do that?" he asked.

"Well," Mrs. Scott said, "the girls smoked, and at that time young girls didn't smoke like that, and I felt—well, I didn't have money for the jacket."

With regard to Andrea's first husband, Mrs. Scott remembered the twenty-two-year-old Wesley Denike as Andrea's boyfriend and not the brother of her older daughter Barbara's boyfriend. When Dunn probed the cause of Andrea's miscarriage of the second baby, Mrs. Scott answered that Denike had been "fresh with her" and then added, "brutal."

DUNN: Did you ever question Mr. Denike about beating your daughter while she was in Cuba with him?

MRS. SCOTT: I didn't want to start any trouble. It was up to her. Because she said that she would work it out her own way for the children.

DUNN: Did they get along OK while they were at your home?

MRS. SCOTT: Well, there was a lot of things that just didn't look right to me. Pushing her when she tried to get in the car with the baby. And he would push her right in. And I'd tell him,

"You know, you shouldn't do that." I didn't want to be the busy mother-in-law. So I figured it was up to her.

DUNN: You intervened on her behalf when you saw him pushing her?

MRS. SCOTT: Yes.

DUNN: But you never asked him about beating your daughter?

MRS. SCOTT: You couldn't talk to him. You couldn't talk to him.

DUNN: Was there any time during the period of time that she was married to Wesley that she said Wesley broke her nose?

Stafford knew Dunn was, as always, probing for a lie.

MRS. SCOTT: Well, she told me he broke her nose, yeah. She was having trouble breathing.

DUNN: What did her nose look like then?

MRS. SCOTT: Well, she had trouble breathing. It wasn't out of shape. I mean it just looked a little large.

"Did she tell you what kind of a picture that was that she was doing when she fell off the horse?" Dunn asked a few moments later, referring to the nudie film.

"Cowboy picture," Mrs. Scott answered.

Dunn questioned Mrs. Scott about a conversation she had with Andrea at a shopping mall when they'd visited Andrea and Mr. Sand at the Springs.

"You said she confided something in you?" Dunn asked.

"Yes. She told me that Robert wanted to do weird sex acts with her."

Mrs. Scott didn't know what kind of sex acts were involved because Andrea didn't say.

"Well, you said she didn't describe the sex, and you didn't ask?" Dunn pressed.

"That's when it all happened in the bedroom," Mrs. Scott said. "I didn't see her. I didn't see him do anything to her while I was in the room with them."

Stafford's next witness was Bob Scott, who also testified about the visit to the Springs.

"Did Robert Sand look like he was in good health to you?" Dunn asked him in the cross-examination.

"In good health?" Scott said. "He didn't look bad. I know for one thing he was a strong boy from the waist up."

"Did you see him get up and walk around while you were there?"

"Well, he tried. He'd get off his wheelchair and get to another chair and fall into it."

Stafford called Yolanda Denike, Guy's wife. She too testified that Andrea had spoken with her about Robert Sand when they went shopping together, and Andrea had told her "not to be surprised" if something happened to her. Dunn took a cross-examination and several recrosses, always going for the lie. It felt to Stafford as if, not just Andrea's, but the veracity of every witness he called was on trial. When Mrs. Denike, testifying about Bob's possessiveness, said Bob and Andrea were always together when the Denikes visited, Dunn jumped on it. What about when Andrea and she went shopping? Was Bob with Andrea then? Mrs. Denike had to admit there were times Andrea was away from her husband.

After the witness stepped down, Judge Moore recessed for lunch at 12:02 and asked that they all return at 1:30.

$$\boxed{7}$$

When court reconvened after lunch, Stafford called Guy Denike, Andrea's tall sturdy twenty-six-year-old son. How had Robert Sand behaved when Guy and Yolanda had visited his mother and Sand at the Springs, the public defender asked.

"He didn't seem like he wanted my mom to go out at all," Denike said. "He wanted her to just to stay in the house right in eye contact with him all the time, and he didn't want to have us down. Every time we got down there, he wanted us to leave. That's the impression that I got."

After she had been married to Sand for a few months, Andrea told Denike that if anything happened to her, there was a letter in the file cabinet safe that talked about how Sand had kicked in the door of the second bedroom when she wanted to be left alone.

He and Yolanda had seen Andrea a week or a couple of weeks—he wasn't sure—after Robert Sand had been killed. Stafford asked if he had observed any injuries on his mother.

"On her arms, she had some bruises."

"On what arm did you see the bruises?"

"I believe they were on the left arm."

"And what did they look like?"

"Like someone grabbed her. Or hit her, or something."

"Why would you say it looked like someone grabbed her? What did the bruise look like?"

"Kind of long and narrow. About so big," Denike said, indicating several inches with his hand.

"Are you positive that you saw her two weeks after the homocide?" Stafford asked.

"Yes, sir. Approximately—yes, sir."

In his cross-examination, Dunn asked Denike whether he had talked with his mother about marrying Robert Sand.

"I said it's her life, and she runs it the way she feels," the witness answered. "She's old enough to do so."

"You figured that she'd already had four marriages, she was pretty experienced in that area?" Dunn said.

Stafford objected that this was argumentative. Judge Moore sustained it.

"When you discussed this with your mother," Dunn asked, "did you make any comments to her about the age of Mr. Sand?"

"Yes."

"Did you say to her, 'Gee, why are you marrying such an old guy?'"

"I just asked her—'Well, he is kind of an older gentleman, and what do you see in him?'" Guy said. "She was telling me that she's tired of being abused by people and that he would treat her nice and that she could help him out because she believed that she could get him to walk correctly."

Dunn asked Denike if he had questioned his mother when she told him of the letter in the safe that would explain what was going on. Guy said he had, and Dunn asked if she had said she was having problems with her health or feeling sick. He said no.

"Did she say she was having any problems with Robert?" Dunn asked.

"I could—anyone that went down there could see there was problems."

"Mr. Denike," Dunn said, "that's not what I asked you. What I asked you was did she say she was having problems with Robert?"

"Yes."

"And what problems did she say she was having with Robert?"

"He wouldn't let her go to church. He wouldn't let her go swimming in the pool. He wouldn't let her go play tennis. He wouldn't let her do a lot of things. A lot of times she would practically beg him to go. He would go along and make sure he was there, present."

A moment later Dunn asked if his mother had told Guy that she loved Robert Sand.

"Yes, she did," he said.

During the remainder of the afternoon, Dunn took up his cross-examination of Dr. Morton Kurland, which he hadn't had time to begin almost a week ago, in the late afternoon on Tuesday, February 21, just before court was adjourned.

While other witnesses could be riled or shaken by the prosecutor's inquisitorial style and persistence—he would generally cross-examine witnesses for the defense far longer than Stafford questioned them in his direct examination—Kurland, an old pro as an expert witness and not unappreciative of a good lawyer driving his points home, gave back as good as he got. Stafford was heartened to see it.

Dunn quizzed Kurland on his interview with Andrea at Indio County Jail before he testified at her competency trial. Was the doctor familiar with the term malingering?

KURLAND: Yes.

DUNN: And what does the word malingering mean to you?

KURLAND: Malingering means a conscious effort on someone's part to feign an illness in order to get some other goal, money or not having to go to work or avoiding school or something like that.

DUNN: Would that include criminal prosecution?

KURLAND: Could easily include that.

DUNN: And when you had your interview with her in February of '83, did you consider Mrs. Sand malingering at that time?

KURLAND: Oh, yes.

DUNN: And in what way did you consider that she was malingering?

KURLAND: I didn't consider she was malingering. I considered that she might be malingering, but I didn't believe that that was the case.

DUNN: Isn't it true that at that time she had reported a substantial number of rapes?

KURLAND: Oh, yes.

DUNN: And didn't you also state that at that time even she admitted that those rapes had not occurred?

KURLAND: She said that she probably was imagining them, yes.

DUNN: Wouldn't that be a marked discrepancy from the person's claimed distress and the objective findings?

KURLAND: Not if you think that the rapes were hallucinations, and then it goes direct to her being disturbed psychiatrically rather than not being raped and not showing evidence of it. That would be more appropriate.

Judge Moore adjourned court at a little after four that afternoon until the following Monday morning.

8

Dr. Kurland was the witness through all of Monday morning and for half an hour after lunch. In redirect examination, Stafford took up the incident at Capistrano By The Sea hospital when Andrea insisted she had been poisoned.

STAFFORD: The notation from the hospital staff is that she could offer no explanation for why anyone would want to do that to her, but continued to hold to that belief that it had occurred. Would that incident be of any significance to you in your opinion that she is a borderline personality type?

KURLAND: Oh, yes. Again it's indication that she has poor reality testing under pressure, and that for reasons which were inexplicable, she believed someone was trying to kill her—at least poison her—even though the evidence was to the contrary.

STAFFORD: Prior to Mrs. Sand going to Capistrano By The Sea, did you ever confront her in any of your interviews with her that there was anything mentally wrong with her?

KURLAND: Indeed I did.

STAFFORD: And when did that occur?

KURLAND: Well, on a specific occasion of her being hospital-ized on one of the alleged rape attempts, I remember her telling me that no one believed her. The nurses didn't believe her, the police didn't believe her, and she didn't think that I believed her.
    And I said to her that's because your story is unbelievable. And it seems to me that you're seriously ill, and that you—I think I even said to her that I thought she was crazy. I used the word "crazy."

She became enraged with that. And angrily told me that if I thought she was crazy, I was wrong and that not only that, but she was going to sign out of the hospital because she wouldn't tolerate being taken care of by someone who thinks she's crazy.

STAFFORD: In your opinion as a psychiatrist, is that consistent with someone who is malingering?

KURLAND: No, that's the opposite of someone who is malingering. A person who is malingering wants you to think they're crazy, leads you to think they're crazy, and agrees with you when you tell them they're crazy.

Stafford asked Kurland if, for a person with the type of character disorder that he characterized Andrea as having, the return from an uneventful two weeks' visit at her mother's home in New Jersey to the scene of the killing of Robert Sand could create enough stress to drive her back into a psychotic state so that she would believe she was being attacked or raped?

"I think it could, certainly," Kurland said.

"Isn't it true," Dunn asked Kurland in the recross-examination, "that if someone is trying to convince another person of a fabrication, the most effective way to do that is to repeat the same story over and over again?"

It occurred to Stafford that this was Dunn's technique in the courtroom: "Andrea is a liar who is only pretending to be crazy," he pounded with merciless regularity into the jury day after day.

"Well, you know," Kurland said, "within limits. But to tell an incredible story sixteen or eighteen times is not reasonable."

"You said a person would have to be crazy to believe those types of stories..."

"Yes," Kurland said.

"Well, isn't it true that whether or not somebody is crazy if they believe the story really doesn't have anything to do with Mrs. Sand?"

"Oh, I think it has to do with intent," Kurland said. "I mean if I know that someone is crazy to believe the story, then I'm crazy to tell it."

Stafford called Sylvia Berger, Robert Sand's tall attractive forty-year-old daughter, as the next witness for the defense. Had she known, Stafford asked, that just prior to his death, her father had written a new will "that provided that if he and Andrea stayed married for five years or less, Andrea would get a third of his estate, and if the marriage lasted longer than five years, Andrea would get a half of his estate," with the remainder going to the witness and her daughter?

Sylvia said she had heard something about it.

"Isn't it true," he said, "that in the interview with Detective Lastar, you made a comment that if Andrea had killed your father, she must have the mind of a 'celery stalk' because she would have gotten over half the estate if she had stayed married to him for a certain period of time?"

At the words "celery stalk," the courtroom had filled with laughter.

"That sounds like something I would say," Sylvia answered breezily and then burst into tears.

Before calling the last witness of the day, Stafford requested that the final, unsigned will of Robert Sand, along with a letter to Sand dated May 5, 1981, from his attorney in Portland, Garthe Brown, be placed into evidence. The will, in an unopened envelope addressed to Robert Sand from Garthe Brown's office, had been found at 6 Brandeis Court in a mail basket in the foyer on the morning of the murder.

Stafford's final witness of the day was Jean Hyams, a registered nurse employed by Riverside County in the Indio jail, who brought to the court Andrea's medical records during her time in custody in order for them to be submitted into evidence. That morning Stafford had asked Dr. Kurland to characterize the drugs that Andrea had been prescribed by the Indio jail medical staff over the last several months, bringing up specifically Thorazine, Lithium, and Triavil.

Kurland characterized Thorazine as an "antipsychotic" and Triavil as similar in its effect. Lithium, he said, was used for manic depressive disorders, "when people have great episodes of excitement and outbursts of uncontrollable behavior." Stafford asked if these drugs were inconsistent with his diagnosis of Andrea as a borderline personality type.

"No, on the contrary," Kurland said. "I would think that if she's been successfully given major tanquilizers and has, in fact, calmed down, that would support the notion that she needed that all the time, and certainly that her behavior is modified by it."

9

On Monday and Tuesday, Stafford finished up his case in chief. Dr. William Harley Jones, a thirty-nine-year-old Palm Desert psychologist with whom Stafford had worked before, and who, like Dr. Kurland, had a reputation as a particularly strong expert witness, testified all day Monday. His diagnosis was in essence and in most particulars the same as Dr. Kurland's, but in addition to interviewing Andrea and reviewing the voluminous file on the case, Jones had gone to Los Angeles in October to interview Guy Denike, and his grandmother, Ellen Scott, who was visiting at the time. Stafford asked about Mrs. Scott's demeanor when Dr. Jones questioned her.

JONES: She was a fairly calm and controlled person when discussing Andrea and her sister. When she got to the point involving the disappearance of her husband, she became very upset, started to cry, and left the room briefly, as I recall. She seemed so upset at the time it was as if the husband had disppeared quite recently rather than twenty-five years ago.

Stafford asked Jones specifically about about Guy's perception of his grandfather.

JONES: [Guy] stated that he believed the grandfather had molested or attempted to molest his brother, that is, the other son of Mrs. Mims. That he said many inappropriate sexual things to the two boys when they were teenagers. And he kept large collections of pornographic material around the house including heterosexual material and homosexual pornography, as well. That there were dildos and obscene statues and whatnot that were displayed in the house.

He stated that when he was young, his mother had been a good mother and had—if there was limited food, she would give the children the food and not eat herself. But later on, the children were frequently on their own when they were in their teenage years.

STAFFORD: The description that Guy Denike gave of his grandfather—was that in opposition to the description that Mrs. Scott gave of her former husband?

JONES: Well, it certainly was. She described him as a quiet, passive, rather saintly figure. I recall her stating that people had told her that at that time he reminded them of a minister.

Citing the larger than usual difference between Andrea's verbal and performance IQs, Jones related it to "a tendency to act out emotional distress in terms of her behavior rather than just an experience on an emotional level...[T]hat kind of difference sometimes is associated with a tendency to not process experience in the verbal manner."

STAFFORD: Dr. Jones, if a person committed an act and was in an actual psychotic state and then came out of it, would there be a possibility that they would not realize what happened during the time that they actually had been psychotic?

JONES: Well, it's very common that people particularly who have delusions and hallucinations don't appear to remember them after they leave the psychotic state.

At the end of the day, in further recross-examination, Dunn asked Dr. Jones what the real difference was between histrionic personality and borderline personality disorder.

JONES: Well, the histrionic personality disorder emphasizes a dramatic behavior—self-dramatization, attention-seeking behavior. Craving activity and excitement, overreaction to minor stresses, irrational angry outbursts. Shallow interpersonal relationships, self-centeredness, vainness and narcissism, dependency needs, possibility of manipulative suicidal behavior. I believe those describe Mrs. Mims by and large. The emphasis on histrionic personality disorder pays a lot of attention to the mode of relating to other people.

The borderline personality disorder, it states in the *Diagnostic Manual*, is sometimes viewed as a level of organization that implies that personality is less organized, less cohesive. Emphasizes impulsivity and unstable interpersonal relationships, problems with emotional control. Particularly with anger. Self-destructive or self-mutilating behavior. Feelings of boredom.

They have a different flavor to them, but in many cases, including the case of Mrs. Sand in my opinion, they're often applied to the same individual. In her case, I believe they do.

Jones knew Dunn was an elder in the Mormon church, a former police officer, a straight arrow not to say a square, and he couldn't help but wonder at the irony—or maybe even the existential aptness—of such a man being handed this case. The jury,

too, mainly older women, were certainly getting an earful. Jones
had been amazed one morning when he came across the phrase
"golden showers" in the conservative *Palm Desert Sun*. That had
to be a first.

As for Chuck Stafford, a charming guy to work with, Jones
had noticed that in the months since he'd taken the case, his hair
had gone from little flecks here and there to totally gray.

On Tuesday, Rick Erwood, Gary Scherotter's associate, testified regarding the rape and assault Andrea reported on the
morning of August 24, 1982, when he and Joe Jones and Gary
and Sherry Scherotter had all gone to the condominium and discovered Andrea tied naked to the bed. It wasn't clear to Dunn
where Stafford was going with this testimony—and the prosecutor knew it had to be unclear to the jury too—beyond just
laying down more facts in the courtroom.

Fred Lastar testified that he had seen a door, off its hinges
with a hole in it, in the garage at 6 Brandeis Court. Stafford asked
the detective whether he recalled Sylvia Berger telling him in an
interview why her father had started a relationship with Andrea.

LASTAR: She was young and beautiful, and she would take care
of him.

STAFFORD: Do you have a recollection of Sylvia Berger ever
saying to you that her father married Andrea Sand because she
would do anything sexually for him?

LASTAR: I believe that's indicated in a report.

STAFFORD: And that basically she was presentable.

LASTAR: Yes.

STAFFORD: And that some of the other women that her father had in fact been associated with were not presentable?

LASTAR: That's correct.

Dunn declined to cross-examine the witness.

Stafford's final witness was Arthur Seay, the supervising investigator for the public defender's Riverside County office assigned to the Desert Division. Seay was the office's handwriting expert. In his opinion, the letter of July 23 had been written by Richard Cordine, but he wasn't sure about the handwriting on the envelope. In his cross-examination, Dunn established Seay did not have extensive training in handwriting analysis and had only testified as an expert handwriting witness four or five times in seven years.

After lunch, Dunn continued his cross-examination, focusing on the handwriting on the envelope, which Seay had characterized as inconsistent with Cordine's. Seay thought there was fifty-fifty possibility that the writing could be by either Mrs. Sand or Cordine.

Dunn drew attention to the postmark on the letter and Seay admitted he'd conducted only a "cursory" examination of it with a low-powered magnifying glass and hadn't noticed anything unusual. Seay also admitted that he had had Lorrie Wright obtain the handwriting exemplars from Andrea for comparison purposes.

"Isn't it true, Mr. Seay," Dunn said, "that it's absolutely critical to a document examiner when he is taking requested exemplars to witness the writing of the person giving that exemplar in order to determine if that person is attempting to disguise their handwriting?"

Seay said he usually tried to do this but wasn't able to take the exemplars himself in this case because of a conflict in his schedule.

Dunn called Dr. Anthony Oliver as his first rebuttal witness. After questioning him on his background and his connection with the case up to now, he told Judge Moore it might be a good time to break until tomorrow. Court was adjourned just before four o'clock.

XV

1

Knowing Anthony Oliver was going to be Dunn's first rebuttal witness, Andrea and Chuck Stafford and Lorrie Wright talked about all appearing in court on Thursday morning with his signature red handkerchief tucked into their jacket or blouse. But in the end discretion seemed the better part of valor.

Stafford requested a voire dire for the first time since jury selection to qualify the witness, and established that, although Oliver was a member of the American Psychiatric Association, he was still not board certified. Oliver explained that he hadn't taken the board certification examination on two different occasions because he had conflicting appointments.

When Dunn took up direct examination again, he reviewed with Oliver that he had gone over a large file on the case, and had had three interviews with Andrea that totaled nine hours.

Oliver's style, it seemed to Judy Campbell, who was in the courtroom that day whenever she had time, was a variation on Bob Dunn's. Impeccably dressed, good looking, and speaking with a precise English accent, Oliver represented a model of civilization in a case where every standard seemed to have been shunted aside. Campbell caught a moment that morning where the doctor described the early sexual relations between Andrea and Robert Sand in language that sounded like it was out of a drawing room comedy.

OLIVER: He wanted her to sit around naked at the dinner table while they ate, and also he wanted her to be naked while she watched television; and, in fact, he would be particularly pleased if she did so in a posture that put her rear end—exposed her rear end to his gaze. So she would spend some of the time watching television—with the television on the couch—rather in a position that a proctologist would wish a patient to be in, as she tried to watch.

She indicated to me that they would engage in sexual relations, usually masturbatory activities, and that the only other activity that he seemed to want to do of the vaguely social kind was to go flying.

Otherwise, she found that they hardly socialized at all, and she certainly objected to that.

Dr. Oliver went on to describe Andrea's later sexual relationship with Robert Sand, as she had described it to him in their recent interviews:

OLIVER: She would be encouraged to simulate killing Derek. Derek was her husband, I believe her fourth husband. And also killing Florence. Florence was Mr. Sand's former wife. And she went through a fantasy of killing them with a knife until, Andrea said, Mr. Sand would climax sexually. And she often became quite upset at the end of these. What I understood she meant was quite agitated and anxious as when going through these.

She would put the knives into her rectum. Insert them through her anus into her rectum while he watched and masturbated to the point of ejaculation.

She would read pornography to him while he masturbated. And he often liked to spank her bottom, her bare bottom. He would do so using his hand, and then he began to use what she described as a wooden paddle, and I understood to be basically a small plank of wood.

Dunn asked if, when she described these activities, she suggested that they were disagreeable or distasteful to her.

"The impression I got," Oliver said, "is that she liked to do whatever pleased him, and that this was not disagreeable to her at all."

Dunn asked if she had described "some type of escalation in this sexual relationship."

OLIVER: She first described it by telling me that she would often need to obtain a climax herself by using a vibrator on herself, Robert Sand sometimes stimulating her breasts to help her reach a climax. And on one occasion, she was tied spread-eagled to the bed for a fantasy—somewhat sadistic fantasy—which involved several men acting in concert together in a form of conspiracy, raping and sodomizing her.

She claimed that Robert Sand solicited a man to in fact sodomize her while he took photographs and masturbated. And she indicated to me that she later cut the photographs up. So they're not available for anybody to see.

And he liked to show her off to other people and watch their reactions. She described occasionally at the Springs Country Club, he would seat her at the table close to the stairs—people would enter the dining room there—and have her in a very revealing low-cut dress, and asked her to expose her breast, and see how people reacted to that. And to this she demurred—she felt that was inappropriate.

Tut tut, Lorrie Wright thought, sitting at the defense table next to Andrea, who was listening quietly. Could this guy be for real? On the other hand, the jury looked awfully engrossed. Oliver was like Alistair Cooke taking them on a brisk PBS tour of sexual depravity, his English accent a necessary, reassuring center of gravity. Now Dunn asked him about the night of the killing.

OLIVER: "The two men out in the parking lot today" [Robert Sand told Andrea]—apparently these were two men that were seen by Mr. Sand by himself when they were at the grocery store earlier that day—"those two men are here with Karen and another couple."

Andrea said something to the effect of "No more games, Bob, please."

And he poked her with a knife.

"Lie still and listen," she told me he said. "Number One Man is going to have a gun." This is Robert Sand talking. "Number One Man is going to have a gun, and when I call him in, you are going to give him the kitty money."

She told me the kitty money was household savings which at that time had reached about $1,200 that were being accumulated to go towards the $2,000 membership fee of the Springs Country Club.

Robert Sand continued: "Number Two Man will have a knife, and you will undress for him. Karen has a knife and drugs, and you are going to give her some of your clothes and jewelry. Lay down on the floor and Karen will suck on your pussy. Number One Man and Number Two Man..."

And Andrea then said their names were being referred to by her husband, Monko and Jose.

"Monko and Jose are going to bite your tits till you come. You are to suck on Monko and Jose's cocks until they climax over your face and chest. Then get them hard again. They will put their cocks into your pussy and asshole and fuck you at the same time."

I asked her at this stage how it would be possible for something like that to occur, and she indicated to me that in fact she had been subjected to such a situation, being sodomized and having vaginal intercourse by two different men at the same time, in Eureka in 1969.

DUNN: Did she give any further circumstances regarding that incident in Eureka where she had had sex with two people? What the surrounding circumstances were that led up to that kind of intercourse?

OLIVER: She mentioned something to the effect that she didn't want to do it at the time. They had threatened some action against the children, so she felt compelled to do this. It has, of course, some considerable significance, those comments.

DUNN: What significance did those comments have to you when she made them?

OLIVER: It is, of course, physically impossible for a woman to be penetrated by two men vaginally and rectally at the same time. It is a physical impossibility.

How would Dr. Oliver know that for sure? Wright wondered. Not that she was about to personally get up and argue with him. But wouldn't Andrea, say, be more of an expert on that particular question? Was it her imagination or were there too many men and not enough women talking in this courtroom?

DUNN: Did that knowledge that you had of the impossibility of that type of sexual act taking place have any significance to you, regarding the statement that she had given to you that she had in fact experienced that type of intercourse previously?

Say what? Wright thought.

OLIVER: Yes, very much. It had a lot to do with her veracity. Clearly.

DUNN: What significance would that have regarding her veracity?

OLIVER: Since it is impossible for such a thing to be done, she's clearly not telling me the truth.

DUNN: The series of events she was describing after these statements that you just testified were made, what occurred next?

OLIVER: She indicated that Robert Sand told her: "If you don't do everything right, another couple will come in, cut you up, drug you, tie you up, and leave you out in the desert with a knife in your pussy and asshole."

In other words, Charles Stafford thought, sitting on the other side of the defendant, Robert Sand wrote the script for the rapes. Was she trying to summon him back to life by acting them out again and again?

After lunch, Dunn closed his direct examination with Oliver's testimony that Andrea was most accurately described as having a histrionic personality disorder, as well as paraphilia, a second diagnosis.

"Paraphilia basically means," Oliver explained, "sexually deviant behavior which is consistent with sexual sadism and sexual masochism."

Oliver could also add to that, he said, antisocial personality traits along with passive/aggressive, dependent and narcissistic traits.

"Doctor," Dunn asked, "do you have an opinion regarding Mrs. Sand's ability to premeditate the murder of her husband on May the 14, 1981?"

"I do," Oliver said.

"What is that opinion?"

"My opinion is that I find nothing to indicate that there would be any impairment of her ability to premeditate."

"Doctor," Dunn said, "do you have an opinion regarding Mrs. Sand's ability to deliberate the killing of her husband on May the 14, 1981?"

"Yes, I do," Oliver said.

"What is that opinion?"

"I find no evidence of any mental impairment that would impede her ability to deliberate."

"Doctor," Dunn said, "do you have an opinion regarding Mrs. Sand's ability to form the mental state of malice afore-thought as regards the murder of her husband on May the 14, 1981?"

"Yes, I do," Oliver said.

"What is that opinion?"

"Again I found no evidence of any mental impairment that would interfere with her ability to harbor malice aforethought."

"Doctor," Dunn said, "do you have an opinion regarding Mrs. Sand's ability to intentionally kill her husband on May the 14, 1981?"

"Yes, I do," Oliver said.

"And what is that opinion?"

"I find no evidence of mental impairment that would inter-fere with her ability to harbor an intent to kill."

"Thank you," Dunn said. "I have nothing further, your Honor."

"Mr. Stafford," Judge Moore said.

Jesus Christ, Stafford thought.

In his cross-examination, Stafford made it known that Dr. Oliver had diagnosed Andrea as having histrionic personality dis-order for the competency trial in February 1983, before he had in fact interviewed her. He also established that Oliver was being paid $6,700 for his services to the prosecution up to that date.

Oliver testified that he tended to doubt the veracity of the sexual games between Robert Sand and Andrea that she had reported—the impossible sexual act being a primary indicator of her propensity to lie—and therefore the potential of those games to cause the stress necessary to drive her into a psychotic state.

He brushed off the severity of the self-mutilations during the rapes and assaults. He felt the same way about the compulsive repetition of those incidents, which Andrea had admitted she had staged, in the face of unanimous disbelief in their authenticity on the part of the police and other officials. He didn't believe that any of it constituted evidence of anything more severe than histrionic personality disorder.

Oliver also discounted the severity of Andrea's current antipsychotic medication.

In the end, it became clear to Stafford that Dr. Oliver didn't see even psychosis itself as necessarily a mitigating or exculpating factor in the murder trial.

"It is perfectly possible for somebody to be psychotic and yet to be still criminally responsible," he said briskly.

2

On Monday, March 5, Dunn presented a parade of further rebuttal witnesses for the prosecution. He began with Dr. Donald Schafer, a board-certified psychiatrist one of whose specialties was hypnosis. Dr. Schafer testified that the results of hypnotizing a subject were not necessarily reliable in terms of truth, although they might later seem to the subject of the hypnosis to have that hard and fast character. In cross-examination, Stafford pointed out that Andrea's testimony in court was inconsistent with what she had recalled under hypnosis about the night Robert Sand had been killed, and instead closely matched what she'd said in a session with Sergeant Richard Hannebaum three weeks after she had been hypnotized. And at that time she hadn't been under hypnosis.

After Dr. Schafer's testimony on hypnotism, Stafford was allowed out of turn to call him as a surrebutal witness to testify on another question in another area of his expertise. Dunn agreed to this provided Stafford assumed a pro-rata share of the expert witness's fee for testimony. Stafford established that Schafer, as both a medical doctor and a psychiatrist, had knowledge and expertise in the area of sexual perversion.

STAFFORD: Based on your experience as a medical doctor, is it physically possible for a woman, if she is placed in a certain position or positions, to be able to be anally penetrated and vaginally penetrated by two men at the same time?

SCHAFER: I understand that it can be done.

In cross-examination, Dunn continued the discussion.

DUNN: Dr. Schafer, wouldn't it be true that the possibility of that happening would depend largely upon how well endowed the male subjects would be who would be performing that type of sex act?

Hunh? Lorrie Wright thought at the defense table.

SCHAFER: I suppose.

DUNN: Isn't it true that the rectal and vaginal orifices on a female are rather close in proximity to one another?

SCHAFER: Correct.

DUNN: And in order for two men to have contemporaneous rectal and vaginal intercourse would indicate that one person would have to be substantially well endowed in order to fit in the space characteristic for that to occur?

SCHAFER: I suppose.

Stafford was having a problem visualizing what Dunn was driving at. The chief deputy public defender took a redirect.

STAFFORD: Dr. Schafer, assuming that a man was lying down on his back and a woman squatted on top of him, and the man's penis penetrated her vagina, and she was looking facially at the man's face, and she moved herself forward dropping herself on the man, and another man came up behind her, would it not be possible for that man to penetrate her anal cavity?

SCHAFER: It would seem possible to me.

Now I'll be able to sleep tonight, Lorrie Wright thought.

Andrea testified that Joe Mims had been with her when she received the threatening letter from Richard Cordine. Dunn put Mims on the stand to testify that, in fact, he hadn't been present.

After the break for lunch, Dunn's next witness was Lieutenant Kennedy, who testified that when he'd interviewed Linda Schrick in August of 1981, she hadn't said anything about Robert Sand making Andrea wear a dog collar prior to their marriage.

Under direct examination by Dunn, Florence Sand testified that Robert Sand had never taken a swing at her, as Mr. Sand's male nurse, David Warner, had testified earlier.

"I never saw him strike anyone," she said. "He didn't strike anyone. That's not the way he operated."

Did the witness know "any reason whatsoever why Mr. Warner would come into this courtroom and lie?" Stafford asked Mrs. Sand.

"I can't think of any reason unless he thought he was going to help me," she said.

Kurt Kohler, the owner of an aircraft management company in Van Nuys who had frequently been Robert Sand's copilot, testified that Sand wasn't able to walk and had other physical problems.

"Bob could not make coordinated movement," Kohler said. "He couldn't reach for a glass of water without the hand detouring on the way. Whenever he tried to crawl or tried to walk or tried to do anything, it was almost a spastic type of motion.

"I'm not a doctor, but there was some short circuit between his brain and his hands. He could fly the airplane smoothly, he could drive the car, but if he wanted to do something, it would not be translated smoothly into a motion. He would control the airplane, but it was not a smooth control."

Kohler testified that before Robert Sand married Andrea, he called him one evening and said Andrea had beaten him.

"Did he say he suffered any injuries from that beating?" Dunn asked.

"Yes," Kohler said. "He said he had been knocked out of his wheelchair, that she had struck him and kicked him, and he had a bloody nose and his hand was scratched. Gouged."

Kohler went on to say that the next day or the day after, he observed a long scratch on the back of Sand's right hand.

In cross-examination, Stafford went back to the incident.

"Mr. Sand supposedly indicated that he had been beaten and kicked; is that correct?"

"Yes."

"And that he had a bloody nose from the incident?"

"Yes."

"And what else did he tell you as to his injuries?"

"That he had a scratch on his hand."

"When you saw him the next day, did you see any evidence on his face of any bruises or redness that would have been indicative of him being struck?"

"Not that I recall," Kohler said.

Stafford asked if Kohler remembered telling Lorrie Wright when she interviewed him that Robert Sand had a habit of exaggerating to great lengths on things.

"I believe I did say that to her, yes."

Stafford told Kohler that Mr. Sand's daughter had testified in court that Sand was as strong as an ox and asked if he would agree with that. Kohler said no.

"He wasn't strong?" Stafford asked.

"Not at all."

"Not strong in his arms?"

"No."

"Or his upper body?"

Kohler said no.

Before dismissing court that day, Judge Moore said that he believed the guilt phase of the trial would go to the jury sometime that week.

$$3$$

The last day of testimony in the guilt phase of the trial, Tuesday, March 6, was enlivened by the presence of the television star Ralph Waite, who had played the father on the long-running show "The Waltons." He was currently being seen on the CBS series he had developed called "The Mississippi," in which he played a riverboat lawyer. A Palm Desert resident for part of the year, Waite told reporters that his interest in the law might spark another project. His current series would be airing for the final time that night.

Most of the day was taken up with the prosecution's last two rebuttal witnesses, both of whom testified about the questioned Richard Cordine letter. An overhead projector was utilized to show their findings to the jury.

George Lewis, the examiner at the Postal Inspectors of Western Region Crime Laboratory who had examined the document in February, testified that, using both a microscope and an ultraviolet light, he had observed that the paper on the envelope in the area of the postmark showed evidence of abrasion. There was supporting evidence of this in the fact that the optical brightener used in the surface of the paper was worn away.

"Was the erasure or the abrasion confined to a particular area of the postmark that you observed on that envelope?" Dunn asked.

"Yes," Lewis said. "Right in a very closely controlled area, just at that area where the date is on the postmark."

Still discernible, however, was the letter B. Since the post office employed a three-letter abbreviation for the months of the year in its postmarks, this limited the month of the postmark to February, while the letter was dated July 23. Lewis also noted that different inks had been used for the address on the envelope and the letter inside it.

Dunn concluded his direct examination by having Mr. Lewis testify that his services, employing state-of-the-art equipment, were available free of charge through the post office to the public defender's office as well as to his own.

J. Kenneth Brown of the district attorney's office testified specifically regarding his analysis of the handwriting in the letter. In voire dire, Stafford brought out that Brown's training in this specialty wasn't appreciably different from that of his own expert witness, Arthur Seay.

Brown testified that forgeries tended to "look drawn. Not free flowing. Often you'll find patches, overwrites, unexplained corrections. Additions of small strokes that a person writing an original signature wouldn't do; and overall they have a drawn, unnatural appearance. Blunt ended strokes, curves that have got tremor in them. Wiggly lines."

Dunn asked him what his impression was of the questioned document.

"First of all," Brown said, "its overall look of what I will say is unnaturalness. It has almost a pieced-together or put-together look to it. The line quality is not really bad, but it shows tremor. It shows some hesitation. It shows numerous overwrites that are not explained and correcting in areas that a normal person would not correct in."

Brown said that forgerers would frequently ignore the most common and simple words, such as "and" and "the" and "I." Using the overhead projector, he first compared eleven I's from the questioned document, purporting to have been written by Richard Cordine, to I's known to have been written by Andrea Sand. The two sets were virtually indistinguishable. Then he compared the eleven I's in the questioned Cordine letter to I's known to have been written by Richard Cordine.

"Each and every one looks entirely different from the I's of the defendant," Brown testified.

Near the end of the afternoon, Stafford called his final two surrebuttal witnesses. Detective Fred Lastar testified that he had interviewed Kurt Kohler over the telephone on June 2, 1981. At that time, Kohler had said he had seen no signs of injuries after Robert Sand claimed to have been beaten by Andrea.

The final witness was Dr. Morton Kurland.

STAFFORD: Assuming that Dr. Oliver made a diagnosis of the defendant that she had a histrionic personality disorder, would you agree with that analysis?

KURLAND: Yes. I would agree that that was a reasonable diagnosis.

STAFFORD: How is it that your opinion that you gave in court differs from simply saying she's histrionic?

KURLAND: Well, I think that in addition to her having a histrionic personality—that is, the underlying personality which she has—there was also a more pathological diagnosis, that is, a worse diagnosis, in which I felt she had a borderline personality in addition.

STAFFORD: Are there some things in this case that you see that are not simply able to be explained by characterizing a person as having a histrionic personality disorder?

KURLAND: Yes. That's my opinion.

STAFFORD: And what things in this case would not be able to be explained by simply saying the defendant suffers from a histrionic personality disorder?

KURLAND: Well, as I've indicated previously, it's my feeling that her behavior is such that she has lost contact with reality on more than one occasion and that this represents a much more severe disorder than simply histrionic disorder.

Judge Moore told the jury they would reconvene the next afternoon at 1:30, at which time they would hear Mr. Dunn's closing summation.

4

Andrea Sand had testified, Deputy District Attorney Dunn reminded the jury in his closing argument on Wednesday afternoon, that her greatest fear in life was that she would end up a fifty-year-old waitress. And it was only months after the death of an aging boyfriend of hers named Elliot, after she discovered that the $100,000 life insurance benefit she was supposed to receive from him would not be paid, that she pursued and then married the sixty-eight-year-old, wheelchair-bound Robert Sand. Sand had told Andrea that he didn't think he had very long to live.

The couple moved to a beautiful home in the Springs in Rancho Mirage, and Andrea had the security, comforts, and luxuries of an upper class lifestyle while Robert Sand paid all the bills.

However, there was one problem, the prosecutor said. Sand didn't seem to be declining physically and instead proved to be a man who was demanding and possessive to the point of being dictatorial. Knowing she would receive a "cool" quarter of a million dollars (the $150,000 bequest in the codicil to Sand's will, plus $100,000 from the sale of the Springs condominium) when her husband died, Andrea grew tired of his demands and decided to hasten the event that would give her complete freedom. She stabbed Robert Sand in the early morning hours of May 14, 1981, and then concocted a story of intruders.

To shore up and bolster this story, Dunn said, Mrs. Sand went on to stage a series of rapes, assaults, and abductions that supposedly were carried out by the same people who killed her husband. Then, two-and-a-half years after Sand's death, when she realized that her alibi and supporting stories "just wouldn't cut it," she came up with a way to blame Sand for his own killing.

"Did you ever get the feeling Robert Sand was the one who was on trial here?" Dunn asked the jury.

Andrea claimed that under hypnosis in September 1983, she had finally realized what happened on the night of the killing. For the first time, she began to tell stories of sadomasochistic games the couple played, which became progressively more and more violent, and eventually, when Robert Sand attacked her one night when she refused to play the game, drove her over the edge into psychosis, and she killed him.

But both the self-defense and the diminished capacity explanations of the crime made no more sense than her previous stories, Dunn said.

Mrs. Sand suffered no visible injuries from the night of intensive combat she had described in court, for instance, and that in itself contradicted her account. But even if her testimony was "100 percent true," Dunn said, she still had no grounds for claiming self-defense. In her own testimony, he said, she had stated that after an initial struggle she broke free, and her husband, Dunn reminded the jury, could not walk.

"That's when the danger ceased to exist," Dunn said. "I asked her, 'Was there anything preventing you from walking out?' and she answered, 'No.'"

Mrs. Sand's other defense of diminished capacity brought on by the "kinky sex games" her husband demanded also had no foundation. If the games in fact existed, Dunn said, they probably originated with Mrs. Sand herself.

"Andrea Sand is a master game-player," the prosecutor said. "She is constantly playing games. Not only has she played games with her personal life, she has attempted to play games with our criminal justice system. And now she is playing a game with you."

There had been many references during the trial, Dunn said, to a photo album that contained hundreds of nude photos of Mrs. Sand. The implication was that the photos were evidence of Sand's sexual kinkiness.

"But how did Andrea Sand describe the photos? As distasteful?" the prosecutor asked. "No, after Sand's death, she described them as an exciting part of their sex life and sometimes pulled them out and showed them to people."

Andrea had also described spanking as a pleasurable part of the couple's sex life after her husband's death.

It was true, Dunn said, that she had testified of more bizarre sexual practices, such as the insertion of knives into her rectum and vagina.

"But did that behavior with knives stop after Robert Sand died May 14?" Dunn asked. "No, when the police officers would come, she would be nude with knives inserted.

"Of Robert and Andrea Sand, who had the problem with sadomasochistic sex?" the prosecutor asked. "Whose sexuality demanded an increased level of sadomasochism?"

Dunn acknowledged that two experts hired by the defense had supported the claim that Mrs. Sand had a serious mental illness. But doctors who examined her before she faced murder charges hadn't found any signs of psychosis. When she filed a workers compensation claim after falling off a horse in 1968, the doctors who examined her then suggested that she suffered from the less serious histrionic personality disorder, indicated by a need for attention and dramatic exhibitions of behavior.

In the end, the real truth about the night of May 14, 1981, came from Andrea's imprisoned pen pal, Richard Cordine, who testified that Andrea told him in July of 1981 that she had stabbed her husband to death.

Not only did this testimony contradict Mrs. Sand's version of the killing, but she told this to Cordine at a time when she was still insisting to law enforcement officials that intruders had done the killing, the same intruders who continued, according to her, to rape and assault her.

As new information came up, Dunn said, Mrs. Sand was, of course, always ready to alter her story to accommodate it. However, when she tried to account for Richard Cordine's statements, she made a critical error. She forged a letter from Cordine, dating it July 1982, in which he wrote that he would lie to hurt her. She then put the letter in an envelope that she had actually received from Cordine.

"But there was a problem," Dunn said. "The postmark on the envelope."

The examiner from the U.S. Postal Service testified that someone had "very carefully removed only that part of the postmark which showed that the letter was written five months after the envelope was mailed," the prosecutor said.

A liar, a forger, and a desperate fortune-seeker, Andrea Sand had contrived an elaborate series of stories, riddled with sex and violence, to disguise the fact that she "viciously and brutally" murdered her aging and crippled fifth husband, Robert Sand, for his money, the prosecutor said.

"I don't get a thrill out of asking people to convict someone of murder," Dunn concluded. "It's very difficult for you, I know. But I'm asking you for a verdict of first degree murder."

After Dunn finished, Judge Moore adjourned court until 9:30 the next morning, when, he told the jury, they would hear Mr. Stafford's closing argument.

$$5$$

Mr. Dunn's argument that Andrea was a fortune hunter didn't make sense, Chief Deputy Public Defender Charles Stafford said in his closing argument on Thursday morning. If money had been her object, she would have waited for her husband to sign his new will, which increased her inheritance from $150,000 to one-third of his entire estate.

To understand what happened, Stafford said, it was necessary to look at Robert Sand himself, his sexual taste for "rough stuff," and the spiraling intensity of the violence of Sand's sexual fantasies.

"The sexual acts in the relationship, and nothing else" Stafford said to the jury, "have the intensity and scope that would push Andrea to the limit to be able to do in a short amount of time the damage she did to Robert Sand."

"It was an interpersonal relationship between two people," the public defender said, "a marriage. The only way to piece together what happened is to look at everything we can know and learn about Andrea Sand and Robert Sand."

Andrea had been scarred by her father's desertion and by her marriage that same year to Wesley Denike, who had raped her and went on to continuously beat her during their marriage. She turned to prostitution, Stafford said, and eventually married the crippled, aging Sand, because it gave her a role in which she felt needed.

Mr. Sand had exhibited past violence, Stafford said, including taking a swing at his former wife, Florence. This supported Andrea's story that he had struck her and threatened her life.

The testimony of Dr. Rene Modglin, the pathologist who had performed the autopsy on Robert Sand, also undercut the prosecution's claim of premeditation.

"The number and variety of the wounds indicated to him frenzy...out of control...overkill," Stafford said. "Does that support premeditation or being provoked, pushed to the other side?"

Mr. Dunn had emphasized that Andrea hadn't mentioned the sexual games until it fit her alibi, Stafford said. But in fact, the rapes that she admitted she staged after Robert Sand's death closely approximated the sexual fantasies Robert Sand directed her to act out for him, including inserting knives into her body.

"She was trying to tell people about what happened to her in the only way she could," Stafford said. And her compulsion to continue acting out the sex games, as well as the severity of the wounds she would inflict on her body, supported the expert psychiatric testimony that she was psychotic at the time of the killing.

The public defender held up a photograph that showed cuts and slash marks on Andrea's legs after one of the rapes.

"Do these injuries go beyond an individual just play-acting?" he asked. "It's a little bit different than someone acting out something or being hysterical. It's a little bit more bizarre than simply having a tantrum."

Regarding the questioned Richard Cordine letter, Stafford reminded the jury that the expert witness for the defense had testified that he believed the letter had in fact been written by Cordine. Cordine's feelings had been hurt when Joe Mims told him not to call Andrea anymore, and that gave him a motive to hurt her. Why hadn't Mr. Dunn sought out a second expert opinion on the handwriting? Stafford asked.

Andrea Sand was provoked by Robert Sand's physical and psychological violence to kill him in self-defense, Stafford said to the jury and asked them to return a verdict of innocent. If the claim of self-defense was rejected by the jury, Stafford said, then the evidence and testimony regarding Mrs. Sand's diminished mental state would justify no more than a verdict of involuntary manslaughter.

After the defense's closing argument, Judge Moore recessed court for lunch.

When court resumed, Dunn asked in his rebuttal why *Mr. Stafford* hadn't called in a second expert witness to testify on the questioned Cordine letter.

The prosecutor told the jury that Dr. Modglin's testimony could also be taken in support of the charge of deliberate premeditated murder.

"He said the fatal wounds in the center of the chest indicated the person had an intent to kill the person being stabbed," Dunn said.

As for the rapes that followed the murder, Dunn said, they were no more than desperate attempts by Andrea to shore up her foundering alibi.

"This is a lady who will go to any lengths to cover her tracks," he said, "to muddy the waters."

The same went for the suicide attempts Andrea had staged in jail; they were, the prosecutor said, only more "desperate attempts to delay the inevitable."

"The inevitable is now," Dunn said. "Today is the inevitable in the life of Andrea Sand."

6

After Dunn's rebuttal, Judge Moore gave the jury its instructions.

"Actual danger or great bodily injury is not necessary," he said with regard to the legal definition of self-defense. "On the other hand, a bare fear of death or great bodily harm is not sufficient."

First degree murder, he explained, comprised premeditation and malice aforethought. Murder of the second degree also involved malice aforethought, but in such cases evidence of premeditation was insufficient.

Manslaughter was an unlawful killing of a human being without malice aforethought. In voluntary manslaughter there was an intent to kill; whereas in involuntary manslaughter there was no intention to kill, no malice.

"With regard to diminished capacity," Judge Moore told the jury, "if you find from the evidence that at the time the alleged crime was committed, the defendant had substantially reduced mental capacity, whether caused by mental illness, mental defect, intoxication, or any other cause, you must consider what effect, if any, this diminished capacity had on the defendant's ability to form any of the specific mental states that are essential elements of murder and manslaughter.

"Thus, if you find that the defendant's mental capacity was diminished to the extent that you have a reasonable doubt whether she did maturely and meaningfully premeditate, deliberate, and reflect upon the gravity of her contemplated act or formed an intent to kill, you cannot find her guilty of a willful, deliberate, and premeditated murder of the first degree.

"If you find that the defendant's mental capacity was diminished to the extent that you have a reasonable doubt whether she was able to form the mental states constituting either express or implied malice aforethought, you cannot find her guilty of murder of either first or second degree."

Judge Moore ordered the matter submitted to the jury for its deliberation, and at 3:15 they retired to the jury room to commence deliberations. At 4:04 they returned to the courtroom, and Moore adjourned until the next morning, Friday, at 9:00.

The jury spent all of Friday deliberating. At 4:30 that afternoon, Judge Moore adjourned court until Monday morning at 9:30.

On Monday morning at 11:30, the jury returned to the courtroom from their deliberations in the jury room and requested that the elements of the crime and the degrees of murder be read to them again, which Judge Moore did. The jury broke for lunch at noon. They began deliberations again at 1:15 and then adjourned at 4:33 until the next morning at 9:00.

On Tuesday afternoon, March 13, 1984, at 3:58, the jury returned to the jury box in Courtroom A. Andrea and both defense and prosecution counsels were present. Joe Mims had also appeared in the courtroom.

"Ladies and gentlemen, have you reached a verdict?" Judge Moore asked.

"Yes, we have."

The foreman of the jury handed the verdict to the court clerk to be read aloud.

"We, the jury, find the defendant Andrea Claire Mims guilty of murder, a felony, as charged in count one, and we set the degree at first degree," the clerk pronounced.

It took a second for Joe Mims to fully comprehend what the clerk had read. Then it hit him. The jury had found Andrea as guilty as the law allowed.

Because the trial wasn't over, Judge Moore admonished the jury not to discuss their decision. He scheduled the sanity phase of the trial to begin on Monday, March 26.

Outside Courtroom A, Dunn told reporters he was "ecstatic" with the jury's decision, which he said "resoundingly rejected" some of the mental issues already raised by the defense that would be the focus of the next phase.

Charles Stafford was unavailable for comment.

XVI

IV.X.

1

Stafford knew well that the first-degree murder conviction in the guilt phase of the trial made it less likely that the jury would rule in favor of Andrea's diminished capacity plea. First degree murder, after all, specifically comprised premeditation, deliberation, and malice aforethought, as if Andrea were capable of planning and executing such an obviously irrational crime. In truth, the chief deputy public defender was appalled that the jury could deliver such a verdict after the testimony they had heard.

Now, his and Dunn's roles were reversed: the defense had the burden of proof in the sanity phase and would present its witnesses first. All he could do was to continue to put the reality of the case, in all its bizarre complexity, before the members of the jury and hope that the lady received justice.

In his brief opening statement to the jury on the morning of Monday, March 26, Stafford told them they would be hearing testimony again from Dr. Kurland and Dr. Jones, and also from a Dr. Proud.

"Did she understand when she was involved in the [murder] that it was, in fact, a criminal act she was doing," Stafford asked the jury, "or did she lack substantial capacity to be able to conform her conduct to what the law required? That is the whole test of whether or not an individual is legally insane or legally sane at the time the offense occurred.

"I think it is quite obvious," he concluded, "that the defendant is very disturbed and that she is, in fact, legally insane."

As his first witness, Stafford called Dr. William Harley Jones again. In direct examination, Jones testified that part of his con-

clusion that the defendant was legally insane at the time of the
murder of Robert Sand was based on the phenomonon of the
many reported rapes. Either Andrea truly believed the incidents
occurred, which implied major delusions and hallucinations and
indicated psychosis. Or she reported the rapes knowing they
didn't occur. Since the stories were so unbelievable, they
couldn't possibly help her cause, and hence this behavior could
only be seen as compulsive with an unsound "mental emotional
basis."

Stafford brought up the antipsychotic medication Andrea had
been prescribed, which had been increased since the murder
conviction. Jones testified that "her functioning seemed to be
better in December and January," when her dosages had been
higher, than when he had first seen her in September of 1983.

Jones also said that Andrea's drawing, depicting the people in
her life as monsters attacking her, which Stafford had brought to
the attention of the jury, was not "inconsistent in any way" with
his diagnosis of Andrea as a borderline personality.

In cross-examination, Dunn went back to Jones's two explanations of the rapes.

"The second explanation you gave," the prosecutor said,
"was that she didn't believe that they'd occurred, which would
indicate peculiar behavior on her part. Is that true?"

"Yes," Jones said. "It suggested a disorder called
Munchausen's Syndrome, where patients report nonexistent
medical disorders in an apparent attempt to gain attention and
sympathy. And continue in a compulsive way to do that. Usually
associated with severe emotional disturbance. That was another
possibility that I considered."

"Did you consider," Dunn asked, "that she was just lying in
an attempt to throw the investigating officers off of her track and
successfully escape culpability for the murder of her husband?"

"I considered that," Jones said.

Dunn wanted to know if it wouldn't be possible for he himself to draw a picture similar to Andrea's.

"I don't know whether it would be or not," Jones said. "Usually nonpsychotic people have a hard time drawing convincing monsters and things of that sort."

"Why is that?" Dunn asked.

"I suppose because they don't have the fantasy basis for those kind of drawings," Jones said.

A few moments later in Jones's testimony, Dunn brought up the medical report from Riverside General Hospital that stated Andrea had admitted to faking mental problems to get transferred from Indio County Jail.

"I never said that," Andrea called out from the defense table.

"I'd ask the defendant to be admonished, your Honor," Dunn said.

"Yes, Mr. Stafford," Judge Moore said.

Stafford looked at Andrea, who was now silent.

The next witness for the defense was Dr. Morton Kurland, who testified again about his diagnosis of borderline personality disorder.

"My whole feeling about the case and this individual," Kurland said, "was that she had poor reality testing altogether and that under pressure she tends to disintegrate."

Stafford asked Kurland whether, based on his review of the materials and his own contacts with the defendant, he thought it possible that her actions or what she said could be just a put-on.

KURLAND: Well, of course, I considered—as I think we discussed earlier—that it was very hard for her, I think, always to tell exactly the truth about things, because I think she's not always sure of what the truth is. I think that in her own mind, it becomes vague.

However, I think the general content of her presentation to me was consistent with this diagnosis and consistent with the fact that this is a person who just slips in and out of reality. And while eveything she says isn't true, I don't think this is a product of conscious planning or lying or figuring out in advance, as much as it is of her not being sure what reality is and in making up what goes along with the moment.

But I don't think that this was a put-on, as you said.

As for the drawing, Dr. Kurland saw it as further evidence of "an extremely deranged person who has tremendous feelings of being attacked, mutilated, put upon, injured by the rest of the world, and that, if they're not attacking her, they're simply sitting by doing nothing."

In cross-examination, Dunn asked Dr. Kurland if he gave any weight to the fact that the drawing was made around the time of the competency trial.

"At that time, I didn't make any comment upon that," Kurland said. "At this moment, I would say that certainly you can make the argument—which apparently you are—that she was trying to look crazy. And if she was trying to do that, she did a great job."

Dunn asked if all people who suffer from borderline personality disorder were criminally insane by the terms of the standard they were using.

"Well," Kurland said, "certainly not all persons at all times, but I think all persons with that disorder who were psychotic at the time and then who committed a crime would fit the standard, that very small percentage."

The prosecutor questioned Dr. Kurland regarding Andrea's statement to Riverside Hospital personnel that the actions that had caused her to be transferred there were a game to keep her out of jail.

"It could mean that that was actually true," Kurland said, "or it could mean that that was a cover story that she was giving to the other people to explain her being in the psych unit, which is embarrassing to lots of people, and they frequently say, 'I don't really belong here,' that 'they're all crazy, I'm sane.' So either alternative is possible."

Judge Moore recessed court for lunch at 12:04 until 1:30.

2

The witness after lunch and for the rest of the afternoon was Dr. Ernest Proud, the psychologist who had written the psychological evaluation for Judge Moore with regard to the guilty by reason of insanity plea. The doctor's report was the most exhaustive assessment of the defendant on record.

Under direct examination by Stafford, Proud said that he suspected, though Andrea denied it, that there had been "some incestual kind of relationship" going on between her and her father before he abandoned the family, and that this had been what actually prompted the father, who "became very much afraid, very hurt by it," to leave.

Stafford asked if this background could be correlated with Andrea's later being involved with prostitution.

PROUD: Prostitution, [and] the men that she married. All of her husbands, as short as most of the relationships were, tended to be real dangerous kinds of people. They were gamblers, people that were high risk takers. They tended to abuse women, their wives. Which isn't all that unusual for a woman, a grown woman that has been molested.

Proud agreed with Jones and Kurland that Andrea's perception of things tended to be "rather questionable."

The public defender asked whether fantasy would play a role in creating her reality.

PROUD: Well, here's a person that's having difficulty dealing with reality and tends to retreat from it as much as she can.

Then she marries a man who cuts her off further from her interaction with reality. From her playing golf, visiting with friends. That's all part of our reality and part of our stability. He cuts her off from this. Doesn't allow her to have friends come over, doesn't like her children coming over, doesn't like her going out...Keeps isolating her further and further and further.

Then he starts creating a reality for her. I think this is a real important key and maybe I'm missing pointing it out. For Andrea, because she tends to withdraw from reality, and she has such difficulty dealing with it anyway, if somebody starts creating a reality for her, she'll start to live it.

For example, when Mr. Sand had said if you go out and golf, if you go out and play, if you go out and ride your bike, you'll be kidnapped and raped: she believed that was true. So when she did go out and ride her bike, she was raped. She created the rape.

Stafford then asked Proud about the night of the murder.

PROUD: It's sort of the old statement, "Look before you leap." Andrea never looks. Andrea leaps. She gets out of control. She just decides to do something, and she does it. She starts getting into something, and she can't stop.

She became very, very fearful of Mr. Sand, and—through that whole incident—she struck out. And the more she struck out, the more fearful she became.

For her, that was reality. All those months of, "This guy is coming to rape you, this guy is coming to cut you up, this person is going to do you harm..." became real at that moment.

When he tried to grab her and she hit him, stabbed him, whatever she did, that was reality for her. She was defending herself. She was no longer able to see Bob Sand there. She was able only to see a person that was trying to make her a victim.

Stafford asked if Andrea was psychotic all the time.

PROUD: When I said she's a borderline psychotic person, that's a person that has trouble dealing with distinguishing fantasy from reality. They're not always sure which one is which. Get confused easily about what they are doing, if it's real or not real. They don't always know. They can't tell a dream from what's really going on. They become one and the same.

That's a borderline psychotic person. They're psychotic, but they're able to generally deal with most of us and hide a lot of that craziness that's going on in their head.

Was there something in Andrea's behavior, Stafford asked, that indicated to Dr. Proud that she wasn't "just feigning and acting out that she's crazy?"

PROUD: The consistency of it, I suppose. Andrea is a very bright woman. If she were faking it—and I've seen many people try to fake mental illness, that's not particularly unusual in the jail—there usually is a misunderstanding about what insanity is, so their behavior will be more retarded than it would be insane. That's typically what most people do to try to feign insanity.

But saying that she was even more sophisticated than that, it's difficult to be insane all the time, even when you're faking it, or even when it's real. It's the consistency that's gone on.

You know, when I do an evaluation on a person that's in jail, I do the evaluation on the person, and then I talk to the sheriff's deputies. These are the people that are watching them. I talk to the other prisoners that share the cell with them. I talk to people they have had contact with on the outside before they went to jail.

There's no feasible way that Andrea Mims could be feigning her mental illness. No possible way.

In cross-examination, Dunn started where Dr. Proud had left off, with Andrea's behavior in jail as reported by those around her. Proud said two deputies told him of Andrea's claim she was raped in jail.

"That was a lie, wasn't it?" Dunn asked.

"That Andrea had been raped?"

"That's correct," Dunn said. "Isn't it true when Andrea said she was raped in jail that she was lying?"

"Lying is a judgment statement," Proud said. "I wouldn't say she was lying."

"Well, was it true that she was raped in the jail?" Dunn asked.

"No."

"Well, don't you think that's significant, that she's saying that things occurred to her in the jail which did not happen?"

"That's why I said that she was insane."

"Isn't it true that she could just be lying? Isn't that another possibility under those circumstances?"

"No."

"That never crossed your mind?"

"Of course it did."

Later in the cross-examination, referring to his clinical interview with Andrea, Proud commented that Andrea was filled with guilt because she had killed her husband.

"Did she state to you why she felt guilty about it?"

"Andrea is a server," Proud said. "She's not a person that hurts other people. She's a person that provides service like a social worker. She sees herself in that role, providing a service for them in taking care of them."

"Andrea indicated to you that she views herself as a social worker?"

"Yeah, more or less," Proud said. "Which I don't think is particularly uncommon among prostitutes. Many of them see themselves in that role, taking care of other people and providing a service."

Dunn brought up the fact that Andrea had told staff members at Riverside General Hospital that she had put on an act to get transferred there from jail. Did Proud think that was significant?

"Now think of it like this," Proud said. "If you weren't mentally ill, would you say that to the staff members? You would be pretty dumb if you would, because they'd throw you out and see through you in a minute."

Dunn asked if Andrea had ever said to Proud that she was attracted to Robert Sand when she met him because he was dangerous.

"No," Proud said. "The real attraction was that she felt sorry for him because he looked like a very lonely old man, and that he had told her he had cancerous lesions on his arm, so she saw her role as taking care of him. Her attraction was really taking care of him.

"She became more attracted to him after they had seen each other for a little while," Proud went on, "and she saw the violence there and the dangerousness in him."

"Did she ever indicate to you why she didn't leave Robert Sand?"

"She loved him," Proud said.

3

On the following morning, March 27, Stafford called two more witnesses for the defense. The first was the nurse from the Indio County Jail, Jean Hyams, who said Andrea's dosage of the antipsychotic drug Triavil was doubled the week before after Andrea complained of "feeling more nervous than usual" and appeared agitated.

Dunn had no questions.

Stafford's second witness was Guy Denike. When he was eight years old, Guy told Stafford, he had been dragged across a sprinkler head while holding onto the leash of a neighbor's dog. His side was torn open and, he realized when he was older, his large intestine was exposed.

When Andrea discovered that he was injured, Guy said, she became frantic, got mad at the neighbor who owned the dog, and wanted to give Guy a bath.

"Did you receive medical treatment?" Stafford asked.

"Yes, afterwards. After I went to the hospital."

"Whose decision was it to get you to the hospital?"

"It was a neighbor," Denike said. "She told my mother either call an ambulance or take me to the hospital. Not to give me a bath."

Guy testified that when he was young, he frequently saw his mother crying in her room. While he was growing up his mother had a succession of interests in alternative health practices like acupuncture and acupressure, in herbs and "just thousands of all kinds of vitamins," and in programs like est and Scientology, he told Stafford. She had once taken him to a numerologist who suggested to him that he change his name.

After Denike was cross-examined, the defense rested. Judge Moore adjourned court at 10:10 that morning until the following morning at 9:30, when the prosecution would put on its expert witnesses.

4

Robert Dunn also knew well that there was only a remote chance of the jury going for an insanity plea after convicting the defendant of first degree murder. In effect, it would amount to a reversal of the decision they'd already made, in light of premeditation, deliberation, and malice aforethought, which might even be said to presuppose possession of one's mental faculties.

On Wednesday, March 28, Dunn presented three expert witnesses for the prosecution, Dr. Otto Gericke, Dr. Anthony Oliver, and Dr. Robert Flanagan. In a brief opening statement to the jury, the prosecutor pointed out that Dr. Gericke had been the director of Patton State Mental Hospital, "where criminally insane persons from the southern part of California are usually sent," for twenty-six years. Dr. Flanagan, also an experienced psychiatrist, was currently the chief of psychiatry at the California State Prison for Women, located in Frontera. Both doctors, then, had a great deal of insight into the psychology of the criminally insane, Dunn said. The jury already knew, of course, Dr. Oliver's qualifications.

"And again thank you," Dunn said to the jury, "and I hope you'll carefully consider the testimony of the witnesses that will testify. And although I haven't mentioned it before, and I don't think it should surprise you, each of these three witnesses will testify that on May 14, 1981, at the time that Robert Sand was murdered, the defendant was sane, was legally sane at that time under the standard that was applicable at that time."

The elderly Dr. Gericke, who was licensed as a psychiatrist in 1934, testified that in two interviews with the defendant, in June 1983 and February 1984, and in reviewing materials on the case supplied by both the district attorney's and the public defender's offices, he could find no evidence of mental illness, but that he did see evidence of a personality disorder, specifically histrionic personality disorder.

In cross-examination by Stafford, Gericke said he doubted that the number and variety of the wounds Robert Sand had received necessarily indicated that the defendant was in a frenzy and out of control.

"I would consider," Dr. Gericke said, "that other actions of hers indicated control: when she was able to wash the knife a couple of times and the board and so forth, showing that she appeared rational shortly after."

Dr. Gericke had not been provided with the police reports and other materials related to the rape incidences, but had seen Dr. Proud's evaluation of the defendant which took into account this material, and didn't feel it was necessary to investigate the alleged rapes.

"You didn't think it was necessary?" Stafford said. "Were you aware of them?"

"Well," Gericke said, "she told me about some of them, and I asked her about them, the fact that a knife was found in her rectum after she was discovered. And she said, 'Oh, well, it was a dull knife.' So I figured it wasn't too important."

Dunn asked his next witness, Dr. Oliver, if the defendant's behavior after the crime was consistent with the possibility that she was in a psychotic state when she committed the crime. Dr. Oliver said that Andrea's behavior offered evidence to the contrary. Her fabrication and distortion of evidence indicated "a very acute awareness of the nature of the act."

Stafford had no questions for Dr. Oliver. Judge Moore recessed court for lunch at 11:20 until 1:30 that afternoon.

Dr. Robert Flanagan had interviewed the defendant in June 1983 at the time of her competency trial and again in February 1984 with regard to his testimony today.

"I think that the diagnosis," Flanagan said to Dunn, "the diagnostic category generally would be character disorder. Some features of a histrionic personality I feel are present, some features of narcissism I feel are present. Perhaps some features of borderline personality present. All are character disorders that tend to merge, one with the other."

In cross-examination, Stafford noted that Flanagan had stated in his report that Mrs. Sand "employs abysmally poor judgment with much evidence of indulgence in fantasies and other forms of intellectualization. This combined with instability of mood renders her potentially a risk at least to her own safety." Was there enough evidence, he asked Flanagan, to indicate that Mrs. Sand was sometimes taken over by her fantasies?

"I believe she has a two-way ticket, so to speak," Flanagan said. "I believe that she does not lose contact with reality to the point where she's no longer able to return to it."

Stafford showed the doctor Andrea's drawing and asked whether it wouldn't be delusional for someone to think of other people as monsters of the type the drawing depicted.

"Well," Flanagan said, "these are very vivid in my opinion for a psychotic delusion. Psychotic delusions are rather vague. These are very vivid, and they show creatures that I would consider monsters with a lot of sharp teeth that are inflicting wounds, injuries. I think this is a graphic illustration, but I don't consider it delusional. This is—fanciful. I think it's symbolic, but I don't see where it's psychotic or delusional."

$$\boxed{5}$$

On Thursday morning, Stafford presented in rebuttal his final three witnesses—Joe Mims, Dr. Michael Leitman, and Dr. Donald Tweedie. The public defender asked Joe Mims about an incident that occurred after he picked up Andrea at Capistrano By The Sea Hospital to take her home.

MIMS: We were driving down the road, and she was upset, visibly upset, and we had gone approximately, let's say two miles or so, and we were on Highway 1, quite a busy street, and I was in the second lane, and she says, "I'm going to jump out." And I says, "No, you're not, Andrea. We're going to have a horrible accident."

She began to say she wanted to go back, and I said, "Okay, let me pull over to the side." So I pulled over to the side of the road, and I said, "Now what's wrong?"

STAFFORD: Did she give you the impression that she was actually going to jump out of the car?

MIMS: She had ahold of the door—the knob.

"Mr. Mims," Dunn began his cross-examination, "have you ever seen the behavior of a spoiled child?"

"I didn't have spoiled children, so I don't know," Mims answered.

"Mr. Mims," Stafford began his redirect examination, "the district attorney has asked you about spoiled children. Do you think of your wife, your former wife, as a spoiled child or a person who's ill?"

"I would not consider her a spoiled child, no," Mims said. "A person that's ill, yes."

"Mentally ill?"

"Mentally ill, yes."

"Thank you, Mr. Mims."

Through Lorrie Wright, Andrea passed a note to Joe after his testimony.

Dr. Michael Leitman testified to Stafford that Andrea had handed him the monster drawing shortly before her competency trial. He said the drawing had been unsolicited by him.

Under cross-examination by Dunn, Leitman said that the fact that Andrea told staff members at Riverside General Hospital that she was acting crazy to keep herself out of jail wasn't necessarily an indication of malingering. It was possible, Leitman said, but other data contradicted it.

DUNN: What other data?

LEITMAN: The fact that she was cutting herself. I don't know many people that would take a knife and play tick-tack-toe on their leg to keep themselves from going to jail. I don't know many people that would lacerate their back and place a knife in their rectum to keep from going to jail.

I think that's psychotic behavior.

DUNN: Because you don't know people like that, you don't feel it's possible she was just manipulating you when she was telling you these things, which later proved not to be true?

LEITMAN: I would say that it's not what one would consider within the normal realm of behavior. Would you consider it within the normal realm of behavior?

Dunn asked Judge Moore to admonish the witness.

"Yes. Just answer questions, Doctor," Judge Moore told Leitman.

DUNN: Do you feel that on May 14, 1981, that Andrea Sand did not know it was criminal to commit first degree premeditated murder?

LEITMAN: Given what I know about her, yes.

DUNN: What basis do you have that she did not know—on May 14, 1981—that she did not know that murder was a crime?

LEITMAN: The personality style that I described earlier, the constant changing of her stories, the creation of a different reality.

If it were true that she were malingering, would her attorney not have been aware of that? The person responsible for keeping her out of trouble?

And would her attorney, who was responsible for her defense, have sent her to see a psychiatrist?

Dunn asked that Leitman's reply be stricken as nonresponsive.

"The motion is granted," Judge Moore said. "The jury will disregard."

Andrea had begun to cry during Dr. Leitman's testimony and
continued, sometimes fiercely, during the testimony of the last
witness, Dr. Donald Tweedie, who said he diagnosed Andrea as a
paranoid schizophrenic.

In his closing statement, Stafford told the jury that the
burden on him in this phase of the trial was a preponderance of
the evidence, and not, as the burden had been on Mr. Dunn in
the first phase of the trial, to prove the case beyond a reasonable
doubt.

"A preponderance of the evidence is quite simple," Stafford
said. "It is when you take all the evidence together and you
weigh it—which side has the greater weight, which side has the
greater probability of truth."

Stafford said the facts of the case contradicted the idea that
Andrea could be malingering, and the public defender pointed
out that one of the most significant aspects of Mr. Dunn's case
was that he wanted them to believe that Andrea was simply
lying. If that were the case, why was Andrea on "antipsychotic
and antidepressant medication to the extent that they're giving it
to her?" he asked.

No longer crying, Andrea folded her head in her arms on
the table.

"In reviewing all the evidence," Stafford said, "it just jumps
out at you that there is something drastically wrong with all the
bizarre behavior that we have."

Dr. Kurland, Dr. Jones, Dr. Proud, Dr. Leitman, and Dr.
Tweedie had all testified that the defendant was seriously mentally ill. The jury's job was to determine whether at the time of
the murder—not before or after it—Andrea had the capacity to
understand that it was wrong.

"To understand the criminality," he summarized, "to appreciate whether or not at that moment in time, when the first stab
wound occurred, when the fifth, when the tenth, when the fif-
teenth, when the twentieth, when the twenty-fourth and
twenty-fifth occurred, whether or not she was able, whether or

not she had the capacity to appreciate criminality, whether or not she had the capacity to conform her conduct to what the law required...

"I contend to you she did not on either point. As Dr. Modglin said, once it started, she would not stop."

When Stafford finished, Judge Moore recessed court for lunch at 11:44 until 1:00 that afternoon.

6

"Ladies and gentleman," Deputy D.A. Dunn addressed the jury as he began his closing argument after lunch, "this is going to be the last opportunity that I have of speaking to you. Although probably you're tired of hearing my voice anyhow after the last nine or ten weeks that we've had an opportunity of standing under the same roof and within the four walls listening to the testimony together. But I'm not going to be lengthy."

The hell he wasn't, Stafford thought, as the prosecutor went to nearly triple the time Stafford had taken for his closing argument. But then in this phase of the trial Stafford had the opportunity of rebuttal that Dunn had had in the first phase.

He covered some of the same ground Stafford had put into his statement regarding the choice before the jury.

"You don't have to worry about lesser included offenses this time around," Dunn said. "Got two choices. Either she's sane at the time of the offense or she's insane."

He asked the jury to consider all the evidence they had heard in both phases of the trial, and to consider the testimony and demeanor of the various expert witnesses they had heard testify.

"You have an advantage over all the witnesses in this case that testified," he told them. "I would just guess conservatively that you probably heard a hundred hours of testimony in this case, and that's a conservative estimate. You've had the opportunity for seven, eight, nine weeks to observe the defendant in this case as she's sitting there, seeing how she acts. Now that's an opportunity that none of these witnesses had, whether they were called by the prosecution or the defense. Some of the people talked to her for a couple of hours. Some of them talked to her for ten or twelve hours. You've had literally a hundred hours or more of seeing how she acts.

"Has she been acting as an insane person, or has she been acting as a manipulative, histrionic person? Now that's a decision you have to make."

It annoyed Stafford that Dunn would go for this when he'd spent a lot of time making a point of the antipsychotic medicine Andrea was prescribed daily, with a big increase in the dosage since the decision came down in the guilt phase of the trial. And even with the increase, he knew she wasn't in good shape right now, suddenly furiously taking notes at the other end of the table.

Dunn made a big point of Andrea drawing her picture around the time of the competency trial. What better time to pretend she was crazy? he asked the jury. Yes, Stafford thought. She had done that all along. When the day drew near, whatever day it happened to be, something was likely to happen. But was that because she was manipulating them or because she was stressed out of her mind knowing the day was coming? And she was communicating with these bizarre acts because she was unable to communicate with words?

"You don't know why that medication was prescribed," Dunn said to the jury. "You don't know if that medication was prescribed because she raised such a fuss in the jail that they finally gave her something just to shut her up."

For years? Stafford thought. But then again, that's what they did with psychotics, wasn't it?

"You have to remember," Dunn said to the jury, "that what Mr. Stafford is asking you to do is to find her not guilty by reason of insanity. That based upon her insanity, she is not culpable for the first degree murder which she committed.

"Ladies and gentlemen," he said, "I'm stating to you right now with all the conviction I can muster that throughout her life—when you look at the pattern of the way she dealt with her life—she did not conform her conduct to the confines of the law. She was a prostitute for over ten years."

"I wasn't," Andrea said out loud, and Lorrie turned to her to keep her from any further outburst. There, Stafford thought, a manipulative gesture for the jury during the prosecution's summary. Like clockwork.

"You remember what she testified to?" Dunn continued. "She discovered she could make more money in one night as a prostitute than she could in a week working as a secretary or another job. And she could conform her conduct to the standards of society if she wished to do it at that time.

"She was doing what she thought she wanted to do, what was best for Andrea Sand, just as Andrea Sand has done throughout her life. Who cares about the rest of the world? What's in it for me? What's best for Andrea? Who cares if somebody else is hurt? What difference does it make?

"That's exactly the same thing that happened on May the 14, 1981. And that evidence supports a verdict of sanity in this case.

"Again, thank you very much, ladies and gentlemen," the prosecutor said.

"Mr. Dunn points to my client with his finger," Stafford said in his rebuttal, "and says you've been able to watch her all during this trial. Does she act like a crazy person?

"When we were selecting a jury, I posed some questions to some of you about making quick judgments about people. We see a man walk down the street staggering, and we make a judgment that he must be sick or he's intoxicated. Isn't that what Mr. Dunn's asking you to do? The reason why my client is somewhat controlled in this courtroom—do you think it has anything whatsoever to do with the medication that she's on?"

Getting sarcastic was a bad idea when you were addressing the decision-making body, Dunn thought. The last thing in the world you wanted was for them to see you as stuck-up, a bantam rooster, as his wife had described Stafford after seeing him in action in the courtroom.

"Andrea Sand," Stafford continued, "on May the 14, 1981, became the ultimate victim by doing what she did. She became the victim because of how ill she is, how she views reality, and how she views herself and how she views other people around her. Because of how disturbed she is, she simply cannot conform to what the law requires. And she does not understand, and she does not have the capacity to appreciate at various times, that what she's doing is criminal.

"There are two tragedies in this case. One, Robert Sand met his death. The other tragedy is Andrea Sand."

$$\boxed{7}$$

In his instructions, after again covering the legal definition of insanity and preponderance of evidence, Judge Moore told the jury "temporary legal insanity or legal insanity of short duration, which existed at the time of the commission of the offense charged, is as fully recognized as a defense of legal insanity of longer duration.

"Uncontrollable or irresistible impulse itself is not legal insanity unless as a result of mental disease or mental defect, a person lacked substantial capacity to appreciate the criminality of conduct or to conform his conduct to the requirements of law.

"In your deliberations, or in arriving at your verdict, you must not discuss or consider the subject of penalty or punishment. That must not in any way affect your decision in this matter."

It was unlikely, Stafford knew, that the jury would be familiar with the procedure in the event that they came to a not guilty by reason of insanity verdict, which was probably for the best. Section 1026.2 of the penal code stated that Andrea could be released after as little as ninety days in Patton State Hospital if it were judged she was no longer insane. At the same time, she could remain committed to the institution to the maximum amount of her sentence, which in her case could be for life. That ninety days could scare people, of course, but Stafford was certain Andrea's problems were severe enough for her to be hospitalized for a long time to come.

The jury, Judge Moore told them finally, must make a unanimous decision.

At 1:50 that afternoon, the jury retired to commence deliberations. At 4:00 they returned to the courtroom and were dismissed until 9:00 the following morning.

At 5:00 that night, after being returned to her cell at Indio County Jail, Andrea cracked the casing of a disposable razor issued to inmates and cut her wrist with the blade. The other women in the cell tried to stop her. The wound missed the major blood vessels but required eight stitches. After it was treated by the jail medical staff, Andrea was taken to Riverside General Hospital for psychiatric observation. She remained there when court reconvened on Friday morning.

At 11:55 in the morning on Friday, the jury requested Andrea's testimony dealing with the evening of the murder. Carol Campbell, the court reporter, was asked to extract it from the record. But at 3:00 that afternoon, she was still working on preparing the transcript, and Judge Moore adjourned court until Monday morning at 9:30.

On Monday, Andrea was present in court again. Campbell read to the jury portions of the testimony by the defendant. Afterwards, at the request of the jury, Judge Moore reread his instructions to them. At 11:44, a lunch recess was taken until 1:00. After lunch, the jury deliberated for the rest of the afternoon and was dismissed at 4:56 until 9:00 the next morning.

The jury deliberated until 3:00 on Tuesday afternoon, when they returned to the courtroom. The jury foreman, J. P. Sundberg, reported a deadlock. Judge Moore gave the jury Wednesday off. When they returned on Thursday morning at 9:00, he encouraged them to keep trying. They deliberated all day Thursday.

The jury deliberated all day Friday, April 6. At 4:45 that afternoon, they returned to the courtroom, having come to their decision. Andrea was present with both Charles Stafford and Robert Dunn for the reading of the verdict by the jury foreman.

"We the jury," Sundberg said, "find that at the time of the commission of the offense, defendant was sane."

Judge Moore began a name-by-name polling of the members of the jury.

"I killed him because he called me a whore," Andrea said and threw a tissue box at the microphone in front of the table where she sat.

"Why didn't you give me the death penalty?" she said and then seemed to lose consciousness in her chair.

Stafford and the bailiff supported Andrea, apparently unconscious, through the courtroom to the jail area. Stafford threatened to break the cameras of photographers who pressed to take pictures.

$$\boxed{8}$$

On Thursday morning, May 3, 1984, before the sentencing, Charles Stafford requested a new trial, contending that "the evidence taken in its totality is not sufficient to establish a reasonable doubt first degree murder," and citing Dr. Modglin's testimony as evidence that the crime was a "frenzied, out of control situation."

Judge Moore said he had followed the evidence "quite con-
scientiously during the course of the trial" and then denied the
motion.

"Are you ready to proceed with the sentencing?" Judge
Moore asked.

"Would the court have any objection if the defendant
remained seated?" Stafford asked.

"No. She may remain seated," Judge Moore said.

"The defendant," Judge Moore said, "is committed to state
prison for the term of twenty-five years to life." An additional
year had been added to the sentence, he continued, for the use
of a knife, for a total of twenty-six years. The judge noted that
Andrea had a credit of 552 days of real time, along with 276 days
for good behavior—more or less routine unless a prisoner
attempted to escape—for a total of 828 days that could be
applied against the sentence. He notified her of her right of
appeal and of the 60 day time limit she had in which to file a
notice of intended appeal. If she didn't have the money for an
appeal, Moore informed her, the appellate court would appoint a
lawyer for her.

"Excuse me, your honor," Dunn said. "I don't want to seem
like I'm being overly picky on this case, but Miss Mata of the
probation department did advise me that the report was prepared
for sentencing on tomorrow. One day less, for a total combined
credit—the day served plus a day of good behavior—of 826
days."

"For a total of 826 days credit," Judge Moore agreed.

Stafford asked that the court find that his client did not have
the present ability to pay for his services.

"I anticipate that she is indigent today," Stafford said, "and
she will be indigent at a later date."

"Well," Judge Moore said, "there is an issue regarding the
estate, and perhaps I should leave that open."

"I anticipate that in light of the conviction," Stafford said,
"that she will not recover unless it is reversed on appeal."

"I suspect that's true," Judge Moore said, "but I think I better leave it open for that reason."

At 9:48 that morning, the proceedings were concluded.

EPILOGUE

In light of the twenty-six years to life sentence, the district attorney's office didn't pursue the attempted murder charge and allowed a disposition of that case without a trial. Andrea pled guilty to a reduced charge of assault with a deadly weapon and was allowed to serve her four year term for it concurrently with the murder sentence.

Joe Mims' marriage in Escondido ended quickly. Not long after Andrea began serving her sentence at the California Institute for Women in Frontera, he started to visit her there. He had heard a program on the radio about PMS and realized that his first wife Dotty had probably suffered from it, and it was probably what was wrong with Andrea, too, if her behavior around her period was any indication. When he saw her at Frontera, he told Andrea what he had heard about PMS, and she said she had always had a hard time with her period and still did. Joe encouraged her to try to get the prison to prescribe estrogen for her.

In the visiting room at Frontera, Joe could only sit and talk with her and kiss her hello and goodbye, but there was no opportunity to get sexual, and Andrea hadn't really been in a situation like that with a man before in her adult life. Over the weeks and months that Joe visited with her regularly and sat talking with her, it made her care about him again.

After he'd been visiting her for the better part of a year, Joe proposed to Andrea. When she said yes, the two began to plan their second wedding. Monday, May 13, 1985, was the day they set and the prison chaplain was to officiate.

The day of the wedding, there was some last minute paper-work that hadn't been handled—the kind of official forms that needed to be filled out every time you wanted to turn around in prison, Andrea had learned. She was a little worried about Joe getting discouraged when she saw him on the morning of their big day. He was standing on the other side of the glass partition between the waiting room and the visiting room.

Andrea looked away for a moment. When she looked back, she didn't see Joe. She wondered where he'd gone. Then a guard pushed past her and into the waiting room, and she saw that Joe was on the floor. A moment later, they were carrying him out-side on a stretcher.

Joe Mims was pronounced dead on arrival at Chino Community Hospital at 11:30 a.m. that morning. He was fifty-nine-years-old. The cause of death was later determined to be a heart attack. The day of Joe Mims' death was one day short of four years after the death of Robert Sand on May 14, 1981.

The Fourth District Court of Appeals upheld the 1984 murder conviction of Andrea Sand in a decision that was filed on October 8, 1986.

Andrea Claire Mims continues to serve her term at the California Institute for Women in Frontera, where she has a record as a model prisoner. She will be eligible for parole in 1997.

ACKNOWLEDGMENTS

This book derives from two sources: interviews with people who figure in it, and official and unofficial records. From time to time, the writer needed to measure opposing versions of an event against one another and make a choice. Then too, occasionally he needed to telescope or otherwise shape a particular sequence in the interests of the narrative. I've never done this, however, if I thought it would in any sense misrepresent the facts of the story.

I'd like to express my thanks to the following people for their help during the writing of this book: Andrea Mims, Robert Dunn, Dr. Morton Kurland, Dr. Michael Leitman, James Hawkins, Judy Campbell, Dan Riter, Charles Stafford, Lorrie Wright, Dr. William Harley Jones, Gary Scherotter, Dr. Anthony Oliver, Fred Kopplin, Elva Kopplin, John Nelson, Rudy Garcia, Dorothy Boerste, Judy Bracamonte, Larry Pedone, Manual Mapula, Chris Brown, Steven Secofsky, Mike Reyes, Richard Hannebaum, Guy Denike, Ellen Scott, Robert Scott, Nina Rhodes, Suzanne Summers, David Chapman, Betty Hawkins, Herbert Hawkins, James Kennedy, Marvin Chesebro, Garthe Brown, Cynthia Sjoquist, Dr. Donald Tweedie, Carmen Mottesheard, Michael Mottesheard, Helen Findlater, Judge Frank Moore, Dr. Laurence Jackson, Rick Jackson, Margie Hill, Richard Erwood, Susan Stedding, Sandy Stuart, Lisa Beck, Vicki Rosenberg, Jon Gilbert, and Carole and Lyle Stuart.

A. S.

ABOUT THE AUTHOR

Aram Saroyan is the author of "lighght," the controversial one-word poem which became the subject of a decades-long government and public debate after it was chosen for a National Endowment for the Arts Poetry Award by Robert Duncan in 1968. His poetry has been widely anthologized and appears in many textbooks. Among the collections of his work are *Aram Saroyan, Pages,* and *O My Generation and Other Poems.*

Saroyan's more recent books have been prose, including *Genesis Angels: The Saga of Lew Welch and the Beat Generation; Last Rites: The Death of William Saroyan; Trio: Portrait of an Intimate Friendship; The Romantic,* a novel that was a *Los Angeles Times Book Review* Critics' Choice selection; and a memoir, *Friends in the World: The Education of a Writer.*

Saroyan was the president of PEN Center USA West for 1992–93. Married and a father, he lives in Thousand Oaks, California. He is the Communications Director of the Job Training Policy Council, a non-profit corporation that distributes federal funds for employment training and placement in Ventura County.